JOHN HAY

John Hay
Courtesy of Brown University Library

JOHN HAY

The Gentleman as Diplomat

KENTON J. CLYMER

Ann Arbor   The University of Michigan Press

Grateful acknowledgment is made to the following for permission to reprint materials:

American Jewish Historical Society, for Kenton J. Clymer, "Anti-Semitism in the Late Nineteenth Century: The Case of John Hay," *American Jewish Historical Quarterly*, 40 (June 1970).

British Library Board, for material from the archives of the A. J. Balfour Papers.

Brown University Library, for material from the archives of The John Hay Library and for the frontispiece of John Hay. Used with permission of the Brown University Library.

Cornell University Libraries, for material from the archives of the Andrew D. White Papers and the Jacob Gould Schurman Papers.

The Houghton Library, for materials from the archives of the Howell, Rockhill, and Hay Papers. Reproduced by permission of the Harvard College Library.

The Henry E. Huntington Library and Art Gallery, for material from the archives of the Huntington Library Collections. Reproduced by permission of the Huntington Library, San Marino, California.

Massachusetts Historical Society, for material from the archives of the Henry Adams Papers, the Theodore Frelinghuysen Dwight Papers, The H. H. Edes Papers, and the Henry Cabot Lodge Papers. Also material from the archives of the Adams Family Papers. Quotations from the Adams Papers are from the microfilm edition, by permission of the Massachusetts Historical Society.

The Missouri State Historical Society, for Kenton J. Clymer, "John Hay and Mark Twain," *Missouri Historical Review*, 47 (April 1973).

The New York Public Library, for material from the archives of the Gilder Papers, Manuscripts and Archives Division, The New York Public Library, Astor, Lenox and Tilden Foundations.

University of California General Library, for material from the archives of the Mark Twain Papers.

University of Virginia Library, for material from the archives of the Richard Harding Davis Papers, Barrett Library, University of Virginia Library.

For my parents

Preface

Forty-one years ago Tyler Dennett published his biography of John Hay. Since that time historians have paid surprisingly little attention to this man whose adult life spans the years from Abraham Lincoln (for whom he was a private secretary) to Theodore Roosevelt (whom he served as secretary of state until his death in 1905). A few articles have recently appeared, and Hay's novel *The Bread-winners* is once again in print, but no in-depth study of him has been published. Hay deserves more attention. A person with strong and articulated opinions on social and political developments in the late nineteenth century, a leading (if often behind-the-scenes) figure in the Republican party, and a man who amassed an unusually large array of admirers in political and literary circles, Hay was one of the key figures in American national life. Furthermore, as secretary of state from 1898 to 1905, he was responsible, next to the president, for guiding the nation's destiny during one of the most critical periods in all of American diplomatic history. It is perhaps appropriate that this work about the author of the Open Door notes appears at a time of renewed contact between the United States and China.

This is primarily a study of Hay's thought, although the first chapter provides an introduction to Hay the man. More particularly it attempts to show wherever possible that Hay's thought, developed primarily in the domestic context, affected his thinking and action in the area of foreign affairs. Although such an undertaking is by its nature elusive and incapable of objective proof at many points, the interrelationships exist, occasionally explicitly, more often implicitly.

Grants from the University of Michigan, the University Research Institute of the University of Texas at El Paso, and the American Philosophical Society were instrumental in bringing this study to completion. I acknowledge their support with thanks. A portion of chapter 3 appeared previously in the *American Jewish Historical Quarterly*, while a portion of chapter 1 appeared previously in the *Missouri Historical Review*.

Numerous persons have generously given me their time and professional advice. I am particularly indebted to Bradford Perkins, who first suggested a study of Hay and who cheerfully and conscientiously read various drafts of the manuscript. Sidney Fine and John Higham also read the manuscript carefully and thoroughly, while Harold K. Jacobson criticized it from the point of view of a political scientist. A special word of thanks is reserved for Joseph F. Wall and Alan R. Jones of Grinnell College, whose inspired teaching led me and numerous others into academic careers. In addition, Professor Wall interrupted a summer vacation to peruse the final draft.

Portions of the manuscript were also reviewed by Wayne E. Fuller, Carl Jackson, and Robert Rockaway. Charles Santaguida did a superb job of tracking down newspaper references for me, Teresa Allen did equally well in checking footnotes, and William Easton Louttit, Jr., of Providence, Rhode Island, who assisted Tyler Dennett and compiled an almost complete bibliography of Hay's printed writings, kindly granted me an interview. I alone am responsible for errors of fact or interpretation.

I would also like to express my appreciation to the many librarians and archivists I consulted for this study, who, without exception, treated me with kind consideration. Mrs. Sharon Wilson typed the manuscript, sometimes under trying circumstances, always maintaining her good humor in spite of incessant demands.

Finally, thanks are due my wife Marlee who has lived with John Hay as well as with me the past few years, and who, in addition to her constant support and encouragement, made several direct contributions toward completion of this study.

Contents

I

Hay among His Friends

In the usual sense of the word, John Hay was a success. At the age of only twenty-two he was assistant private secretary to President Abraham Lincoln. By 1871 he was a well-known author, having written a well-received travelogue, as well as the more famous *Pike County Ballads*, a series of local color poems written in a dialect of the Mississippi river towns where Hay grew up. By 1875 he was a wealthy man, happily married to Clara Stone, daughter of Cleveland industrialist and railroad builder, Amasa Stone. A decade later he and John G. Nicolay were nearly ready to publish the first installment of their massive, ten-volume *History* of Abraham Lincoln. In 1897 President McKinley appointed Hay ambassador to the Court of St. James, the most prestigious of diplomatic appointments abroad. Eighteen months later John Hay became secretary of state and sat at the head of McKinley's cabinet. When McKinley was assassinated in 1901, the incoming president, Theodore Roosevelt, continued Hay in the office where he died in 1905. Had he lived, there is every indication that he would have remained at his high post for the remainder of Roosevelt's second term. Few secretaries of state have enjoyed such a long tenure.

There were many reasons for Hay's eminence. His association with the magical name of Lincoln was a significant political asset in the late nineteenth century and undoubtedly helped make him a power (if often behind the scenes) within the Republican party. His wealth, too, was a source of power. Every election year the party benefited from John Hay's purse, while McKinley personally knew Hay's generosity during his time of great financial embarrassment in 1893. Furthermore, Hay was genuinely distraught over certain developments in the late nineteenth century, and the resulting sense of urgency caused him to devote his considerable intelligence and talents to maintain the social and political status quo.

There were other men, however, just as deeply concerned and with equal or better qualifications who never gained the eminence or political influence of John Hay. Andrew Carnegie and Whitelaw Reid, both friends of Hay, spring to mind. Carnegie and Reid were, of course, more than successful in a variety of ways, and yet each failed to come as close to the center of political power and international diplomacy as did Hay, though both longed to. Hay, in fact, achieved his greatest political appointments in spite of a glaring liability: he had no constituency, for, beginning in 1886, he maintained his official residence in Washington, D.C. But in 1897 it was Hay who walked away with highest honors.

The most important reason Hay succeeded where others failed was his ability to forge and maintain personal relationships with all kinds of people, at least within a broad range of respectable types. "Make all good men your well-wishers," Hay poeticized, "and then, in the years' steady sifting,/Some of them turn into friends. Friends are/the sunshine of life." Hay developed this art to its highest level and was genuinely distressed when a loss of amiability threatened. "I hate to lose my own friends," he once wrote to Reid. "I do not remember that I ever lost one."[1]

Hay's friendships were not limited to persons in select social, intellectual, or occupational groups. He knew the ward heelers of Cleveland and hosted dinners for presidents, was an intimate of James G. Blaine and Henry Adams, Andrew Carnegie and Mark Twain, and knew everyone of whatever reputation connected with the larger newspapers. "He enjoyed a touch-and-go acquaintance with many persons of all sorts who never entered Mr.

[Henry] Adams's door," observed William R. Thayer, a conclusion substantiated by Walt Whitman, who stated that Hay "was much liked by all grades of people in Washington."[2] This accounts, in part, for Hay's political influence and also for his success as a diplomat.

But if Hay was willing to associate with "all grades of people," he preferred of his friends "men who can read." Few men had so many notable friends and acquaintances. "If a man may be judged by the company he keeps," wrote Brooks Adams, "Mr. Hay must be conceded to have always stood high among his contemporaries, for . . . his friends have been more notable than those of any other man of his generation."[3]

Hay, himself a man of some literary accomplishments, particularly valued his acquaintances among accomplished authors. One of his earliest friends among literary men was Walt Whitman whom he first met while serving in the Lincoln administration. The two men never became close friends, but Hay helped out the poet financially on more than one occasion, and in later years as Whitman read Hay's depiction of the Lincoln years in the *Century* the poet longed to see his old friend.[4]

Hay's closest friends, however, were richer and more respectable than Whitman. Whitman knew Hay belonged to another world, in spite of their mutual fondness. A letter from Hay led the poet to remark, "it helps to show how we come on with the grandees—what we pass for in the upper circles. John don't [*sic*] call himself upper circle or anything of that sort, but he is in the elect pit—he belongs to the saved, to the respectables."[5]

Foremost among Hay's earliest literary acquaintances of a more respectable type was William Dean Howells, the author who came to embody the literary traditions and genteel standards of late nineteenth-century America. On his way to Washington in 1861 Hay stopped off in Columbus to congratulate Howells on his first volume, *Poems of Two Friends*, coauthored with John J. Piatt.[6] (Ironically, over forty years later Howells asked Hay to appoint the destitute Piatt to a minor consulate, a request Hay could not honor.) Their acquaintance developed over the following twenty years into a deep friendship marked by exchanges of photographs and presents, family visits to one another's homes, club gatherings, and dinners. "We think of you and talk of you often," Howells wrote to Hay in 1877, "and we congratulate ourselves that in going to Belmont, we shall be two miles nearer Cleveland." Their friendship developed to a point that, during the summer of 1882, the two families vacationed together in Florence, Italy. "Your letter had a powerful effect on Mrs. Hay and me," Hay wrote in answer to Howells' suggestion of the trip. "Our minds were in solution and your letter precipitated them in an eye-twinkle . . . we shall go to Florence. What larks!"[7] This sojourn, and their subsequent contacts over the next several months, helped cement their already close ties.

Hay also enjoyed a remarkable friendship of thirty-eight years with Mark Twain, a relationship that Hay's biographers scarcely mention.[8] The two men met in 1867 and were close friends by the 1870's. Twain recalled his lonely years in Buffalo at this time, a loneliness relieved only by his friendship with David Gray, the editor of the *Buffalo Courier*. Hay had apparently introduced Gray (whom Hay called "the loveliest of his sex") to Twain. Indeed, Twain once attempted to lure Hay to Buffalo, probably with an offer to secure for him a part interest in the *Buffalo Express*, but Hay, after some hesitation, declined. By 1874 they had become good friends, Twain writing, "if I could get John Hay . . . in our neighborhood, I would actually have nothing more to desire in the world."[9]

The Howells-Twain-Hay triumvirate gained symbolic unity when, in 1880, Twain suggested to Howells that they form "The Modest Club" with modesty being the sole qualification for membership. Although Twain mockingly professed that he was the only person qualified to belong, further reflection led him to believe that Howells, Hay, and perhaps a few others might qualify. "I have long felt that there ought to be an organized gang *of our kind*," he wrote.

Howells passed Twain's suggestion along to Hay, who replied, "his idea is as judicious as it is daring. A club which would hold him and you and me, and then reach out for H. [Higginson?] etc.,—and still keep modest—staggers and fatigues the faculty of wonder. I wish he and you would come down here and hold the first meeting of three at my house."[10]

Over the years Hay came to know well virtually all of the nation's leading literary figures and a score or more of lesser lights, and, almost without exception, the friendship was reciprocated.[11] In part, Hay could sustain such a remarkable number of friendships among the cultural elite because of his own carefully cultivated gentility. The testimony of Hay's contemporaries was nearly unanimous on this point—Hay, like his fictional creation Arthur Farnham, the hero of his only novel *The Bread-winners*, represented, as one reporter wrote, "the type and embodiment of that perfection of manners which the American gentleman can show better than the cultivated man of any other nationality."[12] He was, according to his acquaintances, "refined," "cultivated," "well-bred," and "well-mannered." His famous Washington residence, designed by the eminent H. H. Richardson, was exquisitely furnished and served as something of a cultural center in the 1890's.

As a gentleman, and something of a snob as well, Hay disliked philistines, although he thought it was as necessary for political reasons to maintain good relations with them as with the literary lions of the age. But privately he found the "museum of a big house" owned by one of Whitelaw Reid's in-laws "insolent and haughty" and was appalled to learn that the family sometimes dined off jade. Similarly, on his trips to Europe he came to object to the "great change in the appearance of people you meet in first-class conveyances. Formerly," he continued, "everyone you met in a first-class carriage was a person of some distinction. Now they are not even clean."[13]

Perhaps Hay's greatest asset was his proficiency as a conversationalist, a judgment of him shared unanimously by his contemporaries. Elihu Root described him elegantly as "the most delightful of companions" in whom one often found the "expression of a thought that in substance and perfection of form left in the mind the sense of having seen a perfectly cut precious stone." And James Ford Rhodes, a good friend of Hay, chose to devote five pages in his history of the McKinley and Roosevelt administrations to Hay's conversational ability. When Hay died, Rhodes wrote to Mrs. Hay that he doubted "whether there has ever been any better talker in the country" than her late husband. Hay himself was well aware of this talent. When his oldest brother Leonard died in 1904, Hay wrote to the president that Leonard had superior abilities in every way but one—"the gift of expression."[14]

Hay's gentility included wide knowledge of contemporary literature, a factor that helps explain his acceptance by literary men. "He was apt to have at hand some high class French novel or Memoirs," Rhodes recalled. ". . . He had at his tongue's end what we used to call belles-lettres and his conversation thereon was a profit and delight." Hay's upbringing and education contributed to this proficiency. After exhausting Illinois' limited educational resources (by the time he was twelve he had read six books of Vergil in the original Latin), Hay traveled to Brown University where he received a classical education. Professor James B. Angell later recalled that Hay was his best translator ever.[15]

It was during his senior year at Brown that Hay began to associate with literary people, gathering at the home of the strange and mystical Sarah Helen Whitman. Mrs. Whitman, who at one time had been Edgar Allen Poe's fiancée, made her home a salon where young poets gathered to discuss literature, submit their compositions for Mrs. Whitman's critical eye, and quite possibly to smoke a bit of hashish. Hay considered these meetings the most rewarding times of his Providence sojourn and regretted that he came into this circle so late in his college career. So meaningful were his ecstatic experiences at the Whitman salon that Hay deeply resented the necessity of returning to the uncultured West after his graduation. Indeed, to be away from poets and culture drove Hay to despair, and he composed poems debating the advantages of life over death, concluding, in effect, that God was dead and death preferable to life.[16]

Hay felt that his intellect was "losing its edge" in the "well nigh uninterrupted waste of spiritual desolation" that was the West. Sinking into the "slough of barbarism" he felt he could never again be a poet and thought it unlikely he would ever become intimate with literary men and women.[17]

Yet, in spite of these gloomy predictions, Hay achieved fame both as a poet and a writer of prose. In 1871, *The Pike County Ballads* and *Castilian Days* (an account of his sojourn in Spain) thrust Hay into the top ranks of American literature, giving him a life-long reputation and the publicity he needed to enter the company of literary men. It was not until Hay had demonstrated his abilities as an author that his friendship with Howells blossomed. As assistant editor, and then editor, of the *Atlantic Monthly,* Howells read *Castilian Days* in manuscript. He found the book charming and accorded it extraordinary public adulation. "This is high praise for a book on Spain," Howells admitted, concluding his review. "Mr. Hay's volume merits greater."[18] Thereafter Howells constantly urged Hay to submit material for the *Atlantic,* read portions of *The Bread-winners* in manuscript, and urged Thomas Bailey Aldrich, his successor at the *Atlantic,* to accept it for publication. (Aldrich agreed, but he insisted that the author's name be revealed. This Hay was unwilling to do, and so he gave the novel to the *Century.)*

Hay's fame as a literary man was also primarily responsible for his friendship with Mark Twain. Twain wrote to congratulate Hay on his ballads, written in the Mississippi River dialect that Twain later made famous.[19] After the publication of the ballads, Hay never again demonstrated much creativity as an artist (unless his biography of Lincoln can be so considered); yet his literary reputation remained so high that in 1904 he was selected as one of seven charter members of the American Academy of Arts

and Letters. He was chosen over such truly outstanding
authors as Henry James and Henry Adams, both of whom
Hay arranged to have selected on a subsequent ballot.
Hay's selection before these men was unwarranted, egre-
giously unfair to them, and, as George Monteiro states,
"suggests volumes about the nature of the American cultural establishment in 1904."[20] But it also demonstrates the
solidity of Hay's literary reputation and his acceptance by
the cultural leaders of the time.

In addition to his literary acumen, Hay had a remarkable ability to inspire trust and confidence in his actions.
"John is not treacherous: not a drop in his blood," Walt
Whitman stated; "on the contrary he is punctiliously loyal:
I have every right to call him my friend: not deep, not
enthusiastic, but . . . cordial, cheery, hospitable, unequivo-
cal." Alvey A. Adee, Hay's long-time friend, confessed that
he "unbottle[d]" himself to Hay in the 1870's, revealing
his innermost feelings. But Hay sometimes inspired simila
devotion among men he scarcely knew. The reporter Isaac
Marcosson, for example, met Hay only once; yet as late
as 1959 he described Hay as the greatest man he had ever
met—"he could make an obscure person immediately feel
at home in his presence," Marcosson explained.[21]

Hay used this ability to great advantage in his relations
with Howells and Twain and impressed both men with
his genuine interest in their work. He compared Howells
with Henry James and praised virtually everything he
wrote, reserving his greatest adulation for *The Rise of Silas
Lapham*. "It is awfully good," Hay wrote. "I am only
seized with a terror as to how you are going to keep it
up?" Even the one work about which Hay expressed reservations—Howells' adaptation of the Spanish play *Yorick's
Love*—received high praise. It was, Hay felt, too concen-
trated and intense. Yet the play was "magnificent," he
concluded, and Howells' part of the work was "faultless."[22]

In a similar way, Hay professed to believe that all of
Twain's works were marvelous. The "Old Times" papers,
for example, were "perfect—no more nor less. I don't see
how you do it." Twain appreciated Hay's ingratiating

words. "Now isn't that outspoken & hearty, & and just like that splendid John Hay?" he wrote Howells, copying Hay's letter in its entirety. Hay's willingness in his early years to shock the genteel with unorthodox and slightly risqué language also commended him to Twain. Mrs. Hay, who generally kept her husband in line, thoroughly disapproved of his association with the irreverent Twain. One Sunday morning in 1881, Twain recalled, he and Hay

had been chatting and laughing and carrying on almost like our earlier selves in '67, when the door opened and Mrs. Hay, gravely clad, gloved, bonneted, and just from church, and fragrant with the odors of Presbyterian sanctity, stood in it. We rose to our feet at once, of course—rose through a swiftly falling temperature—a temperature which at the beginning was soft and summer-like, but which was turning our breath and all other damp things to frost crystals by the time we were erect—but we got no opportunity to say the pretty and polite thing and offer the homage due; the comely young matron forestalled us. She came forward, smileless, with disapproval written all over her face, said most coldly, "Good Morning, Mr. Clemens," and passed on and out.

For once both Hay and Twain were speechless. "Hay, grown gray in a single night, so to speak, limped feebly at my side, making no moan, saying no word," Twain wrote. Hay finally said, "she is very strict about Sunday," and Twain left.[23]

Even the doughty Mrs. Hay could not dampen her husband's appreciation for Twain's wit, however. This was evident in Hay's participation in the events surrounding the surreptitious publication of Twain's *Fireside Conversation in the Time of Queen Elizabeth*, a title later shortened to *1601*. Twain wrote the skit, he claimed (untruthfully), "for the benefit of a magazine editor who had regretted that modern literature had no Rabelais."[24] It was a ribald account of Elizabethan England which took place, according to Twain, "in Queen Elizabeth's closet in that year, between the Queen and Shakespeare, Ben Jonson, Francis Bacon, Beaumont, Sir Walter Raleigh, the Duchess of Bilgewater, and one or two others. . . . if there is a decent or delicate word findable in it, it is because I overlooked it."[25] Twain sent the piece to Howells in the fall of 1879 and, possibly at his request, sent another copy to Hay sometime later. Hay expressed his gratitude for "that most exquisite bit of English morality." When Hay returned the manuscript to Twain in August, 1880, he included the proof sheets of a printed version. "Here is the Meisterstück," he wrote. "It got into such appreciative hands among the Vampire Club [in Cleveland] that it was read in to rags . . . and then the noble-minded Vampires . . . did have it copied, as you see." What Hay did not report, though Twain must have suspected it, was that he, not "the noble-minded Vampires," was responsible for the publication of *1601*.[26]

Howells and Twain felt that Hay was interested in their work (as indeed he was), but no one believed more deeply in Hay's genuine concern than another prominent literary figure, Bret Harte, who developed, according to his biographer, "a life-long affection, and the highest admiration" for Hay. As he did with Howells and Twain, Hay wrote glowing reviews of Harte's literary endeavors which convinced the author that Hay admired his work. Even Hay's critical comments were tempered in such a way that one might almost wish, as Hay once wrote of Harte's critical abilities, to be the subject of such criticism.[27]

Hay and Harte were well acquainted by 1871 and maintained an informal and jocular correspondence during the 1870's. But the contacts which most endeared Hay to Harte (but not Harte to Hay) developed in connection with diplomacy. In 1878, Harte, in desperate financial straits, had accepted a position as American consul at Crefeld in Rhenish Prussia. He soon found Crefeld's damp climate disagreeable; but of greater importance he concluded that the obscurity and cultural vacuity of Crefeld presented a "ridiculous contrast and anomaly . . . to what is my real standing socially and intellectually in Germany," whereupon he wrote Hay (who had recently become an assistant secretary of state) a petulant and lengthy epistle requesting a transfer. Harte's letter chanced to reach Hay on a particularly bad day. Hay wrote of it to his wife complaining that "the clamorous greedy host" of office seekers had made him "disgusted with human nature." "I have been working a month to get a nice place for Bret Harte," he continued, "& yesterday a letter came from him showing that his ideas were so lofty that nothing I could do would suit him." Nevertheless, Hay replied to Harte with "a long letter full of kindness," and two weeks later Harte received a promotion to Glasgow, where in subsequent years Hay's occasional letters were a great comfort to the lonely author whose literary reputation was declining and who increasingly envied the success and happy home life Hay enjoyed.[28]

With the change of administrations in 1881, Harte, fearing for his position, panicked. But Hay sent him another encouraging and ingratiating note:

I want before my sands run out to say "How?" to you once more, and to assure you of my eternal love and esteem. .... I do not know what Heaven meant by creating so few men like King and you. The scarcity of you is an injury not only to us, but to yourselves. There are not enough of you to go round, and the world pulls and hauls at you till you are completely spoiled.

Such times as I have seen since the 4th of March. You would have got lots of fun out of it. I, only vexation of spirit. They have even asked for Glasgow—never more than once in my presence.

Well, good bye, and good health and good spirits and everything good be yours.

No wonder Harte wrote to his wife that he could not send her Hay's letter. He kept it, he stated, "for reading when I am very low in spirits, and am glad to think there are some two or three men in America who are loyal to me."[29] Although Hay was no longer in the State Department, he played a similar role when President Garfield died and again in 1884. However, Hay was unable to secure Harte's position when the Democrats took over in 1885; nor was he able to have Harte reinstated when the Republicans resumed political control in 1889, although Hay, at Harte's almost pitiful requests, tried on both occasions. Indeed, in 1889 he approached his friend James G. Blaine, the new secretary of state, probably more than once. And although Blaine wanted to help Harte he felt constrained to consider the opinion of the Consular Bureau that the author was "the worst consul thus far recorded."[30]

In subsequent years the two men continued their correspondence and saw each other quite often during Hay's frequent journeys to England, where Harte had made his permanent home. Hay increasingly became an object for Harte's hero worship, a melancholy commentary on the decline of a once widely admired author. But the continued relationship is also striking evidence of Hay's ability to attract and maintain friendships.[31]

Hay's web of friendships probably sustained its greatest strain when Hay became secretary of state and presided over and defended the nation's acquisition of the Philippine Islands. Many of Hay's acquaintances, especially literary men, found themselves in opposition, some in bitter opposition, to American imperialism. Some anti-imperialists criticized Hay personally, of course, among them, William Croffut of the Washington, D.C. Anti-Imperialist League and the satirist, Finley Peter Dunne. (In 1905 Dunne declined an invitation to dine with Hay, reportedly because "it would narrow the field of his antipathies" should he meet Hay personally.)[32] What is more significant, however, was the almost total lack of criticism from such outspoken anti-imperialists as Richard Watson Gilder, Mark Twain, William Dean Howells, and Andrew Carnegie.

As editor of the *Century* Gilder had published Hay's novel *The Bread-winners,* the *History* of Lincoln, and Nicolay and Hay's *Abraham Lincoln: Complete Works.* Their friendship had survived a testy exchange in 1884 over Gilder's support for the Democratic presidential nominee Grover Cleveland, and Gilder appears to have welcomed Hay's diplomatic successes after 1897. Although he disliked American action in the Philippines, the editor could write Hay on his return to the capital after an illness in 1900, "Welcome back! The country—yes, the world, missed you." Indeed, by 1904 Gilder was somewhat reconciled to the American presence in the Philippines. "I shall hope that the little Brown men will ultimately be glad that they have come under the influence of our constitution,"[33] he wrote.

Gilder's direct criticism of Hay was blunted partly because the editor enjoyed having a personal friend at the head of the State Department and partly because he admired aspects of Hay's policies not immediately connected with the Philippines. He fully approved Hay's efforts to further a rapprochement with England, for example. He praised Hay's China policy. And he approved of Hay's efforts to acquire the diplomatic rights to build an isthmian canal, writing to Hay when the first Hay-Pauncefote Treaty was signed, "Added to your flag on the Chinese Wall is now your flag on a neutral canal. . . . May nothing prevent the consummation of this last." But the Senate refused to approve the treaty, which led Gilder to write to Hay, "I am beginning to think that the American Constitution would be greatly improved if the Senate were blotted out of our system completely."[34] Hay shared the editor's sympathies.

Hay's relationship with Gilder illustrates his ability to remain on good terms with someone of a slightly different philosophical persuasion. His relationships with Howells and Twain were more complex and significant, however, both because Hay was much closer to them and because they were more bitter than Gilder in their criticism of American imperialism.

Twain's proposal in 1880 for "The Modest Club" actually symbolized the high point of the three-sided relationship. Thereafter, Hay faded almost imperceptibly, a decline measured more by negative than by positive evidence. After 1883, for example, there is not a single reference to Hay in the extensive Twain-Howells letters, although Hay continued his contacts with both men. And after 1890 the volume of correspondence between Hay and Howells dropped significantly. One letter, which Hay wrote in 1897 about his possible appointment as ambassador to England, was more formal and considerably less frank than his letters of previous years. The letter's conclusion suggested that their relationship had cooled somewhat. "No man's praise is more precious to me than yours," Hay wrote. "I hope, if I do go abroad for awhile, I may have a little of your company over there which I have so vainly sought and desired in these latter years on this side."[35]

Perhaps Howells' growing concern for the less fortunate brought about these slight suggestions of a change in their relationship. In 1883 Howells did not praise Hay's reactionary novel *The Bread-winners* hypocritically. But for some time before its appearance his thought had been evolving away from a staunch defense of the established order while Hay's thought had developed in precisely the opposite direction. "I grudge, a little, the time you made me spend on Bellamy's story," Hay wrote in 1884, suggesting for the first time a conscious difference in their social philosophies. "I think you were overgenerous. No case of lunney [*sic*] diagnosed in the first 3/4 of that book was ever so cured,"[36] he contended.

Differences also developed between Hay and Twain. Politically they had different perspectives. Twain's duties as a Washington reporter in the 1860's had soured him on politicians, particularly congressmen, whom he termed the only "distinctly native American criminal class," whereas Hay early became a staunch Republican partisan. In 1884, Twain chose the mugwump path and voted for Grover Cleveland. Hay, feeling that the Republican party was infinitely more virtuous despite its faults, could not understand the logic of the mugwumps. "I suppose I shall never forgive you for voting for Cleveland," Hay wrote to Twain while thanking him for sending a copy of *Huckleberry Finn*.[37]

At first Twain approved Hay's political involvement, feeling that "the presence of such a man in politics is like a vase of attar of roses in a glue-factory—it can't extinguish the stink, but it modifies it." Nevertheless, he feared that politics would inevitably corrupt even the best men. Perhaps the appearance of *The Bread-winners* or Hay's bitter attacks on the mugwumps strengthened Twain's fears. In any event, he came to feel that politics had trapped

Hay. When he urged his friend Joe Twichell to abandon party politics in 1904, he used Hay to illustrate his point:

I am sorry for John Hay; sorry and ashamed. And yet I know he couldn't help it. He wears the collar, and he had to pay the penalty. Certainly he had no more desire to stand up before such a mob of confiding human incapables and debauch them than you had. Certainly he took no more real pleasure in distorting history, concealing facts, propagating immoralities, and appealing to the sordid side of human nature than you did; but he was his party's property, and he had to climb away down and do it.

It is interesting, wonderfully interesting—the miracles which party-politics can do with a man's mental and moral make-up.[38]

Twain's only misevaluation was that Hay, in fact, believed most of what he said in his partisan speeches.

In addition to their differing views on domestic social and political philosophy, Howells and Twain deeply opposed Hay's foreign policy. Like most Americans, they welcomed the Spanish-American War as a humane effort, a war of liberation. But both men soon found themselves estranged from the administration, particularly with regard to American efforts to pacify the Philippine Islands. Twain, for example, published virtually everything he wrote that attacked the American policy there, despite advice from Twichell that such attacks might damage his book sales. The following inscription he wrote in a book for a friend illustrates the bitterness he felt:

I have rearranged the "Battle Hymn of the Republic" this afternoon and brought it down to date—sample stanza:

I have read his bandit gospel writ in burnished rows of steel,
As ye deal with my pretensions, so with you my wrath shall deal,
Let the faithless sons of freedom, crush the patriot with his heel
                    Lo, Greed is marching on.

Hay's association with the imperialists, as well as his staunch defense of capitalism and the status quo, may help answer the question he posed to Howells in 1902, "Why do I never see you in recent years?"[39]

It is therefore striking that in all the letters between

Howells and Twain during the time Hay was involved with American imperial policy, the secretary of state was never personally criticized, although the policy which he directed was thoroughly dissected. It may be, as one scholar states, that Twain had "a blinding fondness for Hay," which, if true, is further evidence of Hay's ability to maintain friendship. Indeed, in February, 1900, Twain wrote to Hay that he was watching Hay's "onward & upward career with the interest & pride of one with a personal stake in it, & when you say you value my friendship you give me a pleasure which is complete, & which you could add nothing to." Again, shortly before Hay's death, Twain wrote him a loving, anonymous letter indicating that he still felt fondly toward the secretary of state.[40] In spite of the most fundamental disagreements, Hay had managed to retain the respect of one of the most outspoken anti-imperialists. "I am deeply grieved," Twain wrote when Hay died, "& I mourn with the nation this loss which is irreparable. My friendship with Mr. Hay & my admiration of him endured 38 years without impairment." A few weeks later Twain wrote a final tribute to Hay, fiercely defending Hay's claim that he had written *The Pike County Ballads* before Harte's similar poetry appeared.[41]

Howells, perhaps, had more selfish reasons for restraint. Like Gilder, Howells was glad to have a friend in the State Department, and on at least three occasions he attempted to exploit this friendship, asking twice for consular positions for his brother and once for John J. Piatt. But his real reasons were deeper than that. Like Twain, Howells wrote a friendly article on Hay after his death, in which he noted the secretary's services as a statesman: "It was, at least, what we could so perfectly understand that, in any moment of hesitation concerning this or that fact of it, we could say to ourselves that it must be right because Hay did it."[42]

This was the most important of Hay's secrets: the ability to gain the confidence of his associates, even when they strongly disagreed with him. This quality, along with other genteel characteristics, including his knowledge of literary and cultural developments and his own literary reputation, gave Hay an extraordinary influence at all levels of society and proved to be a most valuable diplomatic tool.

Gilder, Howells, and Twain understood, for the most part, that Hay disagreed with them. There was little self-deception on their part. Andrew Carnegie, on the other hand, was considerably self-deceived.

When Hay died, Carnegie wrote sadly to Whitelaw Reid lamenting the passing "of our friend John Hay" who "was one of my inner circle." Carnegie was incorrect. Nowhere, however, is there a more striking tribute to Hay's abilities than in Carnegie's *Autobiography:*

> He [Hay] inspired men with absolute confidence in his sincerity, and his aspirations were always high. War he detested, and meant what he said when he pronounced it "the most ferocious and yet the most futile folly of man." . . .
>
> As a statesman he made his reputation in shorter time and with a surer touch than any one I know of. And it may be doubted if any public man ever had more deeply attached friends. One of his notes I have long kept. It would have been the most flattering of any to my literary vanity but for my knowledge of his most lovable nature and undue warmth for his friends. The world is poorer to me to-day as I write, since he has left it.

Carnegie's own lack of discernment, his uncritical desire to surround himself with men of taste, plus his natural propensity to assume that his friends agreed with him, account in part for his colossal misevaluation of Hay's sentiments, particularly with respect to America's new empire. But Hay's own abilities should not be overlooked. Hay was able to cast an extraordinary spell over the great industrialist. If Carnegie wished to assume that Hay was of his inner circle, that they agreed on critical issues of war and peace, Hay gave him little cause to believe otherwise.[43]

The two men met each other in 1884. In 1887, Carnegie invited Hay (and a host of others) to visit him in Scotland where Carnegie was honeymooning, and by 1898 they were ell acquainted, though not intimate friends. Their con-s were cordial, but sporadic, and did not lead to extended correspondence. With the Spanish-American War, however, their correspondence increased in volume and seriousness. Carnegie claimed that Hay secretly agreed with his anti-imperialist ideals, an assertion resting on one ambiguous letter which Hay wrote to the philanthropist. "I have read with keenest interest your article in the *North American*," wrote Hay in reference to Carnegie's anti-imperialist article, "Distant Possessions—The Parting of the Ways." "I am not allowed to say in my present fix, how much I agree with you. The only question in my mind is how far it is now *possible* to withdraw from the Philippines. I am rather thankful it is not given to me to solve that momentous question."[44]

As American policy toward the Philippines unfolded Carnegie became more and more agitated. He wrote several letters to Hay detailing his opposition to a number of administration policies affecting the islands and threatened that political doom would issue from various quarters if changes were not made. In these letters, however, Carnegie blamed the McKinley administration in general. He directed his wrath particularly at the president, attacking Hay only inferentially and maintaining friendly relations and confidence in him. At the top of his first angry letter, for example, he penned a note, "Strictly confidential[;] I would write this to no one else but you."[45] Carnegie's confidence in Hay contrasted sharply with his bitter dislike of Whitelaw Reid, one of the peace commissioners. Declining an invitation to attend a reception honoring the first anniversary of the "*War* Treaty," as he referred to the Treaty of Paris, Carnegie wrote, "it is a matter of congratulations, however, that you seem to have about finished your work of civilizing the Fillipinos [*sic*]. It is thought that about 8000 of them have been completely civilized and sent to heaven. I hope you like it."[46] The fact that Reid and Hay were in total agreement on this issue distinguishes Hay's influence over Carnegie.

Privately, Hay had no sympathy for Carnegie and resented his intruding letters. Writing to William M. Osborne, Hay concluded that the recent election of 18 demonstrated that "the American people are hard to fool," although "a good many people are trying just now, Andrew Carnegie and Erving Winslow, and some of your other Boston cranks in the foreground." To Reid, Hay was more specific, observing that

Andrew Carnegie really seems off his head. He writes me frantic letters. . . . He threatens the President, not only with the vengeance of the voters, but with practical punishment at the hands of the mob. He says henceforth the entire labor vote of America will be cast against us, and that he will see that it is done. He says the Administration will fall in irretrievable ruin the moment it shoots down one insurgent Filipino.[47]

Hay nevertheless succeeded in maintaining a good relationship with Carnegie, often by ignoring his charges. That Carnegie continued to trust and admire Hay is evident from his selection of Hay to be chairman of the board of trustees of the Carnegie Institution in Washington in 1902. Carnegie subsequently acknowledged, "much were we indebted to him for wise counsel." Hay's opinion of Carnegie remained contemptuous. In 1904 he contrasted the American artistocracy with its English counterpart, writing that "our Rockefellers and Carnegies . . . are deficient in cerebellum." Despite his private contempt, however, Hay not only retained Carnegie's friendship but through a combination of flattery, ambiguity, and tact, also held his confidence. In the spring of 1905 Carnegie provided funds for a new library at Brown University. At his suggestion, Brown officials named the new building the John Hay Library.[48]

With so many friends, Hay sometimes found himself performing a delicate balancing act in order to maintain good relations with all. A very few people questioned Hay's sincerity or noted a rather ugly deviousness that occasionally shone through. One Ethan Allen, for example, thought Hay's marriage to a weathy industrial heiress was "all there is to him." Hay was, he wrote, "as selfish as a dog over a bone, and . . . as mean a puppy as Whitelaw Reid."[49]

Although Allen equated Hay and Reid, it was with Reid that Hay encountered the most difficulty maintaining the balance. Prior to the 1880's there was little if any tension between the two men who had known each other since Civil War days. Indeed, they had worked closely together on the *New York Tribune* from 1870 until shortly after Hay's marriage in 1874. Their correspondence in the last half of the decade indicates that a close friendship existed. In 1880 Reid and Hay exchanged numerous confidential letters about politics, and in 1881 Hay was the first, outside of the immediate families, to learn of Reid's engagement to Elizabeth Mills.[50] During Reid's extended honeymoon, Hay obliged Reid by taking over as interim editor of the *Tribune.*

Hay's editorship generally pleased Reid, particularly Hay's handling of the complicated political situation involving Roscoe Conkling and President Garfield.[51] It was during these months, however, that the first suggestion of friction developed. At Twain's suggestion, Howells requested permission to review Twain's still unfinished novel, *The Prince and the Pauper.* Because Howells was not only editing Twain's work but also acting as his agent, the request was ethically questionable. Besides, Twain's relationship with Reid had been frigid ever since 1873 when the editor refused to provide favorable publicity for *The Gilded Age.*

Nevertheless, Hay agreed to Howells' proposition, thus satisfying Twain, but he explained his decision to Reid in terms designed to give the impression that he agreed, in general, with Reid's low opinion of Twain. Hay thought it would be best for the *Tribune* to carry the review, he explained, but in the future perhaps Reid could engage Bret Harte to review Twain's novels. "That," he wrote, "will be a masterpiece of the Skinner's art." Reid, however, answered rather testily that it was not "good journalism to let a warm personal friend & in some matters literary partner, write a critical review of him in a paper wh. has good reason to think little of his delicacy & highly of his greed. So if you haven't printed it yet, I wld. think of this point before doing so."[52]

Reid's letter placed Hay in an embarrassing situation.

Not only had he already commissioned Howells, but to disclose Reid's objection would doubtlessly have enraged Twain, possibly damaging his good relations with Hay. He decided to stick with his original decision, and, a few weeks later, the extraordinarily lengthy and favorable review appeared.

The affair had placed Hay in an extremely awkward position, yet in the end he managed to maintain good relations with both sides. Howells and Twain were clearly pleased; Reid, while certainly less satisfied with the outcome, did not pursue the matter. Perhaps Hay's suggestion that Harte review future works by Twain served to lessen Reid's complaint. It was a delicate balancing act, but one in which Hay, however brilliant his social abilities, ignored the ethical question raised by Reid. At times Hay seemed more preoccupied with balance than with principle.

In 1889 Hay again played the balancer. The new Harrison administration offered Reid the French mission instead of the mission to London that Reid wanted and Hay had hoped he would get. The president called in Hay and urged him to press Reid to accept what he had been offered. He explained that the *Tribune*'s editor could not be sent to London because of the sometimes anti-British attitude of his paper; either Prime Minister Salisbury would object, or, if he did not, the newspaper would be muzzled since it could not print anything unfavorable to England while its editor was the minister there. "I replied," Hay recorded, "Certainly. . . . Said Reid would not like it, but wd support the Admn with vigor."[53] He agreed to go to New York to try to bring Reid around, and his mission was a success.

Some time later Reid asked Hay to prepare a memorandum of his conversation with the president. Hay did not pass on the one he had prepared for his own files. Instead, he pictured himself as having contested the president's views "one by one, but without making any impression."

He asked me at once to go to New York and lay all these considerations before Mr. Reid. I told him I could not refuse such a request, but that I thought it would be useless; . . . that while he might think it worth his while to go to England I thought he would not care to go to France, but would prefer to stay in New York. . . . The President again asked me to put it, to Mr. Reid, in the light of a personal favor to himself.[54]

Hay thus managed to win the gratitude of President Harrison and at the same time to sustain his friendship with Reid, but the evidence strongly suggests that he had been less than candid in order to do so.

For the next several years Hay and Reid appear to have been on the best of terms, [55] but the infighting for positions that followed the election of William McKinley in 1896 strained Hay's ability to maintain a balance and brought his friendship with Reid almost to the breaking point.

As the Republican party's vice-presidential candidate in 1892 and as editor of the staunchly Republican *Tribune*, Reid had powerful credentials and hoped to secure a prominent position in the new administration, preferably as secretary of state or as ambassador to England. In view of Hay's past encouragements to Reid to seek public office and his occasional intimations that he would never seek an appointment, Reid expected Hay's aid in his quest. Indeed, Hay left the impression, which has become the standard interpretation, that he worked very hard for Reid. "I have done all I could for Whitelaw Reid," he wrote in February, 1897, "and have reason to think he has been offered the place [of ambassador to England] and declined it." To Reid, too, Hay always insisted that if the situation developed to a point where there was a choice between them, he would step aside. "I would not stand in your way," he assured the editor shortly after the election as well as on subsequent occasions.[56]

It appears, however, that Hay assisted the McKinley forces in dumping Reid, and his involvement may have been more malevolent. On December 10, Hay had a long and confidential conversation with Mark Hanna, after which Hay wrote a letter to Reid that was reminiscent of the memorandum he had sent to Reid in 1889. He noted that Ogden Mills, once one of the editor's closest friends, thought that Reid's true interests lay out of the public sphere. And Hanna, he reported, had raised some questions about Reid's health. Hay wrote, however, that he had replied that Reid was "The best man McK. could possibly select as Secretary of State and gave my reasons at length."[57]

Although Hay's letter thus hinted that Reid might be well advised to withdraw from contention, it also indicated that Hay had acted strongly as Reid's defender. Hay's telegram to McKinley two weeks later, therefore, comes as something of a shock:

How would it be to say that his selection for a place in the cabinet or a foreign embassy at his choice had been under consideration [,] that he and his friends had thought it would be imprudent for him to risk the confinement of official work until his health was more completely restored [,] that you then reluctantly gave up the idea of appointing him & recently wrote him a letter expressive of your regard and appreciation & your regret that for the present you were not to have the advantage of his cooperation [.] i [*sic*] think this might be better than printing the letter.

Hay also appears to have authored a press release announcing McKinley's "deep regret" that because of Reid's poor health he could not now offer him a position in the new administration.[58]

How the telegram and the press release came to be written is not clear, but Hay's conference with Hanna on December 10, in which Reid's health was discussed, suggests the following possibility. Early in December, McKinley decided that he did not want Reid to have a high-ranking appointment because of the factionalized state of Republican politics in New York. This decision was relayed through Hanna to Hay, who then suggested (or agreed) that McKinley might reject Reid, whose health had indeed been fragile in 1895. McKinley then asked Hay to comment on his intention to release to the press a letter to Reid outlining his decision. Hay urged McKinley to make public only a summary of his letter to Reid and sent a suggested press release along these lines. In any event, Hay's action did not conform with his pledges to Reid; the press release contained information Hay knew to be false.

McKinley decided to defer a final decision on Reid.
(Indeed, on the same day Hay telegraphed him, McKinley
sent the editor a friendly, handwritten letter in which he
stated that few matters had yet been concluded.) But, as
the president-elect's tentative decision to omit Reid hardened, Hay began to apply increasing pressure on Reid
to withdraw voluntarily, and, at the same time, he thrust
his own name to the fore. On January 22, Hay stressed
the complicated political situation in New York and urged
sympathy for a harrassed McKinley. "Do not think too
much of the pettiness of life and the meannesses—volun-
tary or necessary—of politicans,"[59]he concluded.

In a number of letters to Reid, Hay now hinted that
he might, in contrast to his earlier assurances, accept a
position even if Reid were left out. Still, he continued to
downgrade his own ambitions, leaving an impression of
almost total disinterest and passivity and insisting to Reid
that he had "made no push except for you." In reality,
however, Hay was carefully looking after his own interests.
The same day he wrote to Reid, he persuaded Ogden Mills
to "put the matter in a reasonable light before Reid" so
that he could cause "no further trouble," and he informed
the president-elect that Mills had, incidentally, "expressed
himself spontaneously, as strongly in favor of my appointment." When Reid assured Hay "in the strongest and most
unreserved way" that he preferred Hay's appointment to
that of his political enemies in New York, Hay immediately informed McKinley of Reid's endorsement, although
he claimed he did not want anything himself "which can
cause you a moment's trouble."[60]

Reid, however, had not given up. He refused to acquiesce to Hay's suggestion, conveyed by Ogden Mills, that
he agree in advance to decline certain high positions. It
was for McKinley, Reid thought, to explain publicly why
the president-elect did not want him. The editor was not,
he fumed to Hay, "contented."[61]

Reid's attitude caused McKinley to turn once again to
Hay for tactical advice. Hay drafted a letter for McKinley
to send to Reid explaining that because of Reid's fragile

health, the president-elect thought it unwise to endanger his life with a high ranking position. In the meantime, however, Reid wrote that Senator Stephen B. Elkins thought that Reid's appointment would be politically beneficial. "Elkins' messages have waked him up again and encouraged him to believe he may yet 'Make' the Cabinet," Hay wrote contemptuously to McKinley. Hay, disgusted with Reid's persistence, then drafted a second letter for McKinley to consider in which Reid was offered the English embassy. "I have ceased thinking about Reid," Hay wrote; "he thinks enough about himself for two."[62]

Hay's second draft finally forced McKinley to act. He composed a letter to Reid along the lines of Hay's first draft. He could not appoint the editor, McKinley explained, because of Reid's health. In the final paragraph were the words Hay wanted to see. "And, having been assured that it will meet with your approval, I have in mind the appointment of Col. John Hay, of Washington, for Minister to England."[63]

McKinley then sent this draft to Hay, with a pencilled inquiry on the back:

Dear Mr. Hay
    Will this do? Are you sure it will give no offense? Wire.

Hay wired his concurrence. Then, after making a copy of McKinley's draft, he returned the original along with a letter further praising McKinley's work. "I cannot imagine any man with human blood in his veins, not being pleased and touched by it," he stated. Of the mention of his own name, Hay professed to be speechless. It came upon him, he recalled, "with the force of a great surprise." The next day Hay telegraphed Reid that Elkins' theory was impractical, and that he would soon receive a letter. "I hope you may see your way to answer it cordially," he wrote. Less than a week later, Hay penned his letter to Samuel Mather suggesting that he had done all he could for Reid, that Reid had probably been offered England only to decline it, and that he had not bothered McKinley in his own behalf.[64]

John Hay took pride in his ability to make and keep friends. Using a combination of genuine friendship, favors, and flattery, he had amassed a huge array of admirers and had generally succeeded in maintaining good relationships with almost all of them. He may not have been prepared therefore to receive a bitter letter from Reid in March that attacked McKinley and all the circumstances surrounding the editor's rejection. "The President's letter is . . . everything...delightful, excepting sincere," Reid wrote, correctly summarizing the tone of McKinley's letter, which was essentially Hay's work. Without question, this letter was the closest thing to a personal attack Hay ever received from a long-time associate and friend. "Of course my absence may have been to my disadvantage . . . ," Reid continued, "especially when there are not places enough to go around, when one's friends all want things for themselves, and when one's enemies have nothing but revenge on the absent to console themselves." Reid then zeroed in on the weakest part of McKinley's letter, and Hay's defense of McKinley's action, the question of his health. Reid knew full well that his health was only an excuse. His asthma hardly compared with Hay's multiple diseases, and he took full advantage of the inconsistency. "Still, it amuses me to think what might have been in these piping days of civil service reform, the results of a competitive examination on health for the public service. How would the examiners have rated Bright's disease, for instance, as against a former Bronchitis and Asthma; or Nervous Prostration, or Valvular Disease of the heart?—to refer only to the things you tell me of?" Recalling Hay's earlier letter, Reid took another swipe at his friend. "Like you, I hate to lose a friend—above all to lose him because I trusted him and found it a mistake."[65]

Reid had called Hay's hand, and Hay's felicity of style was not enough, in this instance, to convince Reid of his loyalty. The coolness in their relationship dates from the announcement of Hay as ambassador to England and not, as Tyler Dennett thought, from Reid's actions during Queen Victoria's Diamond Jubilee in the summer of 1897.[66]

The Jubilee celebration was, however, one of several additional causes for strain in the relationship between the two men. In an apparent effort to assuage Reid, McKinley appointed him to represent the United States at the Jubilee. Reid's ostentatious entertaining disturbed the dignified ambassador, who wondered if this experience might "not whet his appetite for further grandness."[67] When, the following year, Hay became secretary of state, his fears were fulfilled. "Reid's famished hunger for office is perfectly insane," he wrote to his wife. To Henry White he related that Reid "begged for a place on the peace commission. When Day's appt. was announced [as head of the peace commission to conclude the Spanish-American War], he asked for Day's place [as secretary of state]. When my appt. was announced he begged for London with tears in his eyes."[68]

McKinley did select Reid to be on the peace commission, but, when he returned from Paris, Reid learned that Joseph Choate had the inside track as Hay's replacement in London. He stormed over to see Hay, who "had to bear the brunt of Whitelaw's voracity for plunder at a moment when he was barely able to walk after a sharp attack of illness." It is unlikely that the state of Hay's health overly disturbed Reid. The interview left Reid unsatisfed, and he wrote Hay a long letter indicating that his bitterness had not diminished.[69]

A few years later Reid vied to represent the United States at the coronation of King Edward VII of England. Hay found Reid's attitude "most humiliating," but President Roosevelt saw fit to appoint him in spite of Hay's objections. Hay feared that Reid would, as he had at the Jubilee, hobnob ostentatiously with royalty. His fears proved true, for in February Henry White was "engaged in the rather ungracious task of declining the large house which the King intended and particularly wished to place at the disposal of the Special Embassy." Instead, Reid desired to lease Lord Tweedmouth's house in Park Lane for £4,000 for six weeks, including servants. Choate and White had to make special efforts to smooth over this potential sore spot with British officialdom, including the king.[70]

Reid sailed in June, received an honorary degree from Cambridge on June 10, and established himself in Lord Tweedmouth's mansion. Due to the sudden serious illness of King Edward, however, the coronation was postponed, and Reid had to depart before the final ceremonies. But, commenting on the "maimed rites" in London, Hay congratulated Reid on his embassy, which "had attracted more notice—altogether favorable—than that of any other Power. . . . The speech you made at Liverpool, and your academic honors at Cambridge were well worth crossing the Atlantic for." His truthful assessment of the king's illness, the deplorable postponement, and the Reid embassy was reserved for Henry Adams:

I heard ill stories of you. I am credibly informed that you shouted with ghoulish glee when you heard that the beloved and revered of the British Dominion beyond the Sea King was suffering from mulligrub, and furthermore that you pranced like a goat at the thought that W. R. one of the best men of his time, D.O. Volente, could not ride in the procession, nor expose the outline of his tibia to the allerhöchst gaze: that you even made a mock of *my* sufferings in sympathy with those Royal and Excellential afflictions. I am afraid you are living too long in Paris.[71]

Reid's appointment, at long last, as ambassador to the Court of St. James in 1905 must have horrified Hay. But his letter to Reid on that occasion was typical of the ingratiating rhetoric he had developed over the decades and is a perfect example of Hay's modes of interacting on the interpersonal level:

I have refrained from saying anything to you about a matter which, as you know, is very near to my heart, wishing to leave the President the pleasure of talking to you first, but I cannot help telling you with what long looked for delight I shall countersign your commission as Ambassador to England. When that is done I shall feel like intoning "my nunc dimittis." It will be the crowning act of a friendship and close association of forty years.[72]

Perhaps it is to Hay's credit that he succeeded in keeping

open the lines of communication with Reid during the difficult years after 1896. A less patient man would have quickly alienated the editor of the powerful *Tribune*, something the administration could not afford. Perhaps it is to McKinley's credit that he selected Hay to keep Reid in line. Hay did not break openly with Reid, although his charms were much less successful with the stubborn editor than with other men. Furthermore, Hay's evaluation of Reid's incessant desire for self-glorification and high office was largely correct. Reid often *did* think "enough about himself for two." His response after Hay received the ambassadorship to England, for example, must be judged petulant at best, especially in light of his repeated entreaties to Hay not to sacrifice his own interests for those of Reid—"don't drop a bone for a shadow,"[73] as he once expressed it.

Nevertheless, Hay was not candid with Reid. In order to sustain his web of personal relationships, Hay sometimes found it necessary to go back on promises and in general to succumb to the devious behavior so often associated with lower level politicians. It was the kind of behavior that made Mark Twain feel "sorry for John Hay; sorry and ashamed."

When Hay died shortly after Reid went to London as ambassador, Henry Watterson, then in London, hurried to see his old friend the ambassador and found him away at a social affair. "The ambassador should not forget the claims and obligations of friendship—and [a] very old and loyal friendship,"[74] Watterson lectured Reid. The ambassador, however, felt less need than Watterson to weep.

II

The Development of
Hay's Social and
Political Thought

John Hay was sixty years old when he returned from
London in 1898 to become secretary of state. Like all
statesmen, he assumed his high office with preconceptions
and opinions that colored his international outlook. But
unlike many secretaries of state in the nineteenth century,
Hay had had some diplomatic experience prior to his
appointment. Immediately after the Civil War he served
as secretary in three American legations in Europe and later
(1879–81) spent seventeen months as assistant secretary of
state. In addition to official positions, Hay wrote editorials
and articles on foreign policy for the *New York Tribune*
in the 1870's, some of his background information coming
from his good friend Alvey A. Adee who was then a minor
American official in Europe and who would later serve as
Hay's assistant in the State Department. In the 1880's and
1890's, the Hays spent considerable time abroad and came
to know many prominent persons in European countries,
particularly in England. Finally, immediately prior to his
elevation as secretary of state, Hay had served as an effective ambassador to Great Britain.

Nevertheless, Hay was not a professional diplomat,
and the preconceptions he brought to the Department of
State were the result primarily (thought not exclusively)
of domestic developments. His ideas about society and the
world owe their derivation more to his lifestyle as a gentleman of considerable wealth than, for example, to his service
as secretary in the Madrid legation. Among these preconceptions was a staunch republicanism, a faith which began

30

to develop shortly after Hay assumed his first public position as assistant private secretary to President Abraham Lincoln, and which became rigid after 1877.

For most of his adult life Hay was a politically active man. The fact that he was also a poet and later a cultivated gentleman has contributed to the impression that Hay regarded politics as little more than a necessary sideline. He had, it is said, "an ingrained hatred of sham and political bunkum" and could not "bring himself to fight fire with fire, as Hanna did, buying votes where necessary, in the interests of better government." When Hay's biographer, Tyler Dennett, ran across an especially partisan assault on the Democrats, he found it "a little difficult to imagine" that Hay had actually written the speech.[1] But in fact, Hay came to equate politics and his own societal values.

When Hay returned to Illinois after graduation from Brown University in 1858, he read law with his uncle, Milton Hay, who had once been associated with Abraham Lincoln and whose offices were next door to those of Lincoln & Herndon. Hay scarcely seemed interested in the events around him. "I am as yet innocent of politics," he wrote, only a few days before the Illinois Republican convention urged Lincoln's nomination for the presidency. "I occupy myself very pleasantly in thoroughly hating both sides, and abusing the peculiar tenets of the company I happen to be in."[2]

Hay took a small part in the 1860 campaign, probably because of his family's Republicanism and connections rather than through any personal zeal for Republican ideals. At the request of one of his Brown professors, James B. Angell, he wrote a series of articles for the *Providence Journal* supporting Lincoln's candidacy. He seems to have played a minor role in the Illinois campaign, and he certainly assisted Lincoln's secretary, John G. Nicolay, in handling the candidate's correspondence. However, when he went to Washington as Nicolay's assistant, he neither knew Lincoln well nor particularly admired him. "I am beginning to respect him more than formerly," Hay wrote in January, 1861, which suggests something less than a total commitment.[3]

Nor did Hay at first express any great sense of concern over the issues being decided on the battlefield; for the most part his diary entries in the years 1861 and 1862 were trivial. What did impress him was personal sacrifice and bravery. He eulogized a young Union soldier killed in 1861 and wrote glowingly of a contingent of soldiers from Rhode Island, some of whom he had known at Brown. "When men like these leave their horses, their women and their wine, harden their hands, eat crackers for dinner, wear a shirt for a week and never black their shoes, — all for a principle, it is hard to set any bounds on the possibilities of such an army," he observed. But of the principle Hay seemed uncertain. Certainly he was not devoted to democracy as a principle, a factor which perhaps explains his ambivalent feelings toward Lincoln. "The right man [is] . . . rarely seen in the right place in a Republic," he wrote scornfully late in 1862 while indicating his preference for the Italian monarch Victor Emmanuel over the republican Garibaldi. He repudiated such sentiments shortly thereafter and began to sing the praises of republicans.[4]

During 1863 and 1864 the republic made a convert as Hay came to feel that Lincoln *was* the right man for the times.[5] "I am growing more and more firmly convinced that the good of the country absolutely demands that he should be kept where he is till this thing is over . . . ," Hay wrote in August, 1863. "I believe the hand of God placed him where he is." This feeling grew into an overriding conviction that Lincoln must be reelected both for the sake of the country and the republican principles which it represented. On the eve of the election in 1864 he wrote to Nicolay, "I have nothing to say till day after to-morrow. God save the Republic!"[6]

Although Lincoln may not, as one student argues, have provided "the form and much of the substance of Hay's later work and policy," he was perhaps the most significant influence on Hay's early adult life and thought. By 1864,

Hay clearly felt that the virtues of republicanism outshone the faults. "As in spite of some rudeness, Republicanism is the sole hope of a sick world," he wrote, "so Lincoln with all his foibles, is the greatest character since Christ." Lincoln had proven the necessity, the viability, and the inevitability of republican principles, and after the war Hay began to speak with a glib optimism about the coming worldwide republican revolution.[7]

Hay's new political and social awareness found expression in his literary endeavors for the next decade. Poems about the Civil War such as "Crows at Washington," "The Advance Guard," "When the Boys Come Home," "Northward," "God's Vengeance," "Guy of the Temple," and "Banty Tim" (the last an open attack on racist feeling in Illinois), were written into the 1870's and illustrated Hay's moral attachment to Lincoln's cause. His European sojourns from 1865 to 1870 resulted in works that were more fervently political and ideological. He had been in Europe less than five months when he wrote "Sunrise in the *Place de la Concorde*," a strong statement attacking the despotism of Emperor Louis Napoleon. The poem referred to "the treasures of forty-eight" and concluded with the stirring and prophetic lines:

> And when in God's good hour
> Comes the time of the brave and true,
> Freedom again shall rise
> With a blaze in her awful eyes
> That shall wither this robber-power
> As the sun now dries the dew.
> This place shall roar with the voice
> Of the glad triumphant people,
> And the heavens be gay with the chimes
> Ringing in jubilant noise
> From every clamorous steeple
> The coming of better times.
> And the dawn of Freedom waking
> Shall fling its splendors far
> Like the day which now is breaking
> On the great pale Arch of the Star,
> And back o'er the town shall fly,
> While the joy-bells wild are ringing,
> To crown the Glory springing
> From the Column of July!

His observations on Spain, published serially and then in book form as *Castilian Days,* spoke directly to the question of political democracy, while trumpeting forth attacks on European despotism.[8]

A few of Hay's poems during this period approached genuine radicalism. "A Triumph of Order," which appeared in the *Atlantic* in 1872, immortalized a young martyr of the Paris Commune, and order was condemned as an end in itself. In "Liberty" Hay suggested that violence might be a necessary part of the struggle for freedom:

> So all in vain will timorous ones essay
> To set the metes and bounds of Liberty.
> For freedom is its own eternal law;
> It makes its own conditions, and in storm
> Or calm alike fulfills the unerring Will.
> Let us not then despise it when it lies
> Still as a sleeping lion, while a swarm
> Of gnat-like evils hover round its head;
> Nor doubt it when in mad, disjointed times
> It shakes the torch of terror, and its cry
> Shrills o'er the quaking earth, and in the flame
> Of riot and war we see its awful form
> Rise by the scaffold, where the crimson axe
> Rings down its grooves the knell of shuddering kings.
> Forever in thine eyes, O Liberty,
> Shines that high light whereby the world is saved,
> And though thou slay us, we will trust in thee!

No wonder that the American radical publication *Liberty,* in its first number, chose the final three lines of Hay's poem as its motto.[9]

But Hay was not as radical as "A Triumph of Order" would indicate. He was a reformer, caught up in the enthusiasm for a kind of spread-eagle democracy more often associated with the years just prior to the Civil War. In his speech "Daybreak in Spain," delivered in the early 1870's, he talked about "murderous revolutionists" as being "men of diseased and hungry minds." He could never, he said, forgive the "madmen of the [Paris] commune."[10]

Yet in "Daybreak in Spain" and even more clearly in the more widely delivered "The Progress of Democracy in Europe," Hay established himself as a champion of reform, democratic progress, and advancement for the lower socio-economic segments of society. Thus, while deploring the excesses of revolution, he did not condemn it out of hand and admitted that "Freedom is an angel whose blessings are gained by wrestling." Every revolution, he stated, even if unsuccessful, undercut despotic authority. The Paris Commune was not pleasant, perhaps not even justified, in Hay's opinion. But it was at least understandable:

If you would go, as I have often gone, among the laborers of Belleville and Meuilmontant, and heard the petty details of their lives of toil and abnegation, and seen the dismal tenements of the dreary suburbs..., the wives and the children dull and weary with that monotonous and colorless life of endless work which runs forever in one level groove on to a nameless grave, you might there understand the atmosphere in which those blind and groping aspirations are born, for a better future ... which the proletaire feels ought somehow to be evolved from the tangled problems of this great new time.

The blame for the Commune, Hay stated, lay primarily with the rulers, not the people. "In spite of all the furious denunciations of ignorance and reaction," he explained, "I deny that the people have ever been so merciless as their tyrants." Brave words, these were, at a time when the public generally denounced the Commune.[11]

Hay's comments were mostly aimed at Europe, but in his poetry, editorial writing, and speeches, he condemned American slavery, racism, and the intolerance of New England Puritanism (lest he be accused of being overly harsh on the Roman Catholic church in Spain), and he even had a kind word for John Brown of Ossawatomie, a champion of "noble thought" who, like other martyrs, died to give "point to a protest and a chorus to a song." Even the famous *Pike County Ballads,* although not explicitly political, were socially democratic, glorifying the common and shocking the genteel. "Pious gentlemen," for example, "wouldn't shook hands" with Jim Bludso, a dirty steamboat engineer who spoke "keerless" and had two wives.

Yet when the *Prairie Belle* caught fire Bludso sacrificed his life for the passengers and crew. "Christ ain't a-going to be too hard," Hay concluded the poem, "On a man that died for men." Similarly, "Golyer," the last of the five ballads, demonstrated that a common man—"no better nor worse than the rest"—had heroic qualities. It was only natural that this uncultured stagecoach driver protected a child during an Indian attack:

> Said he, "When they fired, I kivered the kid,—
> Although I ain't pretty, I'm middlin' broad;
> And look! he ain't fazed by arrow nor ball,—
> Thank God! my own carcase stopped them all."
> And he carried his thanks to God.[12]

In general Hay was on the side of change, reform, and the common people and against despotism and a repressive status quo. Hay's social awareness made him a political figure (in a partisan sense) dedicated to the party of Lincoln. He therefore detested Lincoln's successor, Andrew Johnson, a man, he thought, who "would ruin the best cause a man ever fought for in two weeks stumping." Hay welcomed the nominations of Ulysses S. Grant and Schuyler Colfax in 1868. To Colfax, the Republican vice-presidential candidate, he wrote that his acceptance of the nomination benefited "the ticket, the Republican party, and consequently, as I religiously believe, the cause of liberty."[13]

The corruption and incompetence of Grant soon soured Hay, however. "Grant seems to be doing all he can to destroy the Republican party," he confided to his wife. Not surprisingly, Hay supported the cause of reform in 1872. As a staff member of the *New York Tribune*, Hay wrote anti-Grant editorials, reported from Illinois on the state of anti-Grant movements within the Republican party, and gave strong editorial support to the Liberal Republicans when they bolted from the regular party. Although, in the end, Hay was not able to bring himself to vote for the eccentric Horace Greeley, candidate of the Liberal Republicans as well as the Democrats, he did not like the corruption associated with Grant or the public's seeming indifference. "People merely lift their eyebrows and pass on," he wrote. In later years Hay stayed steadfastly with the regular Republican party, even when he distrusted the leadership, for he felt that it contained, on the whole, the best men. But from 1872 to 1876, Hay was a reformer willing to abandon his party if necessary. Thus, in 1874, Hay voted for the Democratic candidate, Samuel J. Tilden, for governor of New York. This was the last time Hay ever voted for a Democrat. Even so, he was pleased when the Democrats chose to run Tilden for president in 1876.[14]

Hay's democratic enthusiasm had little effect on his later diplomacy, however (although it did influence his opinions on foreign policy in the 1870's), because very shortly Hay changed many of his views. The change is most easily documented in Hay's novel, *The Bread-winners: A Social Study*. *The Bread-winners* was published in 1883, but the ideas expressed therein stretch back to 1877, the "Year of Violence," as Robert Bruce has designated it.

Hay's early works were products of a youthful, even glib, optimism. His novel, in striking contrast, is a bitter book. Instead of praising the open society, Hay expresses serious doubts as to its desirability; instead of lauding democracy, he openly attacks it; instead of sympathizing with the disadvantaged, Hay attacks the newly formed labor unions that were trying to aid the disadvantaged; *The Bread-winners* is, in fact, one of the earliest fictional defenses of unfettered American capitalism.[15]

Among the major revelations of *The Bread-winners* is Hay's challenge to the then widely accepted belief that the United States was great because the society was open. Any man, given some natural talent and a willingness to work hard, could rise to the top. Horatio Alger, Andrew Carnegie, and even Terrence Powderley of the Knights of Labor were agreed that this was the secret of the country's success. Hay did not deny that the society was open; he did question very seriously whether an open society composed of self-made men was good.

Hay's ambivalent conclusion was that "the restless haste and hunger to rise" resulted in "much that is good" but also in "most that is evil in American life." And if he had had to choose, Hay quite probably would have said that more evil than good resulted. To be sure, some societal benefits did result from an open society. Hay's own father-in-law, Amasa Stone, began his adult life as a carpenter and ultimately became a wealthy railroad builder and capitalist in Cleveland, all with little formal education. And in Hay's novel, Mr. Temple rose from steamboat cabin boy to vice president of Buffland's largest rolling mill. As a character, Temple was surely preferable to the indolent union members. Yet, despite his admirable ambition, the industrialist was a philistine. Profanity, dullness, and a general lack of esthetic refinement marked his character. He was "gentleman-like," not a gentleman.[16]

For others in the novel who attempted to rise above their appropriate station, the results were tragic. In fact, the plot revolves about Maud Matchin who possessed "ignoble ambitions" to enter Buffland's aristocracy.[17] Maud's father, a respectable carpenter, felt that his daughter should leave high school and accept work as a domestic. Instead, Maud stubbornly completes her education (barely) and attempts to acquire some culture. The results are deplorable. Although she acquires a taste for literature, Maud remains "vulgar and ignorant." Having assumed the airs that go with a high school education, she refuses to be seen with mere carpenters, thus creating deep dissension within her previously idyllic family. More significantly, she tries to snare the very eligible bachelor Arthur Farnham, who, as a sophisticated and cultured aristocrat will have nothing to do with such a creature. Maud's attempts at romance, however, not only endanger Farnham's chances with a suitable neighbor, they very nearly result in Farnham's death at the hands of Sam Sleeny, a carpenter who burns with jealousy over what he mistakenly perceives as Farnham's affection for Maud.

Hay's heroes were not the socially mobile but those who knew their class and had no desire to leave it. Maud's father, for example, "was contented with his daily work and wage, and would have thanked Heaven if he could have been assured that his children would fare as well as he." At the other end of this stratified society was Arthur Farnham, the real hero of the novel. Farnham, an urbane overly-idealized aristocrat, was "one of those fortunate natures, who, however born, are always bred well, and come by prescription to most of the good things the world can give."[18]

Hay had not entered the upper class through his own aggressive entrepreneurship. Although he did work hard on the staff of the *New York Tribune* in the early 1870's (he frugally insisted he would not marry until he owned two or three shares of the newspaper's stock), Hay's wealth and much of his subsequent influence resulted from his marriage. Nor, after his marriage, was the nature of his new work for his father-in-law taxing. "I am here in a nice little shop where I do nothing but read and yawn in the long intervals of work, an occupation that fits me like a glove," he related to Adee. "My work is merely the care of investments which are so safe that they require no care." Hay doubtless exaggerated the ease of his situation, but, with the significant exception of the time spent on his biography of Lincoln, Hay's married years were not marked by the driving ambition that contributed to the success of Andrew Carnegie, or Amasa Stone, or even Mr. Temple. One reviewer of Hay's novel unkindly (but perhaps accurately) surmised that "the author, after laying the foundations for a long novel . . . reduced it to the proportions of a sketch, perhaps finding the labor involved in the execution of the original plan too great."[19]

The Bread-winners illustrates clearly that Hay preferred a stratified society with minimal interclass mobility, a preference more in keeping with European than with American myths. In fact, the book is filled with favorable allusions to Europe, particularly to England. The homes on fashionable Algonquin Avenue (where Farnham lived) all have well-kept lawns and gardens that compare favorably with their British counterparts. Alice Belding, Farnham's young neighbor and his true love, must be sent elsewhere to receive a proper cultural education, which she does from the French emigré Madame de Veaudrey.[20]

When the novel was published Hay reacted angrily to charges that it lauded aristocracy. He wrote anonymously to the *Century* that such charges were "too absurd to be considered seriously." But only in the narrowest sense was his rejoinder at all justified: Hay did not place much emphasis on accident of birth as a requirement for entrance into the upper class. Indeed, Hay, who considered himself a part of the American aristocracy, could not claim aristocratic lineage, his father being a modest country physician in rural Illinois. But the idea of natural classes, with a wise and prosperous aristocracy at the helm, did appeal to Hay despite his denials. Hay identified with Farnham who "however born" was well bred and came by "prescription" to the best. Indeed, Farnham's house on Algonquin Avenue in Buffland bore a transparent similarity to Hay's own home on Euclid Avenue in Cleveland, particularly the library, in which works of art tastefully surrounded expensive furniture, all dwelling "together in the harmony of varied perfection." All in all, "the whole expression of the room was one of warmth and good manners," perfect for the cultured aristocrat who wore his fine clothes "as easily as any self respecting bird wears his feathers." Hay privately admitted, in fact, that much of the story was set in his own house and garden. One became an aristocrat neither by entrepreneurship nor by birth, but by one's inherent qualities.[21]

Hay's increasingly aristocratic views resulted in his open repudiation of the social democracy found in his early works. *The Bread-winners* is, in part, an explicit denunciation of Jacksonian Democracy. Jackson, Hay wrote bluntly, was "the most injurious personality in American history." Pointedly, the novel's villain is Andrew Jackson Offitt, a name signifying "that the person bearing it is the son of illiterate parents, with no family pride or affections, but filled with a bitter and savage partisanship."[22]

Jacksonian Democracy, so Hay indicated, expressed itself in two despicable and interconnected institutions—labor unions and corrupt city political machines. Offitt, a sleazy and cunning labor organizer, represented the worst element in society. As a boy, Offitt had picked his father's pocket on the way to church, a crime that caused his angry parents to nickname him Ananias after a biblical character struck dead for lying.[23] Thereafter, Hay ascribes to this labor leader Satanic and animal-like characteristics. At one time or another, Offitt is compared to a ferrett, a tiger, a panther, a dog, and a snake. He was, in sum, "a human beast of prey," who when angry "walked up and down the room with his head thrown back, his nostrils distended, a picture of brutal impatience, breathing quick and hard." When he seriously wounded Farnham, he inhumanly felt "pure exultation" and "not a particle of regret or remorse."[24]

Offitt's criminal and animalistic antecedents fitted him well for his tasks. In Buffland, Offitt organized the Brotherhood of Bread-winners, an underground labor organization with ill-defined, anti-capitalistic objectives whose members were, like their leader, dishonest, lascivious, lazy, drunk, profane, and cruel. They were "the laziest and most incapable workmen in the town—men whose weekly wages were habitually docked for drunkenness, late hours, and botchy work." Even the chairs in their hall were of "doubtful integrity," while attempts to order their meetings were hopelessly unsuccessful.[25]

On the other hand, despite their general incapability, the Brotherhood's members possessed enough influence among the workingmen, and, of even greater importance, with Buffland's political machine, that they were able to shut down the city using the radical tactic of the general strike. Furthermore, individual Bread-winners had a devilish ability to corrupt basically honorable men. Offitt, for example, enlisted Sam Sleeny in his cause and even got Sleeny to assault Farnham. Later, when Sleeny had returned to his senses, he murdered Offitt; and Hay, ostensibly committed to the maintenance of law and order, justifies Sleeny's action. The "judicious jurymen" acquitted Sleeny of "the rash act" on the grounds of "emotional insanity"; and Hay praised the verdict as contributing "to the lasting honor and glory of our system of trial by jury."[26]

The Bread-winners was so virulently anti-labor that, as late as 1897, some labor leaders, suspecting that Hay was the author, opposed Hay's appointment as ambassador to England. Hay made some feeble attempts to deny that his novel was against unions as such. The Brotherhood of Bread-winners, he pointed out in the novel itself, was a secret organization, "wholly outside of the trades-unions and unconnected with them." Hay reiterated this contention in the two anonymous letters he wrote to the *Century* defending the novel. Yet in one of the letters Hay maintained that an "inner circle of petty tyrants" governed the trade unions; that strikes inevitably produced violence and murder; and that the whole concept of unionism went against the traditional process of individual bargaining. Furthermore, the distinction between legitimate and illegitimate labor organizations was blurred in the novel itself. Offitt is described simply as an "apostle of labor," and the disclaimer quoted above was not included in the handwritten draft, suggesting that the editors prevailed on Hay to include it at the last minute.[27]

The Bread-winners thus illustrates a dramatic shift in Hay's thinking. In the 1860's and early 1870's Hay was a spokesman for democratic and even radical movements; a decade later he speaks for the conservative elite. How can this be explained?

It is possible to argue that Hay's youthful radicalism was shallow and, consequently, that the change is less dramatic than it appears. Hay's education at Brown University prior to the Civil War, for example, developed, perhaps even instilled, a snobbishness that marked his later life. During his years in Providence, Hay absorbed much of the rarefied culture of the East and rejected the crudeness of the West where he had been raised. It seems significant, in this respect, that Hay's villain, Andrew Jackson Offitt, grew up in Salem, Indiana, where he himself had been born.[28]

Then, too, even at the height of Hay's democratic

enthusiasm his tolerance was not unlimited. For example, in 1869, even while forming the ideas for his most democratic work, *Castilian Days,* Hay wrote an anti-Mormon article for the *Atlantic Monthly* which indicated some of the limits. There are, in fact, noticeable similarities between "The Mormon Prophet's Tragedy" and *The Bread-winners.* The allegedly licentious Mormons, like the Brotherhood of Bread-winners, tended to infect normally upright citizens. Joseph Smith, Brigham Young, "and their fellow blackguards" were "lewd," Hay wrote, and their influence had corrupted both political parties in Hancock County, Illinois.

Very few people urged toleration of the Mormons, to be sure. Hay exceeded some of their critics, however, for the seeds of his later approval (in *The Bread-winners*) of socio-political murder exist in "The Mormon Prophet's Tragedy." Hay did not condone the lynching of Joseph Smith, but he did imply that Smith, because of his provocative sexual ideas, was responsible for his own death. Because of their numbers, the Mormons controlled Hancock County and could thus protect their allegedly licentious behavior. Consequently, Hay explained, "in the mind of any anti-Mormon there was nothing more criminal in the shooting of Smith than in the slaying of a wolf or panther." The mob's action, while distasteful and dishonorable, was completely understandable.[29]

Furthermore, Hay had aimed his attacks on undemocratic institutions primarily at Europe. As one historian has written, to Hay freedom "was concerned with destroying obsolete barriers in other countries rather than eliminating distinctions at home." American institutions and traditions were generally beneficent, the result of a long evolutionary process in an atmosphere conducive to the free expression of ideas. The American Revolution, for example, in contrast to European revolutions, was to Hay "the coolest, most decent, most dignified, most unimpassioned rebellion that the world has yet seen." Indeed, the United States was to some extent a model for struggling European republican movements to emulate. Spanish republicans, he told an audience, wanted "a system of government something like ours."[30]

Hay's latent snobbery, his narrow tolerance, and the Europe-centeredness of much of his democratic fervor, clearly indicated that Hay's radicalism was indeed shallow and unstable. But his switch from democratic enthusiasm to conservative elitism was too sharp to be completely explained in this manner. These factors made a switch more likely; but there were other factors more directly responsible. His marriage in 1874 to a wealthy industrial heiress was doubtless one of them. Hay denied the rumor that he received $1,000,000 on that occasion,[31] but unquestionably his marriage resulted in substantial wealth. Very shortly after the wedding, Hay confided to Alvey A. Adee that his father-in-law wanted him "to go into another line of business which will bring me immediate wealth." The extensive extant correspondence between Hay and Amasa Stone from that time until Stone's suicide in 1883 substantiates this statement. Through Stone, Hay achieved great wealth in investments, especially in railroad stock, bonds, and real estate. He became acquainted with the tycoons of the Gilded Age, such as Cornelius Vanderbilt, Jay Cooke, and Jay Gould. Gould, in fact, was directly responsible for Hay's election to the board of directors of Western Union following Stone's death.[32]

Wealth in itself need not result in a defensive justification of the status quo. Hay's close friend William Dean Howells, for example, married great wealth and still remained sensitive to the needs of the less fortunate. But Hay was soon devoted to capitalism as a moral, as well as an economic, system.

In many ways, Hay was a Brahmin. Educated at Brown University, Hay identified with upper class, literary Eastern culture and shared its aristocratic values. Yet, as a Westerner and first generation aristocrat, he did not share the sense of displacement and uneasiness at rapid industrial development that many true Brahmins did.[33] The financial machinations that upset Howells did not disturb Hay, and the great railroad strikes of 1877 finished off whatever remained of Hay's rather unstable radicalism.

Amasa Stone's business, of which Hay was a part after his marriage, made his opposition to the strikes understandable from an economic standpoint, for Stone constructed railroads and had heavy investments in related fields. In fact, five hundred workers struck Stone's Lake Shore and Michigan Railway. Just how deeply the strikes affected Hay was evident when he wrote to Stone, "I feel that a profound misfortune and disgrace has fallen on the country, which no amount of energy or severity can now wholly remedy." Hay discerned no underlying causes for the uprisings, writing to his father-in-law, "the cause of the strikers is mere insanity." Agitators, coupled with the indolence of many workmen, constituted the immediate and only causes for rebellion. "The very devil seems to have entered the lower classes of working men," he wrote, "and there are plenty of scoundrels to encourage them to all lengths." Later, as secretary of state, he would feel the same way about the Filipino insurrectionists.[34]

In addition to threatening his own material interests, Hay believed strongly that labor disturbances demonstrated a breakdown in traditional morality. Real values were at stake. "I am thankful you did not *see* and *hear* what took place during the strikes," he wrote to Stone. "You were saved a very painful experience of human folly and weakness, as well as crime." Labor organizers, he repeated often, were criminals, for he firmly believed that capital benefited labor by providing employment. It was labor's responsibility to provide an honest day's work. Labor leaders misunderstood, or more probably misconstrued, the proper relationship.[35]

One historian states that the labor unrest of 1877, although upsetting, was quickly forgotten once it was over. But the strikes had a profound effect on Hay, and he did not forget. These labor disturbances were directly responsible for the appearance of *The Bread-winners* six years later. In the manuscript version of the novel Hay explicitly set the story in the year 1877; and portions of the novel read like the letters he wrote during the strikes. The unions, Hay stated in the novel, aimed "at nothing less than the emancipation of the world from its old-fashioned decencies." "We are goin' to make war on capital," screamed the irrational Offitt. "We are goin' to scare the blood-suckers into terms. We are goin' to get our rights—peaceably, if we can't get them any other way," a hyperbole indicative of his portrayal of the debauched values of the Bread-winners.[36]

The novel was, however, more than a handwringing, anti-union tract, for Hay offered a solution. Irish-controlled city political machines tied in with socialistic unions were indeed the deplorable result of Jacksonian Democracy. But if the wealthy and the wise could unite and become involved politically at the lowest level, they might yet ensure their dominance, which, to the extent that it still existed at all, was based on an eroding deference system. Such a system was no longer sufficient when revolutionaries roamed the streets. Like Alexander Hamilton, Hay did not fear power; instead he wanted to use it for class ends.[37] Consequently, in the novel Hay was sharply critical of the wealthy who, after cooperating during the immediate crisis of the general strike, thereafter refused to dirty their hands in petty but necessary political organization:

The rich and prosperous people, as their manner is, congratulated themselves on their escape, and gave no thought to the questions which had come so near to an issue of fire and blood. In this city of two hundred thousand people, two or three dozen politicians continued as before to govern it, to assess and spend its taxes, to use it as their property and their chattel. The rich and intelligent kept on making money, building fine houses, and bringing up children to hate politics as they did, and in fine to fatten themselves as sheep which should be mutton whenever the butcher was ready. There was hardly a millionaire on Algonquin Avenue who knew where the ward meetings of his party were held. There was not an Irish laborer in the city but knew his way to his ward club as well as to mass.[38]

The strikes of 1877 drove Hay far to the right, sharply reduced the limits of his tolerance, and strengthened his Republican faith. Together, all of these changes convinced him to resist social and political experimentation. He pitied the respectable people who saw no danger in the situation, and he extended his dislike of labor leaders to those of his own class who urged political reform, even when the reforms they advocated had little if any connection with labor.

The pejorative connotation of all reform was evident in *The Bread-winners* as well as in Hay's letters. In the novel he applied the word reformer explicitly to labor reformers like Andrew Jackson Offitt. But Hay entitled one chapter dealing with Offitt, "A Professional Reformer," and used the word freely throughout the book without a modifier, which muddled its meaning. The very name Andrew Jackson Offitt confused the political and the social. Even if certain reforms had merit, they could not be countenanced at this time; they would be a foot in the doorway. It was better to keep the door tightly shut. The world was not perfect: philistines like Mr. Temple abounded, due to the disadvantages of a completely open society. But the lesson of *The Bread-winners* was that all members of the upper classes—cultured aristocrats and boorish capitalists—must band together for their common good and preserve the status quo. Thus Hay's hero, Farnham, who looked down upon the superficiality of Temple, fully cooperated with him in order to beat back the mob.

Just how deeply the strikes of 1877 threatened Hay's material and moral interests can be seen in his conversion to active involvement in Republican politics of the most partisan kind. In effect, for some years before he published his novel, Hay was following his own admonition for active political involvement by the wealthy and wise as the best means to maintain conservative control.

Hay can fairly be termed a political reformer and, to a lesser extent, a political independent through 1876. There were, however, indications of a more rigid, partisan attitude as early as 1875. The question of "sound money," for example, began to assume moral connotations for Hay, not unlike those he saw later in the proper relationship between labor and capital. He accused the Democrats of "carrying on a campaign on the bald issue of whether the nation shall be a liar or a thief or not." There were some Republican inflationists, he admitted, and the Tilden Democrats were on the right side. But the preponderance of sound money men were Republicans. Furthermore, he expressed, for the first time, reservations about the desirability of political reform, complaining to Reid about the selection of Henry L. Burnett to chair the New York Reform Club. "There is not a voudou-worshipping nigger in Georgia who is not a safer political guide than the average cultivated man of New York and Boston," he wrote. ". . . Burn this," he added, "for I like Burnett—but Reform Club—Oh Lordy!"[39]

In 1875, Hay did not yet feel that the Republican party was the sole repository of truth. But as he became more and more conservative socially, his partisanship hardened. The strikes drove Hay completely into the arms of the most partisan Republicans. During the Ohio election campaign in the fall of 1878 (Hay had moved to Cleveland after his marriage), he sent a letter to Reid to be published in the *Tribune* urging the wealthy to support Republican candidates. "Without buying a single vote, a million could be spent to great advantage—and would be the best invest-ment ever made," he wrote in a covering letter. Thinking better of the idea, Hay asked Reid not to publish his letter. But the facts remained unchanged, he felt. "Money can carry these elections," he wrote, "and rich men are as blind as moles if they do not see it."[40]

The following spring, with Democrats in control of the Ohio legislature, Hay led a group of sixty-three promi-nent Clevelanders into the Young Men's Republican League. In their application for membership these men declared the Democrats generally devoid of any moral sense. Specifically, like the Bread-winners, the Democrats endangered "the very foundation of public morality" in attempting to effect a coalition "with the Communists and inflationists by adopting their worst heresies." A few weeks later, Hay, demonstrating his continuing concern with so-cial issues that he considered moral, was instrumental in establishing the Cleveland branch of the Honest Money League, of which he became the treasurer. "Reasonable men," he told the initial gathering, would not "stand by and survey with indifference the progress of moral contagion."[41]

In fact, the unconcern of the respectable classes deeply bothered Hay. The principal obstacle in gaining support for the League, he reported, was "the apathy of the honest money men who think the danger is settled. But it is not settled," he insisted. ". . . The danger is real and substantial." If the soft money demagogues won, the country would be in great peril. Therefore, "the men who have some regard for public credit, for the stability of business, for ease and convenience of exchange, for common sense and honesty in finance, have got to bestir themselves. . . . Something surely must be done," he concluded "to defend ourselves against these schemes which threaten our good name, our business prosperity, and the very nature of our commercial and financial system."[42]

Believing that the basic social fabric was under attack, Hay threw himself vigorously into the state campaign that autumn, fearlessly speaking, on one occasion, in the strongest Democratic ward of Cleveland. He made a number of other speeches in the ensuing weeks, blasting the anarchistic Democrats. "These pestilential demagogues and their misguided tools have disgraced us long enough," he stated. Hay's address was reprinted as far away as Cincinnati, where editorial attention was called to it. Hay was following his own prescription for political involvement by a propertied, educated elite to stop the erosion of the "old fashioned decencies." Although the Republicans won the Ohio election, the results discouraged Hay. The 2 percent majority was not really a victory since values as well as political offices were in the balance. "On such an issue we ought to have had a hundred thousand," he stated.[43]

Shortly after the campaign, rumors circulated that Hay would receive the Republican nomination for congressman from his district. Despite his past statements about never holding elective office, the prospect tempted him. He claimed that he did not want the position and told his

father-in-law that he was trying to induce his potential
opponent to run. But he also wrote to former Congressman
Walter Phelps, who had found his own experience in
Washington very satisfying, that he wanted "to stiffen my
backbone a little about running for Congress . . . . If I could
hope to repeat your experience," he wrote, "it might nerve
me enough to go into convention." Not until the end of
March, 1880, did he discourage his friends from urging
his nomination.[44]

His decision not to run for Congress did not mean Hay
was any less concerned about the social and political situation; indeed, the fact that he even considered entering the
race indicated a deeper commitment to political activity
than at any previous time. Partly because he eventually
decided against running, Hay threw himself with great
vigor into the state and national campaigns of 1880.[45] In
July, he accepted the presidency of the Fifth Ward Republican Club of Cleveland, announcing his decision in a
published letter. The Republicans never had a better cause,
he insisted, and he hoped, "for the credit of the country,
that we may never have a worse or more unpatriotic organization to fight against." The Democrats, like Andrew
Jackson Offitt, had "criminal antecedents" and were
"incapable of governing this country wisely and well."
Hay's major campaign effort occurred on July 31 when,
for the first time in its history, the Euclid Avenue Opera
House opened its doors for a political event. Hay addressed
the overflow crowd for nearly two hours amid frequent ap-
plause. Beyond the standard references to bloody shirt issues, Hay's speech was a paean to industrial development.
The Democrats were, he contended, dishonest enemies of
progress.[46]

Not until the campaign of 1896 did Hay again enjoy a
position of such confidence and influence in the upper circles of the Republican party. This was partly because the
Republican presidential candidate, General James A. Garfield, was from Ohio, and partly because Hay actively chose
to make his influence felt. In October, for example, Hay
advised Garfield with some temerity to "beware of your

own generosity" and to stop making so many promises. Later Garfield twice offered Hay a position as private secretary, but Hay declined.[47]

With the Democrats "down below the level of Jackson" during these years, Hay's sense of urgency about moral values, his elitism, and his detestation of reform became more entrenched. Yet, as a conservative elitist with basically Brahmin values, Hay was very close, culturally, to the Yankee reformers. Both looked back to a simpler world where those "old fashioned decencies" were not threatened. Hay, however, unlike the Brahmins, did not feel threatened by the new industrial order; indeed, he was very much a part of it and proud to be so. It seems not to have occurred to him that the new order would itself inevitably produce tension and strain that would demand a revised value structure. If reform even remotely threatened either the new order or the old values, he resisted. "When I pay $14 for a berth in a sleeping car to Cannes and reflect that a party of indignant freemen is forming in America to have justice on Vanderbilt and Pullman for the crime of charging $2—for the same distance," he wrote from Paris, "I cannot help wondering if any damfool in history equals the Yankee damfool who is also a reformer."[48]

As an elitist distrustful of the masses, Hay might well have supported civil service reform as a means of ensuring cleaner and better government. So reasoned his cultural cousins, the Yankee reformers. But Hay looked very dimly upon such reform, at least as it was first enacted in the Pendleton Act, signed by President Arthur in 1883. Hay noticed that in preparing suitable rules for civil service appointments under the new act, the commissioners were to apportion government appointments "among the several States and Territories and the District of Columbia upon the basis of population as ascertained at the last preceding census." This clause meant in practice that each congressional district would have equal representation in the civil service process—"and every true hearted reformer is delighted," Hay commented scornfully. "Three fourths of the districts have not a man fit for Congress, much less for a good clerk,"[49] he added in disgust.

By the time Hay wrote *The Bread-winners* he was a staunchly conservative Republican partisan with increasingly rigid views on issues of social significance. He underscored his opposition to inflationists, labor unions, and political reformers by working in the Republican party at all levels and by stimulating interest in associations spiritually allied to the party, like the Honest Money League.

A strike of telegraph operators in 1883 did nothing to soften Hay's attitudes, for after Amasa Stone's death in the spring of 1883, Hay had assumed a directorship of Western Union. In retrospect, the operators' demands seem reasonable enough—an end to compulsory Sunday duty without extra pay, an eight-hour day and a seven-hour night, and a pay increase. But Hay wrote that the operators had "foolishly given up their means of livelihood at the dictation of a few conspirators, whose vanity and arrogance had blinded them to the plainest considerations of common sense."[50]

The Bread-winners, published serially in the months preceding the strike, and the social philosophy it represented, were being challenged. The novel created a genuine sensation and was widely read; but, contrary to the impression left by Hay's biographers, the reviews were at best mixed. The *Atlantic Monthly,* in a lengthy review, credited the novel with "a good deal of artfulness," but was on the whole critical. Hay's one-sided view of labor and capital was "somewhat inadequate," the reviewer felt, and, as a novel, the work was "by no means satisfactory." But what must have galled Hay the most, although he later denied it, was the reviewer's characterization of Farnham, with whom Hay certainly identified, as "rich, amiable, efficient, but in no way especially fine or admirable."[51]

The *Nation* was less critical, but it too objected to the idealization of Farnham. The *Athenaeum* of London, briefly reviewing the English edition, remarked that "it is by no means one of the best representatives of Transatlantic fiction." The reviewer felt that the British public was growing tired of such "samples of cultivated and uncultivated effrontery which have recently been offered to them so freely in American novels," and condescendingly concluded that "it is not to be expected that such a type would be permanently popular out of its own country." The strongest criticism came from the *Dial* which characterized *The Bread-winners* as "dull, vicious, and disgusting."[52]

In addition, several novels appeared challenging Hay's book, of which the most important was Henry F. Keenan's anonymous work *The Money-Makers: A Social Parable*. Keenan's book, advertised as "an answer to the much discussed *Bread-winners*," contained disparaging descriptions of Whitelaw Reid, Hay (as Hilliard) and Amasa Stone (as Aaron Grimstone). Cleveland was called Valedo, and Euclid Avenue logically became Geometry Avenue. In *The Money-Makers*, Grimstone, like Stone, committed suicide. Near his body lay a pamphlet containing the findings of a jury in the Academy disaster, a clear parallel to the decision of a committee of the Ohio legislature which had found Stone negligent in the construction of a bridge which collapsed, carrying several persons to their deaths.[53]

Hay did all he could to stop the publication and advertising of the book, but he was only slightly successful. Gilder promised Hay that he would take no notice of it in the *Century*, while Appleton & Co., which published *The Money-Makers*, agreed to insist that the offending passages be removed. But the advertising continued and the novel continued to sell. *Vanity Fair*, at least, liked *The Money-Makers*. "The whole story is much better in all its parts than the 'Bread Winners.' 'The Money Makers' is destined to become a famous novel."[54]

In the meantime, the political reformers, including many of Hay's friends and acquaintances, had deserted the Republican party to support Grover Cleveland for president. The mugwump revolt outraged Hay, the more so because he idolized the Republican nominee, James G. Blaine. Had Chester Arthur, whom Hay privately ridiculed, received the nomination, perhaps Hay might not have been so disturbed about the mugwumps. But the notion of freedom from partisanship, so central to mugwump thinking, no longer made sense to Hay. Any break from the Republican fold was sheer madness. "Yes I mean *Hurrah for Blaine!*" he wrote to an incredulous Richard Watson Gilder. "I have never been able to appreciate the logic which induces some excellent people every four years, because they cannot nominate the candidate they prefer, to vote for the party they don't prefer."[55]

A few days later he explained his reasons for backing Blaine, whom the mugwumps anathematized. He characterized Grover Cleveland, the Democratic nominee, as an unlettered "rural sheriff" who would turn out 200,000 experienced, efficient (and Republican) officeholders. "You are working to hand the government of the country over the worst elements of its population," Hay lectured the editor who had published *The Bread-winners* the previous year. "You know perfectly well that the Republican party contains, on the whole, the majority of the better sort. . . . If the contest were between Blaine and Aristidies, I could understand your course," he concluded. "But between Blaine and Cleveland, Blaine is the more civilized. . . . And between the two parties—I cannot conceive how you should feel differently."[56]

Once again Hay took an active role in the campaign, contributing both cash and oratory. He congratulated Blaine on his strenuous Maine-to-Wisconsin campaign swing—a "magnificent personal triumph," Hay thought. No American statesman, Hay wrote, had ever "done anything so brilliant." Privately, however, he feared defeat and blamed the mugwumps. "We are busy trying to elect Blaine," he wrote to Howells. "I don't know how you feel about it—I meet no Blaine men anywhere in the East. Those I saw were so furious at my Maine friend that they bandaged their eyes as to Cleveland and his following." Such men had not learned the lesson of *The Bread-winners.*[57]

Cleveland was elected, and Hay spent the next four years fretting about the mugwumps' shortsightedness. Hay wrote to reformer George W. Curtis asking if there was "anything the President can do which would induce the

Independents to rebuke him in the only way a man of his mental and moral characteristics understands rebuke?" With the nation in peril, Hay stood ready to fight.[58]

But he found the political situation in 1888 "excessively gloomy." Blaine, his favorite candidate, chose not to run, and Hay had no liking at all for Benjamin Harrison, who had received the nomination. Harrison, he contended, was universally regarded as second-rate, and tinged, so Hay implied, with corruption. Still, Hay never for a moment considered bolting the party. "Benjamin ben Harrison got . . . [the nomination]," Hay wrote to Adams, "and I suppose I must vote for him. I will keep myself up to the task by thinking of Cleveland and occasionally reading an editorial from the Nation."[59]

Nor did Hay consider, for long, remaining aloof from the campaign. As the election drew near Hay became more reconciled to the prospect of Harrison's election. He invited the Harrisons for dinner, noted that his election would "save the country, not only from present shames and disgraces, but from the most serious evils and disasters," and gave Mark Hanna at least $1,000 for the campaign fund. Hay regarded the election as more than a matter of the ins versus the outs. Harrison's success at the polls was, he thought, a "glorious victory."[60]

With the Republicans again safely ensconced in Washington, Hay might well have decided to avoid political efforts. In fact, as work on his biography of Lincoln drew to a close in 1890, he began to sink into the rather bored, lethargic existence common to many wealthy men of his generation in the 1890's. "I am a little scared to see how dull I am here," he wrote Adams from Washington in 1890, wishing instead he could join Adams on his tour of the Pacific islands. His letters during the early 1890's, particularly those to Adams, were among the most melancholy of his career. "I am a worthless creature, destitute of initiative," he wrote from his summer home, The Fells. Nor were things much better in Washington. "We try to put a little life into ourselves by abusing the Mugwumps," he wrote, "but all our gaiety rings false." A trip to England in

1893 did not lessen his sense of gloom. "I distrust my own black spectacle," he wrote to Adams. "Things *can't* be so bad as I think." He summed it all up in the following spring: "the enfant de fin de Siecle is hard to amuse."[61]

When Hay returned to Cleveland that autumn he found a situation somewhat comparable to that which had prompted *The Bread-winners.* Tom Johnson, a reformer who had been twice elected to represent Cleveland in Congress, and who was now again campaigning, met with Hay's utter contempt. Had Hay had any initiative left he might well have composed another work like *The Bread-winners.* "I have never known a more gabby campaign," he began a letter to Adams.

Eloquence overflows the legitimate stump and slops the sidewalk. I stop sometimes and listen to the gutter-Ciceros. They are talking finance to the best of their little lungs. Free trade and single tax have the call. Johnson seems to have hired duty orators by the dozen, to blather on street corners. Most of the working men are idle, so that there is always an audience. He is an amazing caricature of the classic demagogue, with a dash of Tammany cynicism. A millionaire monopolist, a frank thief, a glib and jovial liar, best pleased when detected, appealing with tact to the thief that lies . . . in the average citizen's innards, he is almost impossible to beat. If I had the bounding youth and literary vitality of a Tahiti chief, I would make a story of him— and get back the money I blow in every two years, in vain, against him.

Now, however, he was too worn out to write. "I am an ass, and a *dégénéré,* whose initiative is dead," he wrote a few months later.[62]

But Tom Johnson was only one of the disturbing elements in the 1890's, and, despite his melancholy, Hay believed too strongly in his own dictum that the wealthy had to protect their own interests politically to abandon it totally now. Indeed, at the same time he was bemoaning his inability to attack Johnson literarily, he reaffirmed his faith with a classic statement to Reid. "The men who play politics 365 days in the year have an awful advantage over the gentlemen who play *at* the same game in their moments perdus,"[63] he wrote.

More dangerous than Johnson to Hay's interests and values was the farmer's revolt, of which Hay first took apprehensive note in 1890. Not only were their ends dishonorable, but like the Mormons, the Bread-winners, and, later, Emilio Aguinaldo, the agrarian radicals were totally insincere. Jerry Simpson, "the sockless," Hay wrote, "was caught by his coreligionaries drinking fizz with a millionaire democrat" after delivering an anti-capitalistic speech. Unfortunately, these malcontents also had the ability to infect normally decent Republicans. The Democrats, he found, were "ridden by the Farmer's Alliance and bound by dirty trade with the Republican silvermen." They had "gone to the devil," he wrote a few days later, and were "wallowing . . . before the grangers and inflationists." All in all, the ungodly alliance of Democrats, agrarian radicals, and dissident Republicans, Hay wrote, "drips more feculence than any I remember."[64]

Hay could not view such developments without becoming involved. He entered the Ohio campaign of 1891 with vigor, supporting John Sherman and William McKinley. In 1892, he campaigned for Harrison, although without great enthusiasm. (When asked to contribute to the campaign, Hay "abused Harrison for 55 minutes and then got ashamed of myself and surrendered.") Although not as active as in preceding national campaigns, Hay did prepare a speech in which he assured his listeners that never before was "the right side of the argument" so undoubtedly clear. He did not hesitate to condemn the Democrats as silverites. Since Hay could hardly attack Grover Cleveland directly on this point, he decided that the party should "be judged by the acts of their majority in Congress," a majority which was, he maintained, "ready to embark on a stormy sea of reckless experiment." Conveniently ignoring the fact that the most recent government silver purchase was largely the result of John Sherman's efforts, Hay concluded, in sum, that the Democrats had "proposed nothing so radical or so dangerous" since 1860. The voters had best trust to Harrison and Reid.[65]

The people, however, disappointed Hay by electing

Cleveland and Adlai Stevenson. "I shall rely on you to save my neck from the ax of Adlai and the rage of Grover," Hay wrote to the Democratic Adams. Although Cleveland and the agrarian silverites were at opposite poles, Hay had no difficulty hating both. He ridiculed Cleveland's efforts to spur economic recovery by repealing the Sherman Silver Purchase Act. Silver was "only a drop in the bucket," he wrote, thus contradicting his speech of the previous year. The real cause of the depression, he opined to Reid, was the election of Cleveland on a platform of free trade and the abolition of national banks. "The mere threat of a revolution so complete will throw us into confusion for years," he wrote. Hay had absolutely no respect for President Cleveland. "What a vast, diffused, circumambient talent he has for being an ass!" Hay wrote after two years of Cleveland. That summer, on a camping trip with Adams and William Phillips in Yellowstone, Hay named the most inept pack horse Grover Cleveland. "It seems so exactly like the President and his party that it makes even Adams laugh—though Phillips looks grave," he informed his wife.[66]

Piteous as Cleveland was, Hay knew that the real danger came from other Democrats and malcontents—Tom Johnson in Cleveland, agrarian radicals and silverites, strikers and Coxeyites. There was sufficient peril to keep Hay politically active during these years of ennui. "I think I must take office again when we get youalls out,"[67] he wrote to Adams in 1894.

Hay bet on William McKinley as the man most likely to oust the Democrats and restore morality. The correctness of Hay's choice amused Henry Adams years later when he was working through Whitelaw Reid's papers for material on Hay. "The curious form of gambling deserves immortality," he wrote. "Whitelaw, controlling the *Tribune* won all the stakes down to '97; when Hay, by a third gamble . . . won out, and Whitelaw got left. . . . I would give six-pence to know how much Hay paid for McKinley. His politics must have cost." It was a gamble; Hay decided to back McKinley in 1893, and he paid as well. That year McKinley suddenly found himself responsible for the staggering debts of a friend whose business notes he had countersigned. Hay responded with a substantial gift. "I have no words with which to adequately thank you," McKinley replied. ". . . How can I ever repay you & other dear friends!" The following year Hay urged the governor to run for the presidency. "The third of March '97 is a long way off," McKinley replied. ". . . All the same I thank you for your invitation."[68]

Shortly thereafter Hay became actively involved in the Hanna-McKinley operation laying the groundwork for a presidential nomination. Never before had Hay been so deeply involved for so long at so high a level. In the months before the 1896 convention, Hay was an important figure in the McKinley organization. His first significant assignment was in March, 1895, when Hanna asked Hay to assist "the good cause" by visiting James Gary in Baltimore, an influential Republican not completely committed to McKinley. Hay was to resolve Gary's doubts, have John Sherman write him a confidential letter lauding McKinley, and get him to convince another Baltimore Republican to support McKinley. Hay's report, McKinley wrote to Hanna, was "good . . . and the result is as we had expected." McKinley thanked Hay and wrote an endearing letter to Gary commenting on his "valued friend Col. John. Hay." Hanna next urged Hay "to do some Missionary Work" in New Jersey and Virginia. "I do believe you could coax the birds—and things—out of the bushes," Hanna explained. This was an important mission: Hay was to sound out Senator Sewell of New Jersey and ascertain who held real power in Virginia.[69]

During 1896, and particularly until McKinley was nominated in June, Hay maintained a constant correspondence with Mark Hanna and, to a lesser degree, with McKinley himself. Hanna seems to have taken Hay into his confidence almost completely.

Hay's most important assignment was to determine the situation in critical Pennsylvania, where Matthew Quay seemed to be doing what he could to sabotage McKinley's hopes. Quay, it appeared, was working together with New York's boss, Thomas Platt, for Speaker of the House, Thomas Reed. At first, having been misled by Senator Donald Cameron, Hay discounted rumors of Quay's opposition. A skeptical Mark Hanna urged Hay to probe deeper, however, and in the end he confirmed Quay's disloyalty, as well as Cameron's.[70]

Having aided in securing McKinley's nomination, Hay spent a few brief weeks in Europe, then returned to the campaign. Before his vaction he had made several generous monetary contributions to the cause; in August Hay sent McKinley an additional $1,000 and promised similar amounts monthly until November. As Henry Adams guessed, Hay's politics cost a good deal.[71]

Part of the reason Hay gambled on McKinley was personal. He wanted to go to England as ambassador, and although he insisted that McKinley accept his contributions without strings (McKinley would not have done otherwise), Hay did what he could to further his own interests. Beyond purely personal reasons, Hay looked with utter horror on the possible election of William Jennings Bryan. As part of his campaign contribution that autumn Hay wrote a speech, never personally delivered but printed and widely circulated. "The Platform of Anarchy" was the most extreme statement he ever made publicly; it was a condensed, virulent rehash of his themes in *The Bread-winners*.[72] Even more than his 1880 speech, this was a paean to the industrial state. Under Harrison, he recalled, there were "the humming of thousands of looms, the ringing of the hammer on the anvil, the murmur of trade in thousands of marts." It was not unlike idyllic Buffland before Andrew Jackson Offitt arrived. Under Cleveland, by contrast, the fires went out, wheels ceased to turn, and shutters were closed.

The cause of the depression was quite simple, Hay thought. The country was not suffering from poverty, he insisted; "bad politics" lay at the root. The fact was that the "laws of nature" controlled the economy, and neither Cleveland nor Bryan understood that.

But such differences of opinion on how best to run the economy and the government were of distinctly secondary importance. If under Cleveland the wheels of industry slowed, it was more significant that "a decline of values" also took place. And if Cleveland was deplorable, next to Bryan he was a demigod; for "unclean spirits" had captured the Democratic party. "Questions of housekeeping are difficult to consider," Hay continued, "when burglars and incendiaries are seeking to sack and destroy the house. Other questions might well wait . . . until we have put down this shameful insurrection against law and national honesty." Hay's fictional Bread-winners had threatened the "old-fashioned decencies." Now the Democratic-Populist combination was hurling a "frantic challenge against every feature of our čivilization," while the likes of John Altgeld, Ben Tillman and Eugene Debs were the "moral dynamiters" of society. McKinley appeared virtually a Christ figure who would restore the capitalist utopia. Hay's peroration summed up the speech:

Evidently the boy orator has much to learn, among other things these: that to be a patriot one need not be an ignoramus; that a recognition of natural laws is a part of a statesman's business; that the winds of trade know no geographical barriers; that the same law of gravitation rules Niagara and the Ganges, and cannot be changed by a Populist Convention; that commerce and morals are not parochial institutions; that the great commandment "Thou shall not steal," thundered in smoke and flame from a Syrian mountain, still has full force and efficacy wherever there are minds to comprehend and consciences to respect it—from Sinai to Nebraska.[73]

It was a truly amazing performance, and one that might be largely dismissed as political claptrap, except that Hay believed it. His moral world was under its most serious attack yet, and the exaggerations of the speech were in his personal letters weeks before he wrote the address. He described Bryan as "that half-baked glib little brief-less jack-leg lawyer, running around the country . . . denouncing capital and grasping with anxiety to collar that $50,000 salary, promising the millennium to everybody with a hole in his 'pants,' and destruction to everybody with a clean shirt." Bryan, like the rest of Hay's devils, could not possibly be sincere. "Our poorest specimens . . .," he continued, Pierce, Polk, Johnson, Arthur, "loom up like demigods beside this little dog-fennel mountebank." The Republicans had expected to debate Cleveland, he wrote to Adams, but now they actually had to defend him when they found only Populists in the field. "It is as though we had gone out for a tiger and found the warm lair occupied by a skunk."[74]

Nor did Hay make any post-election efforts to unify the country (in contrast to Andrew Carnegie, for example), and he made at least two public statements condemning Bryan and all he represented. Such statements were not likely to reconcile those who had voted for the Democratic candidate, and they indicated how serious Hay considered the threat to basic American values, as he saw them. *The Bread-winners* was fiction, based on essentially local labor disturbances which were only peripherally political in nature. The campaign of 1896, in effect, nationalized the story of the Bread-winners. It was, Hay wrote to Reid, "the revolt of Caliban."[75]

With McKinley in the White House, Hay gradually felt less threatened. "I do not see a ghost of a chance for Bryanism in the next few years," he wrote to Senator Henry Cabot Lodge in 1898. Believing that revolution was no longer imminent, Hay became somewhat more relaxed in his public statements. In an 1899 letter, published as a campaign document in Ohio, he accused the Democrats of unpatriotic behavior for opposing certain aspects of American foreign policy; but, because he felt that "no man regardeth them" and that the country was prosperous, Hay's letter lacked the hysteria of his 1896 remarks.

Hay's greatest contribution to the 1904 campaign was a long July Fourth address on the history of the Republican party. The speech contained a number of implied thrusts at the Bryanites, but there were no wild accusations, no suggestions that Democrats were traitors. The Republican party, he said, did not "monopolize the virtue or the patriotism of the country," and he even made some extremely liberal remarks (for him) concerning labor. Privately, Hay thought President Roosevelt was overly worried about the political situation. "He sees a good many lions in the path," Hay confided to his diary, "but I told him of the far greater beasts that appeared to some people as in Lincoln's way, which turned out to be only bob-cats after all."[76]

Although the hysteria was gone, Hay's underlying convictions were unchanged. He remained a staunch partisan and disliked reformers. He could, it is true, congratulate Theodore Roosevelt for being "a reformer by instinct," but only because Roosevelt attacked the Democratic machine in New York. (Tammany Hall people were, after all, "filthy curs.") Nevertheless, Hay made it clear that the governor-elect was "not a wild ass of the desert," and the suspicion lingers that Hay felt somewhat uncomfortable with Roosevelt's reformist tendencies.[77]

Hay retained his fear of anarchists and his distrust of labor unions despite his attempt in 1904 to woo votes with certain flattering references to labor. Significantly avoiding comment on those portions of President Roosevelt's first message to Congress that dealt with the question of trust regulation, Hay found the " 'anarchy' portion . . . admirable." Two years later, he complimented the president on a Labor Day address in which Roosevelt preached a community of interest between capital and labor and warned labor against succumbing to the appeals of demagogues and anarchists.[78]

Hay's move to the right—economically, politically, and socially—which began in earnest after the strikes of 1877, never reversed itself, although to some extent its intensity ebbed and flowed depending on the immediate social and political climate. Not a technological reactionary like the Boston Brahmins, Hay welcomed the new industrial order and profited by it. But he never believed that the new times called for new values, and he could not comprehend those who believed otherwise. His business interests—railroads and the telegraph—were symbolic of the new technological developments of the late nineteenth century, but Hay was deeply afraid of any challenges to his values and beliefs. His anxiety showed itself in virulent attacks, both public and private, on labor and reformers. Just a few weeks before he died, Hay applauded President Roosevelt's warning to strikers in Chicago that he might call out the army to quell insurrectionaries. "It requires no courage to attack wealth and power," Hay said, "but to remind the masses that they, too, are subject to the law is something few public men dare do."[79]

Hay's views of domestic social and political issues were reflected to some extent in his views on foreign policy. His democratic fervor of the 1860's and early 1870's, for example, influenced the editorials on foreign affairs that he wrote for the *New York Tribune*. His later belief that capitalism was basically beneficient predisposed him to urge protection of American commercial interests in China and elsewhere, and to approve the annexation of Hawaii and the Philippines. Similar considerations make more understandable his strong defense of the seizure of Panama and the construction of an isthmian canal. Likewise, his fear of anarchy and the subsequent stress on law and order predisposed him to endorse America's efforts to crush the Filipinos, despite the fact that some of his best friends in the literary world strongly disapproved. These were not the only factors involved in his foreign policy decisions, but they were significant considerations.

III

Hay and Race

American society in the late nineteenth and early twentieth centuries experienced a fascination with race and ethnicity that has seldom been matched. Lynchings, often of the most gruesome sort and usually perpetrated with little pretext except the race of the victim, reached a peak and constituted the most hideous manifestation of the country's preoccupation with race. Blacks suffered the most, but many Italians, Jews, Mexican-Americans, and others suffered similar fates. On a less violent level, the Supreme Court vitiated the civil rights acts that came out of Reconstruction, and, by the 1890's, a thoroughgoing system of segregation and disfranchisement of black Americans had resulted. Social anti-Semitism was also rampant at many levels of society with hotels and resorts openly advertising their restrictionist practices. The Chinese were also ostracized, particularly in California; in 1882, Congress temporarily excluded most Chinese immigrants, an exclusion eventually made permanent. The Japanese also felt the wrath of Californians although they were not totally barred from immigration until 1924. European immigrants were never totally excluded, but, beginning in the 1890's, there were strong efforts to restrict immigration from Southern and Eastern Europe. The restriction movement, using arguments that were often explicitly racial in character, succeeded in placing immigration on a quota system in 1921 and 1924 with less desirable countries allowed the smallest quotas.[1]

Some of the violence and much of the hatred and

discrimination derived from theories of race held and propagated by the most respected men and women of the age. "One does not have to read very far in the writings of the nineteenth-century social scientists to discover the immense influence of race theories among them,"[2] writes Thomas Gossett. The theories of Charles Darwin and his popularizers were central to this fascination. If individual organisms had evolved to various stages of development, did it not follow that races of men, too, were in different states of evolution? Was it not obvious, in fact, that the white "races," particularly the Anglo-Saxons, exhibited traits superior to other groups of people?

Such beliefs were so widespread that it is the nonracist of those times who attracts especial notice rather than the racist. Even those who ardently disputed the individualistic, laissez-faire doctrines of the Social Darwinists—social reformers and proponents of the Social Gospel, for example—accepted, by and large, theories that placed the races on a superior-inferior scale. Race, it has often been said, was the blind spot of the Progressive movement, and it has long been recognized as an influential factor in American expansionism. One historian has even written that "the concept of race" was "the keystone" of the imperial impulse.[3]

In such a milieu John Hay reached maturity. Although scholars have, to some extent, analyzed his general social thought, none has discussed in any depth his developing thought on race and ethnicity. His thought is intrinsically interesting and significant to students of the late nineteenth and early twentieth centuries. In some ways he merely reflected the general racial atmosphere of his times, in other ways he departed from that feeling. Furthermore, his racial presuppositions affected his international outlook and his actual diplomacy.

Two features stand out. First, in the sense that Hay accepted without much question the general superiority of Anglo-Saxons, he was a racist. But his thought was not static in this respect, and prior to the late 1870's the evidence suggests that Hay's belief in Anglo-Saxon superiority was muted while his views of most other peoples were generous. If others had not yet achieved as much as Anglo-Saxons, they surely had an equal potential. After the 1870's, however, his racial views hardened, something most clearly seen in his novel, *The Bread-winners.* Surprisingly, in light of his intellectual interests, Hay does not appear to have been directly influenced by Darwin, Herbert Spencer, or their popularizers. He was personally acquainted with the popular Social Darwinist, John Fiske, but in virtually none of his writings or private letters does Hay refer to Darwin, Spencer, or evolution. There is nothing, for example, that resembles the intellectual analyses of evolution and race made by his friend Theodore Roosevelt. Hay's racial feelings were not scientifically deduced. He nevertheless believed that Anglo-Saxons were, in general, more capable beings.[4]

The second feature of Hay's thought is that, for the age, his racial feelings were in most respects mild and moderate. He developed unkind opinions of the Irish, American Indians, and Latin Americans. But he was scarcely a Negro-baiter, although he probably thought Negroes inferior; he was not an anti-Semite, although he was not overly concerned with the plight of the Jews; and he thought that Congressional efforts to exclude the Chinese permanently were "wrong & shameless."[5] Perhaps the very fact that he was not a devotee of popular Darwinism made his racial views less than consistent and, in some respects, placed him at odds with the prevailing tenor of the times.

The sketchy evidence available concerning Hay's early, pre-Civil War racial presuppositions indicates a vague, not carefully formulated acceptance of Anglo-Saxon superiority. However, his thought on race was intertwined, in a rather confusing way, with culture and religion. For example, he thought that Roman Catholic countries, especially those under strong Jesuit influence, were unlikely to have progressed as far as Anglo-Saxon, Protestant societies. The Jesuits, Hay contended in a lecture delivered in the late 1850's,"came into opposition with the course of events, the development of modern civilization, the liberty

of the human mind." They created "a vast machine, blood-
less & soulless." In contrast, America—"the young republic
standing in Titanic youth upon the shore of the new Atlan-
tis"—had sprung from the Reformation and held the future.
"The vigor of the Anglo-Saxon mind enlightened by the
large results of the Reformation laid its foundations deep
enough to stand the utmost shocks of fate or time,"[6] Hay
concluded.

Hay's Civil War experiences must have made difficult
such an easy acceptance of Anglo-Saxon superiority. Not
only had "the young republic in Titanic youth" torn itself
apart, but the declared neutrality of the other Anglo-Saxon
power, England, alienated Hay who, like many of his
contemporaries, interpreted England's stance as pro-Con-
federate. "The better classes in England," he wrote, detested the Union army which they termed "a horde of
hirelings enlisted to butcher the gentlemen of the South."
"England said that in English," Hay commented, "and so
we understood and remembered it."[7] Furthermore, the
strong democratizing influence of President Lincoln during
the Civil War may well have caused him to pause and
reconsider his racial views.

During the 1860's, therefore, glib assurances of Anglo-
Saxon superiority are not found in Hay's writings. During
this period, "backward" societies appeared to him to suffer
from institutional deficiencies rather than racial liabilities.
In virtually very chapter of *Castilian Days*, Hay lashed out
at the Catholic church and other allegedly decadent Spanish institutions. But he expressed heartfelt sympathy for
Spanish people and professed to see a great future for them.
If, like his good friend Emilio Castelar, the republican
champion, "the Spanish people can be brought to see that
God is greater than the king," Hay wrote, "the day of
deliverance is at hand." Hay had not written his travelogue
to degrade Spaniards as racially backward. "There are those
who think the Spaniards are not fit for freedom," he wrote
on the flyleaf, apparently replying to those who questioned
Latin abilities. "I believe that no people are fit for anything
else."[8] But later he would implicitly repudiate such an

optimistic assessment of the ability of Latins to govern themselves.

Hay also disliked the repression American blacks suffered. His concern for Negroes lessened somewhat in later years, but his views of Negroes and the injustices they suffered remained more consistent throughout his life than did his views on most other race-related matters.

Slavery disgusted Hay. As a young boy he had stumbled onto a wounded runaway slave, a traumatic incident which instilled in him a hatred for the institution. Although he cannot be compared with white abolitionists and civil rights advocates like William Lloyd Garrison, Theodore Dwight Weld, Charles Sumner, or Albion Tourgee, Hay's anti-slavery feelings were nevertheless genuine. The slavery issue appears not to have commanded much of Hay's attention in the early months of the war; still, as the President's secretary, he heard and recorded many of the debates surrounding possible emancipation. When Lincoln finally decided to issue a limited emancipation proclamation in September, 1862, Hay found the cabinet members jubilant and relieved. "They all seemed to feel a sort of new and exhilarated life," Hay wrote in his diary; "they breathed freer; the Pres^ts Proc^n had freed them as well as the slaves. They gleefully and merrily called each other and themselves abolitionists, and seemed to enjoy the novel sensation of appropriating that horrible name." The enthusiasm with which Hay recorded this reaction, and his suggestion that Lincoln's action freed them all in a psychological sense, indicates that he shared the feeling.[9]

Hay himself wrote that he wanted his "abolition record clearly defined." Although hardly a militant abolitionist in the pre-Civil War sense, Hay contemplated gleefully a proposal of General Henry W. Halleck that former slave owners be imprisoned at hard labor as recompense in kind for selling people into slavery. "That will be rare," Hay wrote, "to see the swaggering lords of lash, lazy & lousy, long-haired & languid . . . in zebra garb and zouave scarcity of *chevelure* breaking stone or digging the first ditch instead of dying in the last."[10]

Hay's concern for blacks did not cease with the abolition of legal slavery. Continuing injustice disturbed him. Reading an account by David R. Locke (who wrote under the pseudonym Petroleum V. Nasby) of the "legal lynching" of a Negro preacher in Kentucky, Hay wrote, "the wit and satire of Locke are growing so earnest and savage that it is painful to read him." Hay had his own chance to be satirical a few years later, although the circumstances were, fortunately, less tragic. Writing in the *New York Tribune* Hay discussed "one of the most beautiful instances of devotion to the Caucasian idea." One Mrs. Todd discovered that her husband, whom "she had sworn to love and cherish, and—if she was a good churchwoman—to obey," was part Negro, whereupon she left him and published the fact, "doing violence to her innate modesty in the interests of ethnology," Hay thought. "On the whole, we are rather inclined to congratulate Todd on his release," the article concluded, "than Madame upon her discovery."[11]

About the same time, Hay expressed his thoughts in poetry. One of his most moving verses dealt with postwar racism in Illinois. "Banty Tim" told the story of Sergeant Tilmon Joy who returned from the war to Spunky Point with a black companion. The White Man's Committee made it known that Joy's friend could not remain in the village, whereupon the sergeant replied:

> I reckon I git your drift, gents,—
> You 'low the boy sha'n't stay;
> This is a white man's country;
> You're Dimocrats, you say;
> And whereas, and seein', and wherefore,
> The times bein' all out o' j'int,
> The nigger has got to mosey
> From the limits o' Spunky P'int!
>
> Le's reason the thing a minute;
> I'm an old-fashioned Dimocrat too,
> Though I laid my politics out o' the way
> For to keep till the war was through.
> But I come back here, allowin'
> To vote as I used to do,

Though it gravels me like the devil to train
  Along o' sich fools as you.

Now dog my cats ef I kin see,
  In all the light of the day,
What you've got to do with the question
  Ef Tim shill go or stay.
And furder than that I give notice,
  Ef one of you tetches the boy,
He kin check his trunks to a warmer clime
  Than he'll find in Illanoy.

Why, blame your hearts, jest hear me!
  You know that ungodly day
When our left struck Vicksburg Heights, how ripped
  And torn and tattered we lay.
When the rest retreated I stayed behind,
  Fur reasons sufficient to me,—
With a rib caved in, and a leg on a strike,
  I sprawled on the cursed glacee.

Lord! how the hot sun went for us,
  And br'iled and blistered and burned!
How the Rebel bullets whizzed round us
  When a cuss in his death-grip turned!
Till along toward dusk I seen a thing
  I could'n't believe for a spell:
That nigger—that Tim—was a-crawlin' to me
  Through that fire-proof, gilt-edged hell!

The Rebels seen him as quick as me,
  And the bullets buzzed like bees;
But he jumped for me, and shouldered me,
  Though a shot brought him once to his knees;
But he staggered up, and packed me off,
  With a dozen stumbles and falls,
Till safe in our lines he drapped us both,
  His black hide riddled with balls.

So, my gentle gazelles, thar's my answer,
  And here stays Banty Tim:
He trumped Death's ace for me that day,
  And I'm not goin' back on him!
You may rezoloot till the cows come home,
  But ef one of you tetches the boy,
He'll wrastle his hash to-night in hell,
  Or my name's not Tilmon Joy.[12]

"Banty Tim" was one of the six *Pike County Ballads* that thrust Hay into the literary limelight in 1871. The 1870's was, as we have seen, an important decade for Hay in other ways as well. He became an assistant editor of the *New York Tribune*, furthered his acquaintances with prominent authors, came to know Henry Adams who would soon become his closest friend, married Clara Stone, and, for the first time, began to accumulate considerable wealth.

The same decade also marked a turning point in Hay's social and political thought; and, in a parallel (though less clear-cut) manner, it marked a significant change in his racial views. In particular he became a bitter foe of Irish-Americans. To be sure, he had disliked the Irish since the New York draft riots of 1863 in which persons of Irish descent were prominent. As a staunch supporter of Lincoln and the Union's cause, he considered such activities treasonous and privately accused New York Governor Horatio Seymour of being a traitor for refusing to enforce the conscription law. Two years after the war his lingering contempt for the Irish led him to write an anti-Irish poem, never published, entitled "Two Fenians." In the poem, Pat MacArone and Micky Macarthy are dirty, sexually immoral, alcoholic, diseased, and venal. They had "squirmed and wriggled" away from England's rule, coming to the United States where they "fed" in the same "doggery." All in all, while the poem had a jocular tone, the two Irish immigrants were portrayed as belonging to a lower order of human beings. A similar theme appeared several years later in *The Bread-winners.*[13]

Hay even questioned Schuyler Colfax's "occasional encouragement of Fenianism." In a letter congratulating Colfax on his vice-presidential nomination in 1868, Hay lectured the politician about the futility of wooing "that solid mass of blind hate and ignorance." Perhaps the grandchildren might "vote for the good side," Hay stated, but for the present "the Irish race is today the bitterest foe of human freedom everywhere but in Ireland. We must do our work, not with their aid, but in the face of their senseless and malignant hostility."[14] It was an odd topic to be included in a letter of congratulation, and it indicates the depths of Hay's feelings on the subject even three years after the end of the Civil War.

These early expressions of anti-Irish feeling, however, were the result of wartime experience and do not entirely explain Hay's later hatred of the Irish. In fact, with the exception of some elements implicit in "Two Fenians," his resentment of the Irish during these years was similar to his dislike of the Jesuits, the Mormons, slavery, and the Catholic church, all of which represented in different ways a throwback to barbarism and a block to democratic institutions.

Indeed, Hay's hope that their grandchildren might yet vote correctly implies that the Irish, like the Spaniards, were culturally deprived, not racially damned, for they were capable of improvement given time and the right environment.

The real turning point in Hay's racial thought was the great railroad strike of 1877. As the strike turned Hay into a partisan conservative dedicated to maintaining the political and social status quo, so it also hardened his racial opinions, especially of the Irish, for large numbers of Irish laborers were involved. Hay was in England six years later when he wrote *The Bread-winners*, and there, too, the Irish were often on his mind. "The great excitement about the Fenians still keeps up," he wrote. "They call them 'The American Irish.' I tell them they sent us the worst element our population has, and I am very glad to have them go back to Ireland where they belong."[15] "Two Fenians," although portraying the Irish in very derogatory stereotypes, was intended to be humorous. *The Breadwinners,* on the other hand, not only reiterated and extended the stereotypes found in the poem, but was bitter and largely humorless in tone.

The distinction Hay made in *The Bread-winners* between the good and the bad rested unmistakably on a racial basis. Without exception, the admirable major characters in the novel—Farnham, Saul Matchin, the Beldings, Mr. Temple, Sam Sleeny—are Anglo-Saxon. A very few admi-

rable minor characters are German. The undesirable figures, on the other hand, are largely Irish. The venal mayor
is named Quinlin. Most members of the hated Bread-winners are Irish as well. Mrs. Belding remarks at one point
that her husband, were he alive, would have made a "little
speech complimenting Ireland and the American flag, and
they would go away." The villian Offitt writes for the *Irish
Harp.* In addition, he is exceptionally swarthy—"dark-
skinned" and "unwholesome looking." His "oleaginous"
face is "surmounted by a low and shining forehead covered
with reeking black hair." His mustache is "dyed black and
profusely oiled." His eyes are green, the normally white
sclera "suffused with yellow and red." He even wears a
black hat and black clothes; and Mrs. Belding recalled that
he was "as black and shiny as a cricket." Being of low-
grade racial stock, Offitt is naturally envious of Sam
Sleeny's "shapely build, his curly, blond hair, [and] his
frank blue eyes." So deep was Hay's disdain for the Irish
after the strikes of 1877 that the death of Offitt in the novel
might be interpreted as Hay's approval of racial-political
murder.[16]

The Bread-winners, therefore, in addition to being a
key document in understanding Hay's changing social
thought, also revealed the existence in his mind of a much
more rigid racial hierarchy than had existed prior to 1877.
Although it is not easy to delineate (except in the case of the
Irish), his general retreat from an enthusiastic attachment
to freedom and democracy was paralleled by a gravitation
toward a more rigid general position on race. In 1890, for
example, a new edition of *Castilian Days* omitted the original flyleaf stating that all men deserved freedom. In its
place Hay wrote a preface acknowledging that his
prophecies remained unfulfilled, his hopes baffled by "the
swift progress of events." Although he claimed that the
work could not be seriously amended without "tearing the
book to pieces," a subsequent edition, published in 1903,
omitted not only the flyleaf but six chapters as well, some
of which included strong pleas for democracy.[17]

In the years following 1877, Hay's personal correspondence is sprinkled with racial slurs, particularly dur-

ing his term as secretary of state. Japanese were usually "japs," Chinese often became "chinks," and, most regularly of all, Latins became "dagoes" and worse. In the months preceding the Panama revolution of November, 1903, Hay and President Roosevelt outdid one another with epithets directed at the character of the Colombians. To Hay the Colombians (who had refused to give in to American pressure) became "greedy little anthropoids" and "poor creatures" with the minds of "jack rabbits."

To the extent that there were any exceptions to the general direction in which Hay's thought on race and ethnicity moved, they were his conceptions of Jews and blacks. In fact, Hay was admired (at least on the surface) by some segments of the black community, and he became something of a hero to many Jews because, as secretary of state, he took strong stands on issues of interest to Jewry.

Hay was not noticeably anti-Semitic, a surprising fact in view of his close friendship with Henry Adams, one of the most vitriolic of the patrician anti-Semites. There is some evidence that Hay accepted the nineteenth-century stereotype of the Jew. In 1868, for example, he hoped that one of his friends was "getting [as] rich as a Dutch Jew." And, in 1903, he wrote to his wife that a "jew from the East" had bought out a newspaper owned by his friend "poor Joe Bishop." In fact, he added upon reflection, "it is perfectly wonderful how they run to newspapers. Think of the 2 Pulitzers, Ochs . . . . and now this jew who has bought the Advertiser, and now [that] I think of it Villard who bought the Evening Post—yes, and Einstein who bought the N.Y. Press."[18]

But the existence of such stereotyped expressions do not necessarily establish an anti-Semitic outlook. Hay may have regretted that "a jew from the East" had bought out "poor Joe Bishop" but he was not terrified, or even outraged, as Henry Adams would have been, to think that Jews controlled so much of the press. Rather, the phenomenon was something to be wondered at. Hay even closed his letter humorously, noting that only the *Tribune* and the *Herald* remained in non-Jewish hands, "and both of them owned by Scotchmen, who are said to be double-jews."

Hay, then, appears to have accepted the stereotype without feeling threatened by it. The existence of anti-Semitism did not drive him to open defense of the Jews—otherwise he could not have survived the company of Henry Adams. But neither did he take it seriously. Indeed, he privately chided Adams for his irrationality. As they prepared to tour the Nile together in January, 1898, Hay found Adams "clean daft over the Dreyfus affair. He believes all Jewry is banded together to get him free," he wrote. "The Jews are all the press, all the cabinets, all the gods and all the weather. I was amazed," he concluded, "to see so sensible a man so wild." By March, Adams was still fuming, convinced that Dreyfus and Jewry generally were responsible for all evil. With barely concealed sarcasm Hay wrote that Adams "now believes the earthquake at Krakatoa was the work of Zola and when he saw Vesuvius reddening the midnight air he searched the horizon to find a Jew stoking the fire."[19]

In sum, Hay was very much like his anti-Semitic friends. He accepted most of their values, lifestyle, and attitudes, and his racial attitudes were, in general, similar. Furthermore, he appears to have shared with many gentiles of the Gilded Age a stereotyped image of Jews. Yet he was not anti-Semitic.

One possible explanation may be that Hay was not a dispossessed aristocrat, like the true Brahmins, shoved aside by new forces. Hay was a newly arrived aristocrat who did not share the antipathy for capitalism felt by the Brahmins. If Adams and other patricians despised Jews because they represented "the supreme expression of a commercial, bourgeois society,"[20] Hay felt comfortable with the very business culture they resented so deeply.

Hay included influential Jews among his professional associates, most notably Oscar Straus, whom he consulted from time to time about diplomatic matters in the Middle East. Hay's popularity among Jews, however, developed primarily from his responses to the plight of Jews in Russia and Eastern Europe. In 1902, Jacob Schiff urged the State

Department to protest Romania's treatment of her 400,000 Jewish citizens. Although Hay was reluctant to appeal openly and directly to the Romanian government, he nevertheless entered a strong, if private, protest. Hay's note (actually drafted by Adee) was a noble effort. It reviewed the various disabilities and discriminations under which Romanian Jews were forced to suffer, wrongs which, Hay stated, were "repugnant to the moral sense of liberal modern peoples." Then, to bring more pressure on the Romanian government, Hay openly asked all of the signatories of the Berlin Treaty of 1878 to urge Romania to right her ways.[21]

Yet Hay was himself only tangentially concerned about the Romanian Jews. The diplomatic protests were undertaken mostly for domestic political consumption; it was hoped the stand would be advantageous to Republican candidates. As Hay informed Adee in a letter marked "Please burn *promptly*," "The President is greatly pleased . . . and the Hebrews—poor dears! all over the country think we are bully boys."[22]

The highly respected rabbi, Joseph Krauskopf, of Temple Keneseth Israel in Philadelphia, took issue with Hay's note. Krauskopf admitted in a sermon that the note was "laudable and well intentioned," but the thrust of his remarks was critical. The note, he stated, was "self-protective," which impaired its noble sentiments and invited "failure for the United States and disappointment for the Rumanian Jews." Indeed, Krauskopf inferred that he wanted the United States to intervene militarily in Rumania.[23]

Basically, Hay's calculation appears to have been accurate. Krauskopf's sermon was delivered after the elections, perhaps intentionally. Prior to the elections, other rabbis praised Hay. Rabbi Bernard Drachman of the Congregation of Zichron Ephraim in New York, for example, viewed Hay's "noble plea" as a restoration of the American tradition to respect basic human rights. To those goals Drachman pledged the "enthusiastic loyalty" of all Jewish-Americans. Indeed, copies of Hay's note were read in some of the synagogues the Saturday immediately preceding the elections. And at least one prominent New York politician urged President Roosevelt to send Hay to campaign in the Jewish areas of New York. "The mere fact of his presence & words of cheer & advice," he wrote, "would arouse more enthusiasm than all the meetings we have had. The appreciation of the Hebrews for Mr. Hay's splendid defence in their behalf in the Roumanian matter, has evoked a tremendous outburst of gratitude."[24]

The Romanian incident demonstrated well Hay's working relationship with prominent Jews, as well as the popularity he was building among the Jewish community. The same year another matter arose that promised to test that popularity. For some time American Jews had been badgering the administration to respond to Russia's refusal to honor the passports of American Jewish citizens. The *American Israelite*, Hay wrote in August, 1902, has "been beating us black-and-blue for our laches in not going for Russia," and he finally suggested to Adee the outlines of a protest note. But it was clear that Hay was thinking more of the political benefits that might derive from such a protest than of the justice of the issue. "Even if Russia does nothing," he concluded his letter, "we shall have a good note to print next winter."[25]

Nothing came of this matter, however, for before Adee got around to drafting such a note the outrageous Kishenev massacre of Russian Jews occurred on Easter Day, 1903. The massacre changed the issue from one of honoring passports to whether the United States should formally protest the slaughter. Because Hay did not act immediately, he received much criticism from American Jews. But he effectively finessed the criticism, partly by writing an aggrieved letter to Jacob Schiff in which he wondered why he should "be required to defend myself against any accusation of neglect of duty in such a matter." He deftly explained why he could not act publicly at this time and permitted Schiff to show his *"private and confidential"* letter to Oscar Straus "or to any friend who may inquire." He also contributed $500 to a Jewish relief committee based in New York.[26]

Hay's most effective counter, however, was his willingness to meet privately with several prominent Jews, at
which time he listened to their suggestions. The meetings
eventually produced a mutually agreeable approach. Hay
successfully argued that a protest note would only exacer-
bate relations with Russia and would be of no use to the
Russian Jews. Instead, at a meeting on June 15, Hay and
President Roosevelt agreed to a suggestion by a B'nai B'rith
delegation consisting of Oscar Straus, Leo N. Levi, and
Simon Wolf that the State Department undertake to forward
a massive petition to the Russian government. On June 26,
Hay made the decision public by releasing a letter to Simon
Wolf formalizing the decision. But the administration
could not, Hay added pointedly, "tell you what reception
your petition will meet with at the hands of the Russian
government."[27]

As Hay expected, the Russian government refused to
accept the petition, telling the American representative in
St. Petersburg that if the petition were delivered in person
to the foreign minister, he would hand it back at once
without looking at it; and if it were sent along with an
official note, "he would at once place it in another envelope
and return it ... unopened, unread." Hay immediately
informed the press, then sent letters to the Jewish leaders.[28]

Sometime later Hay received the "murdered petition"
into the State Department archives. The deposition was
accomplished amid as much publicity as possible, a move
agreed upon by Hay and Roosevelt in consultation with
Straus and Levi. "It gives me pleasure to accept charge
of this significant document and to give it a place in the
Archives of the Department of State," Hay stated.

Although this copy of your petition did not reach the high
destination for which it was intended your words have attained
a worldwide publicity and have found a lodgment in many
thousands of minds. This petition will always be memorable,
not only for what it contains, but also for the number and weight
of the signatures attached to it, embracing some of the most
eminent names of our generation, of men renowned for intelligence, philanthropy, and public spirit. In the future when the
students of history come to peruse this document, they will

wonder how the petitioners, moved to profound indignation by intolerable wrongs perpetrated on the innocent and helpless, could have expressed themselves in language so earnest and eloquent, yet so dignified, so moderate, and so decorous. It is a valuable addition to public literature, and it will be sacredly cherished among the treasures of this Department.[29]

During the latter stages of this crisis, Henry Adams, in his cynical, churlish manner wrote to Mrs. Hay, "I'm so glad John loves the Jews." Actually, love had little to do with Hay's action in any of his diplomatic activities on behalf of Jewry. He acted only under pressure in all three instances. Although he was glad to reap whatever political benefits might accrue from his actions, he would have preferred not to have been bothered at all with matters of this sort. Certainly he was mildly sympathetic to the Jews of Russia and Romania, but he much preferred to deal with other questions. Indeed, Hay found the whole matter of the Kishenev petition to be a dangerous irritant in Russian-American relations. He was having trouble with the Russians regarding China and hoped to come away from the massacre affair without further embittering relations between the two countries. "It seems advisable to me to close the petition incident as soon as possible," he wrote to the president, a sentiment he had expressed on other occasions as well. His actions and desires in this matter were understandable and, indeed, probably represented sound diplomatic thinking, but he was not in any sense overly concerned with the persecuted Jews of Eastern Europe.[30]

As he had done with so many other people, however, Hay convinced most of American Jewry that he shared their fervor. When he died in 1905 the Jewish community mourned, issuing extravagant praise. In Philadelphia, Rabbi Krauskopf and his congregation consecrated a memorial window to Hay. In contrast to his critical remarks at the time of the Romanian incident, Krauskopf now praised Hay for his "spirit resolute in the defense of the wronged, a tongue fearless to speak the truth, even when truth speaking is dangerous, a hand ready to strike a blow for justice and right." The window likened Hay to the prophets of old. Rabbi Krauskopf explained:

The attitude of noble defiance, the fire of the prophet's soul gleaming from the eyes, the face burning with righteous indignation, the right hand keeping back the weaponed horde in eager pursuit of a downtrodden people, the other hand holding the charter of his right of protest, and extending in protection over refugees seeking our shores of freedom—these tell the story of a prophet of our day, of an emancipator and redeemer of the twentieth century, the story of John Hay.[31]

In the same spirit a Detroit lodge of the B'nai B'rith prepared to erect a monument to Hay in Washington, D.C., and several hundred Jews from both the United States and Great Britain signed a memorial address which was presented to Mrs. Hay. "As the world champion of Justice," the address stated, "he stood ready to inaugurate a new diplomacy—a diplomacy of humanity—which will forever mark an epoch in the affairs of nations."[32]

Even Oscar Straus, who should have known better, looked back in 1913 and incorrectly credited Hay with discarding "traditional diplomatic methods" in favor of "sincerity and directness" and of emphasizing "the principle . . . that national wrongs are of international concern." Hay was, Straus concluded, "a personality whose visioned eyes windowed the soul of a prophet, whose lips worded the majestic imagery of the Psalmists, and whose patriotic heart throbbed with the divine spirit of the Golden Rule."[33] Actually, there was nothing Hay wanted less than to initiate a new diplomacy based on moral crusading.

In sum, Hay was not an anti-Semite. He did not feel threatened or outraged by the new, industrial, business culture that many of his contemporaries associated with the Jew, and there was little if any shift in his opinion of Jews during his life. But neither was he a philo-Semite, and the praise he received was misplaced. He felt neither threatened nor much concerned.

With regard to blacks, there appears to have been a noticeable change in Hay's thinking during the later decades of his life. But the change was subtle, not dramatic. The best example of Hay's concern for blacks occurred in March, 1879, almost two years after the strikes of 1877, when several thousand Negroes engaged in a migration from the deep South to Missouri, Kansas, and Nebraska.

The trek, resulting in deprivation and suffering that was heightened by the resistance of white settlers in the West, received major newspaper attention in the North, and sympathy meetings were held to raise funds for the refugess. It appears that Hay was among the leaders in the relief effort in Cleveland. As a member of the committee involved in the effort, Hay spoke to a large gathering. "They are cold and hungry—that is all we need to know for the present." he said. "It is our business to give them something to eat and wear—before discussing the question of how they came on our hands." He even acknowledged a corporate guilt for their plight. "We are not free from responsibility in this matter," he continued. "The ancestors of these people were brought here by our ancestors. The whole nation—not a part of it—shared in the shame and profits of slavery through a long course of compromising years." The North freed them, he went on, "and we cannot altogether stop our ears to their cry by saying we are not our brother's keepers. Especially in this Western Reserve of Ohio is this plea impossible," he reminded his audience. "You did too much to make these people free, to look upon their distress with coldness now." As for those whites responsible, by their racist behavior, for forcing the exodus, "it were better that a millstone were hanged about their necks and that they were cast into the depths of the sea."[34]

Hay's views on blacks in the 1880's can be ascertained from his biography of Lincoln. Since shortly after Lincoln's death, he, together with John G. Nicolay, had begun gathering materials for a definitive account of the Lincoln years. Completed between 1885 and 1890, the massive biography demonstrated that Hay's views of slavery and Negroes were apparently unchanged. The authors treated slavery as an anachronism; it was, they wrote, a "relic of barbarism," a "reactionary obstacle in the pathway of modern civilization, and its political, material, philosophical and religious development." The biography was less clear about the inherent capabilities of black people. But the tone suggested that Negroes, much as Spaniards, had at least the potential for achievement comparable to Anglo-Saxons.

Slavery might have debased them temporarily, the authors implied, for Negro soldiers were not immediately success-ful because "the full manhood which springs from liberty and individual self-assertion still needed to be aroused and stimulated." A few pages later, however, even this qualifi-cation was gone. "One point of doubt about employing negroes as soldiers was happily removed almost impercep-tibly by the actual experiment," they wrote.

It had been a serious question with many thoughtful men whether the negro would fight. It was apprehended that his comparatively recent transition from barbarism to civilization, and the inherited habits of subjection and dependence imposed upon him by two centuries of enslavement, had left his manhood so dwarfed and deadened as to render him incapable of the steady and sustained physical and moral courage needful to armies in modern warfare. Practical trial in skirmish and battle, however, proved the gallantry and reliability of the black soldier in the severest trials of devotion and heroism. Within a year after Lin-coln's order of enlistment the black regiments had furnished such examples of bravery on many fields that commanders gave them unstinted praise and white officers and soldiers heartily accepted them as worthy and trusted companions in arms.[35]

Hay retained his interest in Negroes for the rest of his life. Shortly after his death, the *New York Times* reported that he had invested a very substantial sum, perhaps $1,000,000, in a model tenement program designed to aid the poor, especially Negro poor, in Washington, D.C. Former Surgeon General of the Army George M. Sternberg headed this philanthropic enterprise that benefited some 194 families, mostly "respectable colored tenants," until Sternberg's death in 1915. Although no corroborating evi-dence of Hay's involvement has yet come to light (and Sternberg's widow made no mention of Hay in her account of her husband's life), Hay may well have been involved. Not only was he sympathetic to the blacks, but Sternberg was a close friend of President and Mrs. McKinley. He once visited the Philippines at the president's request, and he treated Mrs. McKinley (a semi-invalid) from time to time. Those who invested in Sternberg's project, moreover, had not donated their money, for there was a return (albeit a small one) on the investment.[36]

Despite such manifestations of genuine concern, other evidence suggests that Hay's assessment of blacks changed. Even his speech in 1879 on behalf of the emigrating blacks, although unquestionably noble, was paternalistic. Black people, he had noted, were generally "the most domesticated race in the world, a people as devoted to their old plantations as so many cats." Then too, Hay may have used the occasion for subtle partisan advantage, since those he condemned were presumably Democrats. Hay asked for compassion for the victims, and political vengeance for their oppressors, but he did not address the issue of real equality.

In 1892, Hay did come out strongly for political equality when he publicly defended Henry Cabot Lodge's so-called Force Bill which attempted to ensure voting rights for Negroes in the South. Although Lodge's bill deserved a strong defense, Hay's speech was frankly intended as political oratory. It was, in fact, his contribution to the campaign of 1892. He might well have been more concerned with the benefits that would redound to the Republican party from Democratic opposition to Lodge's efforts than with equality per se.[37]

In the 1890's racial slurs pertaining to Negroes appeared in Hay's correspondence for virtually the first time. In October and November, 1898, for example, he "struggled with the nigs in the cloak room," met a Haitian diplomat whom he termed "a bright little nig," and wrote to Henry White about the "coons" in Liberia. In 1900, he wrote to his son, Adelbert, that he planned to work Alvey Adee, John Bassett Moore, and William W. Rockhill "like Guinea niggers," and, in 1903, he reported jocularly to President Roosevelt that his other son, Clarence, had a pet raccoon named Rastus that followed him around in the woods like a dog.[38]

Symbolic of Hay's lessening concern for Negroes was his reaction upon learning of the incredible double life led by his long-time friend Clarence King. The enigmatic and brilliant King had for some years maintained a common-law marriage with a Negro woman in New York. According to

Tyler Dennett (who does not specify the nature of King's double life), King's name "was never again mentioned over the 'Five of Hearts' teacups."[39] The contrast between Hay's reaction in 1873 to Mrs. Todd's divorce of her racially impure husband and his attitude toward King's later action is revealing.

While Hay maintained a paternalistic interest in Negroes, his concern seems to have lessened subtly after the 1870's. Certainly he never became an outspoken advocate of civil rights during the very period those rights were being steadily undermined. Yet, for the most part, Hay confined his unflattering racial references to private letters. And he was popular, at least superficially, with some blacks. On at least two occasions, for example, he received invitations to visit Tuskegee Institute. More revealing was the establishment of the John Hay Normal and Industrial School in Alexandria, Virginia, in 1894. The philosophy of its founders, Robert and Magnus L. Robinson, was in line with that of Booker T. Washington, and the school's purpose was to train black youngsters for "acceptable" jobs, a mission that ensured the support of white philanthropists.[40]

Hay's reaction to this unsolicited honor, which included school stationery with his portrait prominently displayed in the left-hand corner, was one of embarrassment. He did contribute to the school from time to time, checked into its status on one occasion, and advised friends to contribute when they asked him, though he generally claimed to know little of the school's function. He received invitations to address the students but always had other commitments. When, in 1902, an opportunity to change the school's name arose, Hay jumped at it. "They called their school at first after my name," he explained to George B. Cortelyou, who had written asking whether he should contribute, "and I got so tired of answering questions about them that I induced them with coin to change the name from John Hay to William McKinley."[41] Thereafter the institution bore the title, The William McKinley Industrial School.

Not surprisingly, Hay also cast off his previous suspiciousness of England so that by the time he became ambassador to the Court of St. James in 1897, he was an outspoken champion of Anglo-American friendship. His advocacy of a rapprochement with England was based, in part, on racial-cultural considerations.

Outside of the time he spent abroad as a minor diplomat in the late 1860's, Hay's first sojourn to Europe took place in 1878, a trip that included a quiet month in England. However, his first chance to meet prominent Englishmen did not occur until 1882, when Henry Adams arranged a number of introductions. "I know none of the great people," Adams wrote modestly, "but am fairly intimate with the literary crowd."[42]

Hay looked forward to this vacation with some trepidation. "I never promised myself that much of a spree in my life," he wrote to Howells shortly before he sailed. "I feel a little superstitious about it now—as if it were too good for the likes of me." But the trip exhilarated him, and to Adams he was effusively thankful for the introductions, adding, "we hope to be in England next summer."[43]

The main reason Hay desired to extend his stay was that he had arrived too late to take full advantage of the London social season that summer. "If I am able to spend a month or two of the early summer in London," he explained to his father-in-law, "I can meet and make the acquaintance of a considerable number of the leading men of letters and science in London, whose acquaintance and perhaps occasional correspondence will be a pleasure and advantage to me, the rest of my life." Hay pursued this goal vigorously, feeling confident enough the following March to ask the American minister to have Mrs. Hay presented at a drawing room. Hay knew, he wrote, "a few . . . fahig people who would doubtless stand sponsors, if needed."[44]

Besides the joys of new friendships, Hay admired the English countryside and the city of London. London, he wrote, "is one of the most wonderful phenomena of the world." Significantly, Hay felt that the most notable aspects of the city were the contributions of aristocracy and wealth. "It shows on every hand the results of vast accumulated wealth, almost beyond calculation," he wrote approvingly. "A numerous idle class, accustomed to luxury and unlimited expense, make their influence felt everywhere."[45]

Hay was thus introduced to English society with which he soon became almost as familiar as with American society. The English, to be sure, had their faults. There was the numerous "smart set," a name applied to British philistines, and, of course, there were the inevitable common people. But there was also an unusual percentage of fine gentlemen who welcomed good company and conversation. These Hay sought. Late in 1883, after Hay's return to America, Adams took note of Hay's new status by urging him to purchase a share in a new Washington theater, "so that you can use the place for your English friends."[46]

Hay returned to England the following summer for a brief stay after Adams ordered him to "go to England and be happy. Come back and bring us gossip of the great." Hay found England particularly pleasant this time. The beauty of Richmond Park captured him as he drove with Clarence King. "This beautiful England!" he exclaimed to his wife. "There is nothing equal to it in this world. Sometimes I feel like settling down here for good and all—but then I know we can't." The Hays next visited England in the summer of 1887, staying with friends acquired in 1882 and 1884 and making new acquaintances everywhere they went. By now Hay could move easily in the "better" social circles, although Adams nevertheless continued his paternal watchfulness.[47]

All in all, England appealed to this increasingly conservative gentleman for its culture, its manners, its orderliness. "We saw some of the prettiest country we have ever seen," Hay wrote to Adams, "and the establishment wore an air of decency and order, of industry and intelligence which was extremely agreeable."[48] How different from Cleveland, upset as it was with labor disorder, and agitated, so Hay believed, by shiftless Irish trade union organizers.

So cosmopolitan had Hay become that there was even

some talk that he would become minister to England under President Benjamin Harrison. Although Hay did not receive the appointment, he was sufficiently acquainted with the British elite to have been well received in London. He knew, for example, the outgoing British minister in Washington, Lionel Sackville-West, whom the Cleveland administration had asked to leave for allegedly interfering in America's domestic politics. Hay wrote to the minister expressing his "shame and disgust at the unexampled meanness and cowardice with which you have been treated by the present administration." He also held a dinner for the new minister, Julian Pauncefote (whom Adams called Punchfoot). Hay and Pauncefote later became close friends, but at the time the new minister did not impress Hay or one of Hay's guests, who later averred to Adams that "Punch was stupid."[49]

Shortly after the Pauncefote dinner, the Hays sailed again for England, and, again, it did not disappoint them. "I wish you were here," Hay wrote to Adams from Kirkcaldy, Scotland. "I have rarely seen a place so beautiful. The park gates are near the station and all the long drive up the hill the road is bordered with a flame of rhododendrons and azaleas and the jargoning of the sweetest singing birds I ever heard."[50] As Adams had predicted, the Hays were lionized, and their social schedule was extensive. In the week preceding June 23, 1889, for example, they dined with Lady Metcalf on Monday and followed with lunch the next day at Mrs. Dorothy Tennant's. That evening they dined with a large party at the Andrew Carnegies where they met the Gladstones, the Robert Lincolns, the William Harcourts, John Morely, and a host of other distinguished people. On Wednesday, Hay dined with Sir John Puleston, after which he drove with his wife to Lady Salisbury's party at the Foreign Office. On Thursday, Cecil Spring Rice dined with them, and, on Friday, they were at Lady Jeune's with William H. Mallock, author of *The New Republic* and George Earle Buckle, editor of the London *Times*. On Saturday, they went to the Joseph Chamberlains, where they found Mrs. Endicott, Deputy-Speaker Courtney, Mrs.

Robert Peel, Sir Henry Drummond Wolff, and a number of others.

The following Monday, the Hay's planned to attend a reception in Grosvenor Gallery, and, on Tuesday, they expected to attend a function at Windsor castle and then dine with the Munro-Fergusons. On Wednesday, they were to attend a military tournament and dine with the Murray-Smiths, after which they hoped to attend a soiree at Lord Huntington's with tickets secured by Lady Jeune. On Thursday, they would dine with the Sir William Farrars and Friday they were to be with Lord and Lady Wolseley at Greenwich; and so it went, day after day.[51] Yet John Hay professed to be disturbed over Whitelaw Reid's distasteful hobnobbing with the great!

Before he became ambassador to England in 1897, Hay traveled twice more to the island, including an extensive sojourn from August, 1893, to July, 1894.[52] The patterns established in the 1880's continued, Hay visiting prominent men, charming them with his wit and good manners; Mrs. Hay more concerned, at least outwardly, with being seen at the proper functions. Hay had come to love the country, its culture, and, for the most part, its people. Spiritually akin, so he believed, to the cultured English aristocrats with whom he associated, Hay had rejected democracy in favor of the stratified society he outlined in *The Bread-winners.*

Many of the men with whom Hay became acquainted in the 1880's and 1890's were outspoken advocates of Anglo-Saxonism and, often, of imperialism as well. James Bryce, Joseph Chamberlain, Arthur Balfour, Rudyard Kipling, and Cecil Spring Rice were only five of the many staunch supporters of Anglo-Saxonism whom he knew well. Hay first met Spring Rice, for example, in 1887 when Anna Roosevelt introduced them. Kipling, who later wrote the famous poem, "The White Man's Burden," was one of the few new English acquaintances Hay made in the 1890's. The author gladly accepted Hay's invitation to visit him in New Hampshire in 1892. Unfortunately, the details of the Hay-Kipling relationship cannot be fully reconstructed since Kipling destroyed all but one letter from Hay, but other evidence indicates the two men were good friends. Without doubt, Hay discussed the future of the Anglo-Saxon race with these men.[53]

In 1898, Spring Rice, in his outspoken, enthusiastic manner, urged Ambassador Hay to use his influence to see that the United States retained possession of the Philippine Islands as a result of the Spanish-American War, then in progress. It was necessary, he wrote, to "secure what we can for God's language." Hay was more discreet than Spring Rice, and he seldom invoked the Diety as a justification for racial imperialism. But at heart he did not disagree with the Englishman. The racial theme in Hay's letters and speeches was usually subtle but, when combined with occasional explicit references, the theme was clear. When Hay called for "A Partnership in Beneficence" in 1898 in which the two peoples would be "ministers of the same sacred mission of liberty and progress, charged with duties which we cannot evade by the imposition of irresistible hands," or when he wrote to Henry Cabot Lodge that "the interests of civilization" were "bound up in the direction the relations of America and England are to take in the next few months," or when, later the same year, he told representatives of an Anglo-American league (headed by James Bryce) that a cordial friendship between the two countries was "a necessity of civilization," or, in 1900, when he wrote in reference to the Boer War that "the fight of England in South Africa is the fight of civilization and progress, and that all our interests are bound up in her success," he was not thinking only of advancing the concrete material and strategic interests of his country. His diplomacy was based in part on racial grounds intertwined with cultural factors. As Bradford Perkins has written, the concept of race in the 1890's, as applied to Anglo-Saxonism—hardly a scientific term, especially when applied to the United States—implied simply "a community of outlook." Hay and other leaders in both the United States and Britain clearly believed in the superiority of that Anglo-Saxon community of outlook.[54]

Beginning in the late 1870's, Hay's overall views of race and ethnicity gravitated toward a more rigid posture. Although he was never entirely consistent and was not the fawning Anglophile that some contemporaries alleged him to be, he had come to feel that Anglo-Saxons were alone capable of efficient government and that the "backward" races were not likely to improve in the near future. Racial and cultural considerations were only in part responsible for the direction of his diplomatic thinking, but such factors were more important than they would have been had he been secretary of state in the 1860's or 1870's.

IV

Setting the Stage: Hay's Views on International Questions, 1865–97

John Hay's ideas about society and politics in the United States influenced his thought concerning international relations to a significant degree. His first opportunity to consider seriously questions of international affairs arose shortly after the Civil War when he was appointed secretary of the American legation in Paris. Subsequently he served as chargé d'affaires in Vienna and as secretary in Madrid, returning to the United States in 1870. An enthusiastic defense of American republicanism and a corresponding disgust with European monarchism emerged during these years, an attitude derived in large part from his conversion to the republican faith during his service with Lincoln. Clarence King, Hay's long-time friend, aptly summed up Hay's thought during these years by comparing him to John Randolph of Roanoke. Randolph, King wrote, "used to say he would go a mile out of his way to kick a sheep. Col. Hay goes farther than that sometimes to kick a King."[1]

Although Hay lambasted monarchy in numerous letters, his critical remarks were more often humorous than bitter, for he firmly believed that monarchism represented a cause as lost as secession. From Vienna, for example, he wrote to John Bigelow:

I am very glad I came. Vienna is worth while for a year. It is curious & instructive to see this people starting off in the awkward walk of political babyhood. They know what they want & I believe they will get it. The Aristocracy are furious and the Kaiser a little bewildered at every new triumph of the Democratic

92

& Liberal principle. But I don't think they can stop the machine now–though they may get their fingers mashed in the cogs. I don't think the world ever seemed getting ahead so positively & quietly [?] before. Two years ago–it was another Europe. England has come abreast of Bright. Austria is governed by Forty-Eighters. Bismarck is becoming appalled by the spirit of Freedom that he suckled with the blood of Sadowa. France still lies in her comatose slumber–but she talks in her sleep & murmurs the "Marseillaise." And God has made her ruler blind drunk, that his Helot antics may disgust the world with despotism.

If ever in my green & salad days, I sometimes vaguely doubted, I am safe now. I am a Republican till I die. When we get to Heaven, we can try a monarchy perhaps.[2]

Spain provided Hay with his best chance for close observation of the clash between old and new. "I had never seen the Republic and the monarchy in the Ring," he wrote to a friend explaining his decision to accept the Madrid post. Spanish civilization was much closer to the Dark Ages than other European societies, Hay felt, and thus it provided a severe test for any optimistic philosophy. With its antiquated culture, Spain's politics were naturally corrupt and anarchic, in Hay's view, and the young diplomat felt that lack of principle existed nowhere to the extent it did in the Spanish government. Spanish politicians, he wrote to Bigelow, retained "the speech of Don Quixote, but the heart and stomach are Sancho's." After three months in his new post, Hay could not recall a single instance where any leading Spanish official had "committed the indiscretion of telling the truth." Individual officials were charming and amiable, he thought. "They only suffer from that utter elimination of the moral principle from their nature."[3]

Such reprehensible traits resulted in strained diplomatic relations. Being insincere themselves, Spanish diplomats expected insincerity from others. "It is this which renders their diplomacy so annoying and vexatious," Hay observed in *Castilian Days.* "They take all you say as a ruse to cover your real intention." Ingrained lying, when combined with a high sense of Spanish honor, inevitably produced paradox and made it unrewarding to press even the most legitimate claims, particularly where money was involved. For example, when Spain finally released the *Lloyd Aspinwall,* an American ship seized illegally on the high seas and held for four months by Spanish authorities resident in Cuba, Hay thought that this was only "the first act of a disagreeable quarrel. . . . They have given her up, with a very ill grace, but we shall have trouble getting the indemnity."[4]

Centuries of benightedness, moral turpitude, political corruption, and diplomatic evasiveness made it difficult to espouse a progressive philosophy. Hay recognized the dilemma in *Castilian Days.* "The only question asked in Spain and in the world," he wrote, "is, not whether the republic is needed there, but whether it is possible." Hay was not easily discouraged, however. "The theory that the Latin Races are incapable of self government is a very convenient one for Latin aristocrats," he wrote to Charles Sumner, "but I expect before I die to see it practically contradicted." In essence, Hay believed that all peoples were outgrowing the need for monarchy. He ridiculed those who declared otherwise; logic led to the republic.[5]

Although Spain's medieval traditions were deeply ingrained, Hay thought he discerned real changes in Spanish society after the republican revolution of September, 1868. For example, Spaniards were now investigating spiritual phenomena forbidden by the church. Politically, the republicans brought a breath of fresh air, despite internal dissensions and occasional relapses into more traditional Spanish molds. On certain fundamental issues they formed a "solid phalanx," favoring individual rights and autonomy for the Spanish colonies, opposing the rule of violence and superstition, denouncing the "slavers of Cuba and the thought-stranglers of the Vatican." Caught up in his own rapturous rhetoric, Hay proclaimed that the voice of the republic "rings out in the Cortes in strains of lyric beauty, that are only heard in the fresh and dewy dawn of democracies. . . . The current cannot be turned backward. The record of these two laborious years of liberal effort has not been written in water. . . . Spain, the latest called of the nations of Europe, is not condemned to everlasting punishment for the crimes of her kings and priesthood." There is a Jeffersonian leap of faith in such statements. But *Castilian Days* clearly demonstrated that Hay thought he saw the future. "The people have the right to govern themselves, even if they do it ill," he wrote in the concluding chapter.[6]

The Spanish republican Hay most admired was Emilio Castelar, with whom he became close friends. Hay corresponded with Castelar throughout much of the 1870's and editorialized about him in the *New York Tribune*. "He is the only man I have ever seen who produces, in very truth, those outstanding effects which I have always thought the inventions of poets and the exaggerations of biography," he wrote in *Castilian Days*. A gifted orator since the age of sixteen (he was thirty-two in 1870), Castelar devoted his abilities and great energy to the cause of spiritual and particularly political freedom. "During all these eventful years," wrote Hay, "he has not for one moment faltered in his devotion to liberal ideas. In poverty, exile, and persecution as well as amid the intoxicating fumes of flattery, he has kept his faith unsullied."[7]

Shortly before Hay left Madrid, Europe stumbled into the Franco-Prussian War–"the most infamously unjust and causeless war that ever was made," Hay opined. The war would set back reform initially, he feared. But Hay, who never claimed republicanism would arrive without difficulty and setback, left Spain full of hope. "I leave Europe in a grand and imposing time," he wrote to his family. "The greatest historical drama of our age is now being played. I hope that the war will not last much longer and that it will result in a lasting peace with freedom."[8]

For the next five years, while serving as an associate editor of the *New York Tribune*, Hay's faith in the ultimate triumph of democracy remained strong. The establishment of a republic in 1873 appeared to corroborate his belief. "The faith of all of the Republicans of Spain has been justified by ways [all?] could have foreseen," he editorialized. Adee, who witnessed this parliamentary revolution, was fairly ecstatic, even writing Hay two letters in one day. "We recognized the Republic today amidst a blaze of soldiery in the streets and the bands playing 'Yankee Doodle,'" he wrote in one. "I would not exchange these last five days and their memory for ten years of life."[9]

Despite Hay's conviction that republicanism was inevitable, he feared the reaction of the European powers to Spain's experiment in democratic government. Considering his later attachment to things English, it is significant that Hay particularly disliked Britain's attitude toward the fledgling republic. "Nowhere is . . . injurious distrust so openly manifested as in England, where it takes on the form of overt sympathy with Carlism," he wrote, condeming English efforts to send arms to the forces of reaction. Also significant, in light of Hay's later attitudes, were his reasons for singling out the British for criticism. In contrast to the amoral Germans, for example, who aided the Carlists for reasons of trade only, the immoral British assisted them "simply because they dislike Republicanism."[10]

Clearly, during the late 1860's and into the following decade, Hay allied himself with a deep American tradition extending back to the Puritan's sense of mission. Thomas Jefferson and other American philosophers expressed similar notions; indeed, Jefferson could well have written portions of *Castilian Days.* The Young Americans of the 1850's who cheered Louis Kossuth on his triumphal tour of America continued the tradition, and Abraham Lincoln, clearly the most immediate influence on Hay, demonstrated the necessity and viability of republican government. Hay's final editorial on Spanish affairs in 1875, by which time monarchist forces again ruled Spain, indicated that he still possessed a republican faith:

It is difficult to understand and impossible to sympathize with those florid hopes, wherewith so many people, in England and France, especially, greet the accession of Don Alfonso to the throne of his mother. . . . The maddest hope is that which fires the usually temperate brain of our British cousine [sic]. Some of the soberest English papers take it for granted that civil war and conspiracies will now immediately cease.[11]

Although he was certainly a democratic enthusiast, Hay's specific policy recommendations to achieve republican goals were considerably less clear. The Young American phenomenon, Norman Graebner states, "represented a national self-consciousness, nothing more. Its objectives were vague, its means nonexistant. Europeans, to the extent that they responded to American sentimentalism, might better have anchored their hopes and fears to forces purely European." Graebner's generalization describes the Hay of this period rather well. He sympathized with the republicans and was outraged by their opponents. In 1868, for example, Hay objected strenuously to the behavior of the American consul in Rome, J. C. S. Abbott, who allied himself with the papal forces against the Italian republican patriot, Garibaldi. Abbott "would suffer immediate decapitation if the Senate heard of it," he opined to Mrs. Bigelow. When Abbott published an article in *Putnam's Magazine* which referred to the "insane adventure of Garibaldi," Hay was indignant. "I have just been blushing and swearing by turns over that miserable, measly, crawling, lying apology." Had Putnam perhaps permitted its publication sight unseen? "Perhaps decent people–not very well informed–may read that vile trash and believe it. It is too horrible, to think of the public conscience being so debauched." Outraged as he was by anti-republicanism, Hay seldom suggested positive action. Even in 1873, for example, when it became evident that European monarchies were actively aiding the Carlists forces in Spain, he never advocated American assistance to the other side. Like the Young Americans, Hay's beliefs represented only an attitude, not a program for action.[12]

Cuba, the one big diplomatic question on which Hay expressed himself during these years, illustrated his lack of a viable and consistent program to attain the democratic goals he so loudly espoused. The Cuban rebellion was an involved affair made all the more complex by the unstable conditions in the mother country. From the beginning, Hay was convinced that, at least as long as the monarchy held power in Madrid, Cuba was lost to Spain. "I am afraid

Cuba is gone," he wrote to Nicolay. "This government wants to sell but dares not, and has no power to stop the atrocities on the Island."[13]

Hay's statements implied that a new government in Spain might be able to control the volunteers and enact reforms or otherwise dispose of the Cuban problem. As time passed, however, Hay came more and more to feel that no Spanish government could retain Cuba and that the island was destined to become part of the United States. By 1873, he was convinced that even his beloved Republicans, then in power, could not keep Cuba despite their good intentions; but if Cuba was certain to become part of the United States eventually, Hay saw no reason at that time to force destiny.[14]

Soon, however, Hay implied that America might have to take a more active role in the Cuban situation. He found the rebellion "monotonous. . . . The Spaniards make no headway against the insurrection, and the insurrection seems powerless to do more than sustain itself in the mountains and forests." Hay therefore concluded that only "some now unforeseen shock from the outside world could loosen the grapple in which Cuba and Spain hold each other."[15]

Unknown to Hay, the possibility of an "unforeseen shock" had already occurred with the seizure off Cuba of the *Virginius,* a ship flying the American flag. The Spanish volunteers swiftly courtmartialed and executed fifty-three persons, including several Americans. Since Americans did not then know that the *Virginius* was actually a Cuban vessel illegally flying the American banner, a genuine war scare developed. The affair left Hay in a rather embarrassing position, for having editorially praised the recent accession of the Spanish republicans, he did not wish to endanger their still uncertain control by attacking Spain. On the other hand, American rights had to be upheld. Furthermore, Hay reasoned, Cuba was a millstone about Spain's neck, and the *Virginius* affair might prove to be a blessing in disguise. It could give the United States a chance to provide the "outside shock" needed to resolve the revolution by forcing the Spanish government to come to grips with the Cuban problem. "No one went before us in welcome to the enfranchised democracy of Spain," Hay wrote. "But we recognize the false position in which they are placed by the lamentable state of affairs in Cuba, and we conceive that we are fighting their battle when we force them to join issue finally and decisively with the Casino Español."[16] This was a delicate balance, but it was the best Hay could do under the circumstances.

In keeping with the objectives of saving the Spanish republic, securing justice for the *Virginius*'s victims, and hopefully resolving the Cuban civil war, Hay's initial editorial was emotional but, at the same time, cautious. "This is an outrage of the highest grade which can be inflicted by one country upon another," Hay began ". . . Our neighbor's house is on fire, and we cannot hope to escape the fire. . . . We have delayed interfering long enough. . . . Whatever others may do, we cannot afford to do nothing." Despite such provocative language, Hay backed away from advocating immediate military redress. He hoped that no "*brutum fulmen*" would be launched, suggesting instead a demand for full and immediate reparation and punishment of the guilty.[17]

In the days following the capture, Hay's position moderated steadily, and soon the possibility of using the *Virginius* affair as the "outside shock" disappeared from his editorials. Hay retreated to his long standing belief that history had destined Cuba to become a part of the United States. The United States should therefore prepare for the inevitable, he felt, instead of dissipating energy in cries for revenge. The State Department should negotiate "with the greatest discretion," and Americans should give "hearty approval to any solution of the question which shall save our interests and honor without bloodshed." Hay immediately approved the protocol subsequently negotiated by Secretary of State Hamilton Fish and the Spanish minister, Admiral Polo de Bernabé.[18]

The *Virginius* sank in eight fathoms off the North Carolina coast while being towed to the United States, thus ending disputes as to the proper ownership. The civil war in Cuba, however, continued without respite into 1874. Spain could not control the volunteers, the volunteers could not quite defeat the rebels, and, although the rebels could harass, they could not win. "We have restricted ourselves to giving the news from Havana and from the interior more fully and accurately than any other paper," Hay wrote, "and to stating from time to time that each side was too strong for the other to beat it, and too weak to beat the other."[19] The time might come when the United States would truly have to provide the impetus if destiny did not choose to impose itself. But for the time being, Hay could suggest nothing more positive than to wait for Cuba's inevitable drift toward America's orbit.

After 1875, Hay's interest in foreign affairs diminished as he settled into a life of leisure. Railroad investments, labor strife, domestic politics, and the collection of material for his long-delayed life of Abraham Lincoln occupied his attention. In 1879, Secretary of State William Evarts offered him the position of assistant secretary of state. Hay at first declined, but after a long talk with Whitelaw Reid, he agreed to take the post.[20]

Hay seems not to have viewed his new position as an opportunity to evaluate or investigate the nature of international relations. Indeed, the fact that the appointment involved diplomatic work was mostly fortuitous and rather unimportant, for Hay considered the office primarily a reward for his political contributions. In return, Hay rewarded his friends.[21]

The new assistant secretary of state also felt he was duty bound to serve the public, a reflection of his adopted Brahmin ethics. The office afforded him no pleasure, he wrote, except that he was "doing a public service honestly." Office seekers constantly besieged him, and by June, 1881, the petty pressures were so bad that even the service ethic held little sway. "I have only one aspiration in life," he wrote to a friend, "and that is to . . . get out of office and stop the head ache." No doubt Hay's tenure in the Department of State was significant in giving a future secretary of state some knowledge of the inner workings of the department. But essentially the office was simply one among many that he might have received. Hay was in tune with the general American apathy toward foreign affairs during this period.[22]

But, in the 1890's, foreign affairs attracted the attention of a number of prominent Americans, particularly the issues of national assertion and expansion. Hay was not an early theorist of either. Although he apparently approved the attempted annexation of Santo Domingo in 1868, his earliest sentiments clashed with expansionist ideas. How could one who had advocated self-determination in the clearest language accept imposition of government from the outside? Such ideas were too reminiscent of the practices associated with the European autocracies he detested. In such a mood he composed a sonnet, "Hawai" [*sic*]:

> Thou little isle, afloat in western sea,
> Alluring bait to many a great power!
> Oh, may we long postpone the evil hour,
> When, in our zeal for making others free,
> We join thee with us. 'Tis a foolish plea,
> That thou, who seekest shelter like a flower
> Behind the greatness of a massive tower,
> Still our advance guard in the world should be,
> Far be it from our principle of state
> On distant reefs and islands to display
> Our power of nations. It would take the might
> Of untold fleets to guard thee, day and night.
> Nay, islet, keep thou in the distance, pray
> And if thou fain wouldst join us,—watch and wait.[23]

Although Hay's swing to the right had sharply reduced his democratic fervor and instilled in him an admiration for commercial and industrial capitalism, he appears to have retained a certain poetic and sentimental view of the Pacific islands and was somewhat distressed at the effects "civilization" had upon them, effects which Adams brought to Hay's attention in 1890. His agreement with Adams was tenuous and partial, however. Significantly, he avoided taking up Adams' implied challenge to discuss the advantages and drawbacks of advancing commercialism. And, in 1893, when Hay discovered that the Cleveland administration had tentatively dropped plans to annex Hawaii, he was livid. "They deserve no toleration in the Hawaiian matter," Hay wrote to Reid, whose *Tribune* had treated the new administration with restraint. ". . . I can see no reason, except the fact that Blaine and Harrison favored it, to account for this stupid and senseless opposition of Cleveland and Gresham." When the administration did, in fact, reject Harrison's treaty of annexation, Hay professed to feel a sense of national disaster. "This Hawaiian business is too painful," he wrote. "I feel as if it had happened to all of us."[24]

It is not entirely clear why Hay reversed his earlier sentiments and came to favor annexation of the islands. Perhaps part of the reason lay in his blind antipathy toward anything the Democratic president attempted. Indeed, he immediately grasped the political potential of what he viewed as Cleveland's blunder. "Their hauling down the flag, by the instrumentality of a confederate, will be one of the most effective points on the stump for a year or two,"[25] he predicted, almost gleefully, to Reid. There may, however, have been reasons deeper than mere partisanship for Hay's strong response to Cleveland's actions, reasons which, if not yet fully formulated, became important later when Hay was charged with responsibility for American foreign policy.

Hay's early belief that all men had a right to freedom was by this time muted. If his views of American society had become more conservative by the 1890's, he was even less democratic with respect to nonwhite lands. He accepted without much question the common belief that Anglo-Saxons were intellectually superior, a bias which his increasingly frequent trips to England, his love of English traditions and culture, and his many friends from prominent English families fortified. His belief in self-government for all had changed to a conviction that Anglo-Saxons were most capable of good government, and he later used this argument to defend British imperialism in both North and South Africa, as well as American acquisition of the Philippine Islands.

Quite possibly Hay's friendship with two famed exponents of Anglo-Saxon superiority and imperialism, Rudyard Kipling and Cecil Spring Rice, contributed to this conviction. Hay met Spring Rice in 1887, and by the time President Cleveland decided against annexation they were close friends. Hay met Kipling a year before Cleveland rejected annexation of the islands. Whether Hay discussed the Hawaiian situation with these men remains speculative, but there is little doubt that Hay, by and large, agreed with their racial assumptions. Hay later relied on Spring Rice's racially motivated advice regarding annexation of the Philippines, and it is probable that Hay felt similarly that American annexation of Hawaii would benefit the natives.[26]

It is also probable that Hay thought annexation would benefit Americans materially, though the lack of hard evidence makes final conclusions impossible. His evolution to the right included a staunch defense of capitalism which, perhaps, explains his refusal to mention, much less discuss, Adams' allegations regarding business exploitation in the Pacific islands. Hay disagreed with Adams' attack on American capitalism and probably came to accept commercial exploitation of the islanders as inevitable (if somewhat sad), natural, and therefore good for all parties in the long run. As Walter LaFeber has made clear, most businessmen, especially in the 1890's, saw expanded markets as the way to alleviate the periodic depressions of the late nineteenth century which were caused by overproduction.[27] On the other hand, the desire for expanded markets does not necessarily result in a commitment to formal acquisition of overseas territory; indeed, the opposite is often the case.

Another factor may have entered Hay's mind as he considered the Hawaiian case. Hay believed stongly in national honor and integrity, a belief partially derived from his Civil War service for a president determined to uphold the integrity of the nation at all costs. *The Bread-winners,* too, called for strong, honorable, honest government, and proposed that revolt against legitimate governmental authority could not be tolerated. As a close observer of the domestic scene, Hay knew that the United States of the 1890's had developed into a power to be reckoned with. Indeed, his personal financial interests—railroads and the telegraph—epitomized the nation's growing strength. Hay may have felt that the United States should begin to act in the world like the great power she was.

Hay's assertive, mildly nationalistic outlook appeared to conflict with his sentimental attachment to Britain. Some people, in fact, thought that Hay's attachment to England was almost obsequious and blinded him to the genuine national interest. Theodore Roosevelt, for example, wrote in 1896, "[George Washburne] Smalley has been here for a week; worshipped by John Hay, of course. He is more English than the English, and has not the faintest idea how the people of the United States really feel."[28]

Roosevelt's assessment of Smalley was absolutely correct, but his implication that Hay was also a fawning Anglophile was not, even though Hay admittedly admired the British. Even in some cultural matters Hay preferred American standards. He much preferred Howells and James to any English authors, for example, and he readily acknowledged the existence of British philistines, including, he privately thought, the royal family and the Prince of Wales particularly.[29] His attitude toward his predecessor in London is even more revealing.

Hay disliked Thomas F. Bayard because of what he regarded as Bayard's undignified obsequiousness. In London in 1894, for example, Hay observed on the Bayards' faces "the most serene and transparent happiness that has ever been seen in the Legation here. When I saw them Saturday in the Royal Procession at the Foreign Office treading on the trains of H.R.H.'s too happy to do anything but smile, I felt proud of my country that still nurtured the almost lost faculty of enjoyment." When Hay replaced Bayard in 1897 he attended a farewell banquet for the outgoing ambassador where he delivered a short speech, gracious on the surface, yet filled with double meanings. Hay felt, for example, that "it would be most injudicious for any immediate successor of Mr. Bayard to attempt to rival his brilliant career. . . . Such an attempt would end in nothing but disaster." And he concluded that "it would not be inappropriate to speak of Mr. Bayard not so much as Ambassador to England, as Ambassador to the English," possibly a reference to Bayard's efforts to undercut his own government during the Venezuelan affair of 1895.[30]

Hay was pleased with his performance. Bayard "had a bitter blow yesterday," he reported to the president. Bayard "spoke an hour in his usual blundering gushing style. I spoke five minutes. . . . *The Times* printed *four lines* of his speech, and printed my remarks *verbatim* calling editorial attention to them. The fact is, they are sick to death of him, and his vapid flattery." Senator Lodge appreciated Hay's remarks at the dinner, which he read "with delight. It was a masterpiece of delicate irony & nothing cruel for he hasn't the wit to understand it. In fact I approve all your doings both your silver speech & golden silences."[31]

Hay's assessment of Bayard was not entirely fair. Both men worked diligently to bring about better Anglo-American relations. But it does illustrate that Hay hoped to carry on his diplomacy in a dignified manner consistent with national honor. In contrast to Bayard's penchant for accepting a multitude of speaking engagements (he was formally censured by the House of Representatives for attacking the protective tariff in one of his addresses), Hay determined to attend a bare minimum of engagements, "and resolutely to avoid slobbering over the British."[32]

Indicative of his nonsentimental approach was the nationalistic tone and substance of many of his dispatches. His recommendation on the proper American response to Queen Victoria's Diamond Jubilee, for example, reflected this concern. Many states, Hay reported, were preparing to spend large sums on the occasion. "It might not be advisable to pass by without notice an event of so much interest and significance, and one which so strongly engages the feelings of all the people of the British empire,"[33] Hay reported to Washington. Respectable powers should make clear to the world their proper status.

Similarly, Hay took pride in British uneasiness about America's growing economic power. In September, 1897, for example, he forwarded a blue book on the economic state of the British colonies that showed that Americans were capturing an increasingly larger portion of the colonial trade. "The whole report," Hay wrote in summary, "is valuable and timely, and the facts contained in it are most encouraging to American industries."[34]

On the other hand, Hay hoped to forge strong and lasting bonds with Great Britain. His motives were partly of a cultural nature, as his public speeches and private letters during 1897 and 1898 indicate beyond doubt. But the cultural motive did not conflict with Hay's tough-minded, nationalistic approach to Anglo-American relations. Britain, after all, provided a powerful model, complete with empire. Furthermore, a good case could be made (as Hay did) that the strategic interests of the two countries required a rapprochement. The far-sighted British government early recognized the value of a friendly United States in the event of future conflict with the continental powers; the United States, now more deeply involved in world politics, did not wish to alienate what was still the most powerful country on earth, especially since Britain was doing all it could to avoid conflicts in America's baliwick, the Western hemisphere.[35]

Because, as ambassador, Hay was at first thwarted in his attempts to improve Anglo-American relations, his early months in London were not entirely happy. He found himself occupied much too often with "petty anxieties," and he grappled "with futilities too trivial to think about, much less talk." A more important reason for Hay's unhappiness was Washington's decision to relieve him of major responsibility in each of the three important areas of Anglo-American concern in 1897. John W. Foster assumed responsibility for the discussions surrounding the pelagic sealing dispute with Canada, Edward O. Wolcott headed a commission that hoped to achieve a bimetallic agreement with England, and Whitelaw Reid represented the president at the Queen's Jubilee. In all of these matters Hay played a role, but in each it was largely confined to matters of protocol and was of a distinctly secondary nature. He even thought fancifully of resigning. Although he never seriously considered such a course, Hay did not like the plethora of American diplomats in his baliwick. "Never since dead-beats began to go on Embassies, were there so many American diplomats in London at any one time as now," he complained in July. ". . . When it comes to individual withering, it is I who am champion witherer."[36]

Considerations of personal pride were only part of the reason for Hay's unhappiness. More to the point, Hay thought the special American diplomats, with the exception of Wolcott, were incompetent or inept and therefore made difficult any rapprochement. This was particularly true of the negotiations surrounding the sealing dispute, in which Hay felt that Foster pursued a course devoid of form, taste, and politeness. As a gentleman, Hay believed good relations were more easily and securely established when diplomats carried on their business with the good manners that characterized his own discussions. When Foster exhibited a pushiness unbecoming a patrician gentleman, Hay objected.

By the time Hay became ambassador, the seal dispute had had a history dating from the first administration of Grover Cleveland. American sealers, who plied their bloody trade on the Pribiloff Islands off Alaska, felt threatened by Canadians who slaughtered the animals at sea (a practice known as pelagic sealing), sometimes sixty or more miles from the islands. When American revenue boats seized the pelagic sealers from time to time, diplomatic crises developed. Indeed, in 1890 relations were so strained that Great Britain warned the United States in language constituting a virtual threat of war, and English naval vessels in British Columbia were completely overhauled, coaled, and supplied with ammunition.[37]

Contradicting its traditional position regarding freedom of the seas, the American government developed the intriguing theory that since the seals bred on the Pribiloff Islands they were American property and could not be taken by others even when they strayed beyond the traditional three-mile limit. At times the United States also insisted that the Bering Sea was a closed body of water, not subject to the usual limits of territorial water. When an arbitral commission decisively dismissed these contentions in 1893, the government fell back on two propositions which had been advanced before, namely, that pelagic sealing was inhumane, and that its practice, even as restricted by certain regulations imposed by the decision in 1893, was severely diminishing the seal herd, possibly to the point of imminent extinction. England refused to accept the American contention, claiming that the seal herd was not in any danger of extinction and that American land sealing on the islands was responsible for what little diminution there might be.

Shortly after Hay's arrival in London, Britain agreed to consider an American proposal for an international conference regarding the seals. Secretary Sherman then appointed Foster to negotiate the terms for such a conference, Hay's role being merely to extend his good offices.[38]

Foster's first action alienated Hay, for the interloper drafted a sharp note to Britain and persuaded Sherman to send it on May 10. Foster was an expert on seal negotiations but lacked the tact and persuasive abilities that Hay thought so important. Foster's dispatch criticized at great length the British government's refusal to halt pelagic sealing and, in harsh language, accused it of deliberately delaying publication of a report prepared by one of its experts. The delay, Foster alleged, prevented the American government from considering the report before the opening of the seal season.[39]

Although some of Salisbury's dispatches had been nearly as harsh as Foster's, Hay at first refused to present the instruction as ordered. Instead, he met informally with Joseph Chamberlain, who suggested that in return for a halt to pelagic sealing, the United States might consider compensating Canadian sealers, a formula eventually employed when the dispute was settled in 1911. Chamberlain's suggestion impressed Hay, who cabled Sherman inquiring if he could delay presentation of the note until Foster arrived in London. Foster, however, persuaded Sherman to instruct Hay to present the note at once.[40]

The May 10 dispatch and the subsequent order to present it without delay represented the worst possible taste, Hay thought. "I wish you were here," he wrote in frustration to Adams.

I need some discreet person to listen to about an hour's steady cussing. There is nobody here with whom such profanity would be safe. I said when I started I could stand it a year—I begin to doubt it. It is utterly inconceivable the things they do and the things they say.

I have this week twice kicked at my orders—a thing beyond reason and utterly unjustifiable. But—I really must not talk about it.

Adams, fearing that Hay might resign in a huff, replied in a soothing letter that insanity in the State Department was quite normal and that it would be foolish to step down.[41]

Foster's dispatch appeared to have no ill effect on Anglo-American relations, however, and, on July 1, Hay received instructions to renew his efforts to induce the British government to agree to a conference of powers interested in protecting and preserving the seal herd to be held in Washington the following October. Hay carried out his instructions the next day, and, although Salisbury did not commit himself and still disagreed with the American premise that there was danger to the seal herd, Hay was quite optimistic.[42]

The May 10 instruction arose to haunt Hay, however, for just when agreement seemed possible, the *New York Tribune* published the document *in toto*. Beneath multiple headlines the *Tribune's* article proclaimed that the instruction showed "at length England's policy of procrastination, her continued failure and refusal to support this Government in its efforts to prevent the extermination of the seal herd." Hay reported to the State Department in correct terms about the "anger and resentment aroused in the press of England" by the publication of the instruction. To the president he was more blunt. "Everything was going on prosperously, until Wednesday night I received the news that the instruction . . . had been published in New York," Hay lamented. ". . . Today the British lion is standing on his head and lashing his tail around a lot." Because the British government had known the contents of the dispatch for two months and had apparently ignored its objectionable tone in discussions during that time, Hay hoped it would "not now go back on the almost completed agreement, in deference to the rub a dub in the papers." But, although Hay hoped for no ill effects, Foster's dispatch clearly disturbed him very deeply:

As I am writing to you, at your kind suggestion, in perfect confidence, I will say I foresaw all this rumpus from the moment I read the dispatch. It was an admirable paper in its facts and arguments—but the tone was very unusual. I therefore wired the Department of State, asking permission to hold it over a week until Foster arrived. I felt sure I could convince him that a very slight change of phraseology would not weaken but rather strengthen it. I received in reply a peremptory order to present it at once. When Foster arrived he told me that *you* had thought the tone of it rather severe, and that he had said he had meant to have it so. It is certainly not your style—you have the rare gift of being strong and courteous at the same time.

To be "strong and courteous at the same time" well described Hay's approach to diplomacy, at least when he dealt with "civilized" nations, of which the most civilized was England.[43]

But in spite of the publication of the Foster dispatch, the British government agreed at the end of July "to a meeting of experts nominated by Great Britain and Canada and the United States, in October next." Hay acknowledged Salisbury's note the following day, adding that the United States expected experts from Russia and Japan to attend as well.[44]

The agreement was reached, Hay felt, with needless difficulty, the result of Foster's methods. As Henry White wrote to McKinley's secretary, "the whole matter of the agreement reached . . . was entirely due to the admirable tact, good management and personal influence of Mr. Hay." Foster's note, he continued, was a "heavy handicap . . . to the ambassador's negotiations."[45]

Hay's accomplishment was not as significant as it first seemed, however, for late in September Britain decided not to attend a conference that included Russia and Japan. Britain's decision surprised Hay, who had all along assumed that Russia and Japan would attend; indeed, they had already been informed of the conference. Hay remonstrated with Foreign Office officials, still thinking that Britain would eventually agree if managed tactfully. "I believe they will come in at last, if we firmly but courteously insist," he wrote to the president in a most revealing letter. "I hope you will excuse me for talking about it—but in the present state of our relations with England the *form* is of unusual importance. The tone of the press betrays quite uncommon sensitiveness; they think Lord Salisbury did not sufficiently resent our note of the 10th of May. It would be seriously embarrassing for him to yield to any demand of ours now, which was not most courteously expressed." The form of communication, matters of taste, and good manners deeply concerned Hay and were intimately related to his desire to bring about an Anglo-American rapprochement. If England did not attend the conference, Foster was clearly to blame, Hay felt.[46]

Late in October the international conference met in Washington as scheduled. But England was not there, ingenuously claiming that Russia and Japan had no sealing experts. England's refusal irritated Hay, who called this behavior "tricky and tortuous." He nevertheless felt that the root cause of the failure was neither England nor Canada but the lack of manners exhibited by General Foster and subsequently by the American press. "Expressions of American newspapers saying that England has 'backed down,' were telegraphed over here and viciously commented on by the English papers," Hay wrote to the president. "The government was attacked for its cowardice, and probably did not like it."[47]

The seal dispute lingered on. From October 23 to November 6, American, Russian, and Japanese experts met and recommended outlawing pelagic sealing. The recommendations were binding, however, only if England agreed. Throughout December and January, Hay tried valiantly to gain British support. Britain stalled, then refused on the specious grounds that informal discussions were then underway between the United States and Canada. Although Hay contradicted Britain's contentions, Salisbury soon delivered a final and definitive refusal to adhere to the convention.[48]

As the months and years passed, the seal dispute waxed and waned. Occasionally, as in 1899, the parties were very near agreement, only to be hamstrung by more or less unrelated matters like the Alaska boundary dispute. The matter was not finally settled until July 7, 1911, when representatives of England, the United States, Russia, and Japan agreed to prohibit pelagic sealing operations. Canadians engaged in the business were handsomely compensated, a solution that Hay and Chamberlain had agreed upon fourteen years before.[49]

As a strong democrat in the 1860's and early 1870's, Hay had hoped for worldwide democratic revolution, and, as an American diplomat, he worked with republican elements in those nations (particularly Spain) to which he was assigned. Immediately thereafter he expressed similar democratic views in his editorials in the *New York Tribune.* His changing international outlook more or less paralleled his changing social views. His turn away from democracy, his concommittant devotion to capitalism and order, his increasing Anglo-Saxonism combined with nationalistic pride, and a largely unsentimental desire for strong Anglo-American bonds all found expression in his later international outlook. These later strains were still nebulous when Hay assumed his duties as ambassador in 1897. They developed during the early months of his tenure and became more evident when he was confronted with the great national crises of the following years.

V

The Spanish-American War and the Acquisition and Governance of the Philippines

The seal dispute detracted from Hay's otherwise pleasant stay in England, and its development was an important concern in Anglo-American relations. Of far more significance, however—for Anglo-American relations and for America's position in the world—was the Spanish-American War of 1898.

After his initial concern with Cuba in the 1860's and 1870's, Spanish-American relations seem not to have concerned Hay in the slightest for twenty years. When the Cuban revolution was vigorously renewed in the 1890's, however, he could not ignore it, for the sympathies of most of his friends forced the issue upon him. Theodore Roosevelt wanted to intervene, and Henry Cabot Lodge, who knew much less about Cuba prior to the 1890's than did Hay, was a staunch interventionist by early 1896.[1] Although he was friendly with Roosevelt and Lodge during these years, Hay was probably more influenced by closer friends with strong opinions—Henry Adams, Clarence King, and Henry White. King and Adams, who visited Cuba in 1894 and 1895, turned passionately in favor of the Cuban rebels, and White reported from London that England would not object to American intervention in the island.[2]

From 1895 through 1897 Hay concealed his views for the most part and seems not to have shared the fervor of his interventionist friends. It is not even clear if he favored American intervention at all. Late in 1895, for example, he expressed his sympathy for the Spanish minister, who was being attacked by "our unbridled and licentious press,

113

because he tries to serve his country, and wants ours to obey the laws." And when Adams straightforwardly asked Hay his views about Cuba, Hay seems not to have replied.[3]

Nor were his opinions much clearer by the time the *Maine* exploded in Havana harbor on February 15, 1898. At that time Hay was vacationing with Henry Adams on the Nile. News of the explosion made Adams "turn yellow,"[4] but Hay was strangely unperceptive about the implications.[5] His return to England was so leisurely that, in addition to indicating a lack of interest, in retrospect, it amounted to professional negligence. The Hays remained in Cairo until March 5. Mrs. Hay wrote that they were "so busy sightseeing that we have not had much time for writing."[6] They might have stayed even longer but, as Henry Adams explained when they left, "the Hays got a little nervous for fear of overstaying their leave in these nervous times."[7] They did cancel a proposed visit to the Holy Land and proceeded instead to Athens. Hay's concern was still not urgent, evidently, for he spent several days sightseeing with Minister to Greece William Rockhill. "There are only two steamers leaving a week," Mrs. Hay explained to her mother, "and as one was tomorrow we decided to stay till Friday."[8] Hay finally resumed his duties on March 21; he had asked for a sixty-day leave and, despite the *Maine* incident, he was away the entire time.

Even at the time Hay's extended vacation attracted critical attention. Theodore Roosevelt could not "understand how John Hay was willing to be away from England at this time," while Henry White, who became burdened with delicate and important diplomatic maneuverings, wrote Hay that the Spanish ambassador was "most anxious" to discuss matters, something Hay should have suspected.[9]

During the few remaining weeks until war was declared, Hay's views were not bellicose. In contrast to Roosevelt's fear that the president was too peace-loving, Hay admired McKinley's courage in risking his popularity in the effort to prevent war. "You and I had better have no opinion about the Spanish War, except the President's,"

Hay ordered his apprehensive wife. "He has done everything man can do to avert it—If it comes now, it is not his fault."[10]

Hay's strong ties to the business community may account in part for his reluctance to espouse the cause of war. Most American businessmen opposed a war as likely to upset an economy only recently improved after a long depression, a pacifistic viewpoint which the more outspoken jingoes detested—"the craven fear and brutal selfishness of the mere money-getters,"[11] as Roosevelt expressed it. But Hay was more sympathetic to business needs. In January, 1898, for example, he cordially congratulated the president on his speech to the National Association of Manufacturers in which the president expressed his faith in the steady but gradual recovery of business. McKinley hoped for an increase in foreign trade (as did virtually everyone else during the decade); and war might well have hindered the slow recovery. "It is a pity we have so many men among us who do not and who cannot believe in the American people and in their glorious destiny," Hay wrote to President McKinley, a statement liable to misinterpretation as jingoistic cant if not read in the context of the president's speech and the country's business situation when it was still not certain if the recovery would be complete or lasting. His European experiences, Hay went on, had rooted in his soul "a confidence and trust in our future, which is beyond and above any temporary or personal disappointment"—a clear reference to the recent depression. "The greatest destiny the world ever knew is ours."[12] Hay's letter was chauvinistic, but he was primarily expressing his faith in the American economic system and doubtlessly hoping that the increased international trade McKinley predicted would forestall future depressions. He was not urging war nor was he yet suggesting territorial aggrandizement.

On the other hand, Hay was not irrevocably opposed to war with Spain, for if his business instincts suggested caution, his humanitarian, racial, and nationalistic feelings operated in the opposite direction. For example, late in

August, 1897, Hay forwarded to Sherman an article from the pro-American *Daily Chronicle* which gave, in Hay's words, "one of the most striking pictures I have seen in print of the desperate condition of things in that island." The article indicated that Spain's policies, particularly as implemented by General Weyler, were self-defeating, and the *Chronicle*'s reporter painted a vivid picture of brutality, sickness, famine, and economic chaos. "Traveling by rail, dozens of bodies lay by the track, the train disturbing the vultures from their gruesome feast,"[13] he wrote. Might the time not come when the United States, consistent with what Stewart Woodford called the "natural and logical result of successive conditions,"[14] would have to recreate order in Cuba?

The humanitarian aspects of Hay's thought on Cuba dovetailed nicely with his considerations of race. To Herbert W. Bowen, Hay commented irritably about "the excitable people of the [Iberian] peninsula" who could not be convinced "that all their disasters do not come directly from our fault."[15] Perhaps Hay thought of Cuba two days later while speaking before the American Society in London. Beginning with his oft-stressed theme that antagonistic Anglo-American relations would be "madness," Hay went on to emphasize particularly their common tradition of rationality and order. Lawyers especially appreciated the need for good Anglo-American relations, Hay continued, because of "that intense respect and reverence for order, liberty, and law which is so profound a sentiment in both countries." Americans, he continued, were "the fortunate heirs of English liberty and English law."[16] The implication was that Anglo-Saxons, not "excitable people," were most capable of rational government. The contrast with *Castilian Days* is striking and significant.

Whether for cultural or strategic reasons (the two often become hopelessly intertwined), Hay was well aware that American tension with Spain provided an opportunity to reverse popular dislike of England if that country would support American efforts to resolve the situation in Cuba. A possibility along these lines arose as early as June, 1897, when McKinley formally protested to Spain regarding her manner of conducting operations in Cuba. Shortly thereafter, Hay received instructions to discuss Cuba with America's new ambassador to Spain, General Stewart L. Woodford, who was to stop by London on his way to Madrid. Secretary Sherman asked Hay to acquaint himself with influential British opinion respecting Cuba and gave him substantial leeway to impress upon Woodford his own impressions and ideas.[17]

Hay did not report his conversations with Woodford in any detail, but Woodford sent McKinley a personal account of his London sojourn which indicated that Hay believed the Cuban situation could result in improved Anglo-American relations and increased American prestige. Annexation of Cuba might thrust America to the ranks of the great powers. Indeed, had England been confronted with a Cuba, Hay felt, she would have intervened long ago. After "full consultation" with Hay, Woodford wrote that he was certain

that the British people do not yet take any active interest in Cuban affairs. They are only concerned in seeing that their commercial and business relations are not disturbed or injured. They probably expect that Cuba will eventually come under the control of the United States either by a virtual protectorate or by actual annexation. I do not believe that recognition of Cuban belligerency by the United States would be followed by any protest or unfriendly action on the part of England. The British Government probably would do only what it might deem necessary to protect the commercial and financial interests of British subjects in Cuba.

Annexation by force might provoke protests, but should it come as the natural and logical result of successive conditions I think it would be accepted as inevitable.

I have gone into no details because my judgment is based upon all that I have seen and heard, rather than on any special facts. I think Ambassador Hay concurs in my views.

It may be only an impression, but after nearly a week in London, I fancy that the English people are mildly surprised that Cuba has been allowed to remain a Spanish possession so long. England would probably have found some good excuse for occupying Cuba long ago, had Cuba been as near to any English possession as she is to our Southern coast.[18]

All of these developments led Hay to venture, without specific instructions, an informal discussion about Cuba with Lord Salisbury. Although the prime minister talked with "considerable reticence" about the matter, he did acknowledge "the deplorable state of affairs in Cuba," and (as Woodford had discovered) hoped that tranquillity and prosperity would soon be restored. Hay's conversation with the prime minister probably justified the optimistic interpretation he ascribed to it when he stated that it "deepened the impression I already had, that we need apprehend no interference from England, if it becomes necessary for us to adopt energetic measures for putting an end to the destruction and slaughter now going on."[19]

But, consistent with his cautious approach, Hay never directly advocated more "energetic measures," although his letters and dispatches continued to emphasize the deplorable Cuban situation, and the clippings he forwarded almost invariably stated that American intervention was either necessary or inevitable. A week after he wrote to the president, for example, Hay transmitted a Reuters dispatch which contained, he wrote, "a very ·strong and evidently intelligent statement of the actual condition of affairs in the Island of Cuba." The statement, datelined October 1, attempted to shatter Spanish illusions about the effectiveness of their pacification program. "Not a single Province of Cuba is in any degree pacified, nor is the state of things any better than it was two years ago. Matters are, indeed, worse." The Cubans, the agency reported, were the better organized, more effective fighting force, and would stop at nothing less than independence. The war had so ruined Cuba's finances that "the only chance for rehabilitation of credit lies in protection from a strong nation like the United States," something all classes in Cuba, except the Spanish troops, agreed was necessary.[20] If, in 1897, Hay was not on record positively urging American intervention to end the civil war, he clearly would have had little objection to such an action.

After Hay returned from Egypt the following March his dispatches continued in a similar vein. Within ten days of his return he sent several optimistic communications concerning the state of British opinion. After the results of the American investigation of the *Maine* disaster were released, for example, Hay reported that most leading journals in London generally favored the United States. The *Chronicle*, which Hay selected to forward to Sherman, complained of the "brutality and incapacity" of the Spaniards and "assumed" that the United States would recognize Cuban belligerency. There was not an Englishman living, the paper stated, who would not ask its government to intervene in an analogous situation, and there was no British government that would not have intervened long ago. "Whatever may have been our differences with the United States," the article continued, "the heart of our people will go out to the great attempt to be made to liberate an American colony from a cruel yoke." Spain, the *Chronicle* concluded, "will fight alone."[21]

Clearly, Hay did not actively push for war as Theodore Roosevelt did, but like most Americans, he deplored the desperate plight of the Cubans and came to feel that war was almost inevitable. As he told St. Loe Strachey, editor of the British publication, *The Spectator*, "the positions of the United States and Spain were like two railway engines on the same track, neither of which would give way, and both of which were advancing. You might delay the collision, but you could not prevent it, unless one train was cleared out of the way of the other, and to this neither side in control would agree. Therefore, a collision had to come."[22] Hay saw, in addition, certain diplomatic advantages which might develop from a war with Spain. If war came, Hay was fully prepared to exploit it in an effort to strengthen Anglo-American ties.

When, on April 5, Hay learned from Secretary of State Sherman that war was almost certain, he set aside whatever doubts remained and pressed for the advantages he believed could be gained from a Spanish-American conflict. He immediately wrote a famous letter to Senator Lodge, commenting on the extremely friendly feeling in Britain. He even intimated that the United States could borrow the British fleet.[23]

In part, Hay urged an Anglo-American rapprochement for purely pragmatic reasons. Like any good ambassador, Hay attempted to gain the friendship of a powerful state at a time when hostilities with a third state seemed likely. Thus Hay lectured Senator Lodge on the value of British friendship, "I do not know whether you especially value the friendship and sympathy of this country in the present state of things,—as it is the only European country whose sympathies are not openly against us. We will not waste time discussing whether the origin of this feeling is wholly selfish or not," he continued. "Its existence is beyond question."[24]

But Hay envisioned more than immediate advantages. As he told the American Society that summer, the new found amity between "the two great branches of the English-speaking people" had been "too-long delayed." But "now that the day of clear and cordial understanding has come which so many of us have long desired and waited for, may we not hope it is to last for ever."[25] The long term advantages were largely cultural. Americans, he stated in April, were "knitted . . . to the people of Great Britain by a thousand ties, of origin, of language, and of kindred pursuits." Recalling a pageant the previous summer in which a naval vessel flew both the American and British colors, Hay concluded, "may we not hope that the lesson and the inspiration of that spectacle may last as long as those banners shall float over the seven seas, carrying always in their shadow freedom and civilization."[26] Senator Lodge grasped Hay's thought well. "The ties to which you have alluded so fiercely . . . are evident to all," he wrote. "Race, blood, language, identity of beliefs, and aspirations all assert themselves."[27]

Anglo-Saxon superiority entailed responsibilities to the world. Thus in April Hay called for "A Partnership in Beneficence." Although the speech served an immediate diplomatic purpose (it was delivered only after Hay consulted "with men at the head of affairs here"),[28] it expressed his long-held convictions. "We are joint ministers of the same sacred mission of liberty and progress," Hay stated,

"charged with duties which we cannot evade by the imposition of irresistible hands."[29] In May, he wrote to Lodge
that "the interests of civilization" were "bound up in the
direction the relations of America and England are to take
in the next few months," and, in September, he told representative of the Anglo-American League that a cordial
friendship between the two nations was "a necessity of
civilization."[30]

In a narrow sense, Hay accepted the burdens imposed
on the white race to uplift those less well endowed. In
an address on July 4, for example, Hay spoke of "the
breaking of fetters, the freeing of those who sat in darkness,
the lifting of cruel burdens from the shoulders of the
poor."[31] But Hay meant much more by "civilization." He
meant virtually every benefit of Anglo-Saxon culture. This
included, for example, capitalistic trade. In "A Partnership
in Beneficence" Hay commented that "all the nations of
the world will profit more or less directly by every exten-
sion of British commerce and the enterprise and enlighten-
ment that go with it."[32] Because Hay was speaking to an
English audience, he emphasized British trade; but he
really meant Anglo-Saxon trade and had no intention of
omitting Americans from his general considerations. As he
later explained to the American Society, the United States
and Britain would peacefully compete and by so doing
would spread wide the benefits of civilization. Such competition, he stated, "threatens no one; it injures no one;
its ends are altogether peaceful and beneficent." The two
nations would, he continued, compete "in the arts and the
works of civilization, and all the people of good-will on
the face of the earth will profit by it."[33]

It is difficult to assess Hay's contribution to the rapprochement. One historian credits him with "creating and
directing British support for the United States throughout
the war."[34] Certainly relations improved. Hay even found
it necessary to have printed in London's newspapers an
announcement that applications for service in the American
armed forces were "becoming too numerous for individual
replies." And, on an official level, Hay found British neu-

trality distinctly benevolent. For example, when Adee asked Hay to procure authentic texts of any manifestoes or circular notes which Spain had sent to the European powers, Hay sent the information, adding that the source must be kept confidential.[35]

No single individual created the rapprochement; indeed, the British government had decided to conciliate the United States many months before the war. Yet those Englishmen who desired stronger Anglo-American bonds thought Hay's tenure crucial, and when he left they paid him tribute. The *Saturday Review* commented on Hay's "courtesy and high ability. . . . Not since the departure of J. R. Lowell . . . have we felt such keen regret at the loss of the American ambassador to Saint James's." Balfour felt "awfully sorry" about Hay's departure and commented that Hay knew "more people than the Staals or Deynes [?] who have been here for twenty years." Even the London *Times*, which was not especially pro-American, spoke glowingly in retrospect of Hay's contributions as ambassador. "If it be possible to speak of any envoy from one country to another as ideal," the *Times* editorialized, "the word may be used of Mr. Hay. He knew England, and before he had been in this country a year England came to know him and to like and respect him."[36]

Shortly before he returned to the United States in September, Hay received the most direct evidence that important Englishmen appreciated his efforts to forge strong Anglo-American bonds. James Bryce and other representatives of the Anglo-American League called on the ambassador to express the League's appreciation for Hay's "eminent tact, judgment, and courtesy," while an honorary address commended his "great service" in the cause of Anglo-American friendship. Bryce himself commented that Hay's "genial character and manners won our hearts."[37] Such sentiments fully corroborate Henry Adams's summation of Hay's tenure in London: "in the long list of famous American Ministers in London, none could have given the work quite the completeness, the harmony, the perfect ease of Hay."[38]

The outpouring of compliments rather overpowered Hay, whose early unhappiness in the position had been transformed during 1898. "So long as there is life in my heart I can never cease to be grateful for every hour I have been permitted to live here,"[39] Hay wrote to the English statesman Arthur James Balfour, permitting his sentimental attachment to the island kingdom to surface briefly. So overwhelming was the evidence of good feeling that Hay fleetingly questioned if his promotion was a sound move. "It seems a pity to throw it all away and go home just now," he confided to his wife, "but that is not to be discussed," he added quickly. "There was no refusing such a summons."[40]

The Spanish-American War focused American attention on Hawaii and the Philippine Islands. Hay's opinions about what to do with these Pacific outposts further demonstrated his Anglo-Saxon prejudices as well as his beliefs in the goodness of commercial expansion and in the proper role a great power should play.

Hawaii was the initial concern. Grover Cleveland had thwarted a previous attempt to annex the islands, an action that Hay deplored; but McKinley's election assured another look at the Hawaiian matter. In the summer of 1897, the new president presented a treaty of annexation to the Senate. From London Ambassador Hay sent Secretary Sherman the *Times'* leading article which predicted, Hay wrote in his summary, that there would be no European objections.[41] Although the *Times* thought the United States would be unwise to venture into a colonial experiment, Hay may well have agreed with and welcomed the article's observation regarding European indifference. In any event, he persuaded Whitelaw Reid, then in London as America's special representative to the Queen's jubilee celebration, to support the treaty in the *New York Tribune.* Hay also reported personally to the president that no diplomats in London had objections to American annexation; Hawaii, they felt, lay " 'wholly within the sphere of our influence.' "[42]

As the possibility of hostilities with Spain increased,

Hay had occasion to discuss the implications with Cecil Spring Rice, then British ambassador to Berlin. When they talked over the matter in March and April, 1898, Spring Rice urged the ambassador to press for immediate annexation of Hawaii lest Germany rush in with demands after the war. Impressed, Hay cabled the State Department, "excellent authority in German matters suggests prompt annexation Hawaii before war closes as otherwise Germany might seek to complicate the question with Samoa or Philippine Islands." Expressing his appreciation to Spring Rice, Hay wrote, "I cannot fathom the stupidity of those senators who, preserving the Cleveland tradition, still fight the annexation, but *gegen die Dummheit,* etc."[43]

Hay's reliance on Spring Rice was significant, for the Englishman was an outspoken advocate of Anglo-Saxonism who detested Germany. Upon receipt of the news of Admiral Dewey's victory at Manila, for example, Spring Rice exclaimed to Hay, "let us try while we can to secure what we can for God's language," adding that "it was the divine instinct ingrained in the race which has brought us to where we are."[44] Hay may not have agreed with Spring Rice's excesses, which sounded like Lyman Abbott's subsequent contention that the Navy had used "God's projectiles" while laying "hold on the muscles of the Almighty."[45] But he had no objection to Spring Rice's race pride or his complementary hatred of Germany. Hay was so much influenced by Spring Rice, whose opinions supported his own desire to achieve a world dominated by Anglo-Saxons, that when the German ambassador in London called to discuss the Pacific situation, Hay told him bluntly that the Hawaiian question was not a matter for discussion by European powers.[46]

The Philippines constituted the larger portion of the Pacific problem and were more directly related to the war. Just when the Philippines entered the scope of American vision is a question that has long intrigued historians. Some have argued that prior to actual hostilities only a small group of imperialists advocating the "large policy" had longed to secure the islands for strategic and economic reasons. Others have suggested that the desire to secure at least a portion of the Philippines as a convenient base from which to penetrate the China market was not confined to the "large policy" advocates but was a fundamental assumption of most decision-makers in the administration, including the president.[47] Although Hay was not as ignorant of the Orient as some historians have stated, it does not appear that he gave much thought to the Philippines until Dewey's victory in May, 1898, although they played some part in his conversations with Spring Rice, and he was unquestionably well aware of the threat posed to American interests in China by European states. Even so, it is not likely that Hay had any fully formulated notions about what to do with the archipelago at the time of Dewey's victory. Most probably he agreed with Adams who wrote to him, "I hardly see my clue. . . . I had prepared myself for a new deal, and don't quite feel as though I knew the value of the cards or the players."[48] Indeed, the following week, when Hay played a role in early (and informal) British attempts to end the war, he offered no advice to Washington with respect to the Philippines, in contrast to his efforts to gain annexation of Hawaii.[49]

However, Hay was by now a staunch defender (if less vocal than some) of Anglo-Saxon expansion, and it was not long before he was favorably disposed to the retention of a coaling station in the Philippines. Henry Adams, traveling in Europe, advised Hay to try to end the war as quickly as possible, suggesting complete American withdrawal from the Philippines, with the exception of a coaling station. Hay agreed. "I have your yesterday's letter," he responded, "and it was a great balm to my self conceit to know that I hold the same views you express as to terms [of] peace. I had drawn up a little project which was yours almost verbatim." Hay feared the Senate, however. "I have told you many times that I did not believe another important treaty would ever pass the Senate," he continued. "What is to be thought of a body, which will not take Hawaii as a gift and is clamoring to hold the Philippines."[50]

Hay's fears of German ambitions may well have spurred his thought toward a policy of total retention. As early as June, rumors surfaced that Germany was unhappy at American intentions to establish a foothold in the islands. Salisbury himself reassured Hay, and even Spring Rice ("the same diplomat whom I have heretofore quoted as to German affairs") dismissed the rumors.[51] But the following month an interview with Count Hatzfeldt, the German ambassador in London, confirmed Hay's suspicions. Germany, Hatzfeldt said, wanted a "few coaling stations" and recognition of her claim to the Carolines, evidently hoping, as Spring Rice had once warned, to receive these in exchange for acquiesence to American control of Hawaii. Hay properly replied that he could not discuss the matter since nothing definite had been decided, but his private reaction to the German request was disdainful. He told St. Loe Strachey of the affair, and the journalist later wrote, "I can well recall his contemptuous imitation of the manner of the request: 'You haf so many islands; why could you not give us som?' I asked Hay what he had replied. With a somewhat grim smile he answered, 'I told him,"Not an island—not one!"' "[52]

A few days later, Spring Rice related his renewed fears of German ambitions in the Pacific. "They hated Teddy as author of the proposal that the Americans should go to the Philippines," he wrote to Hay, warning that "it would be a great mistake to suppose that the idea of a [German] coaling station in the Pacific was given up. It is difficult to tell Germany she shouldn't have one."[53] Spring Rice's letter, following Hay's unhappy interview with Hatzfeldt so closely, produced a predictably vehement reaction which Hay vented in a letter to Lodge. "I have been under great obligations the last few months to Spring Rice, who knows Germany as few men do and has kept me wonderfully au courant of facts and opinions there," he began.

The jealousy and animosity felt towards us in Germany is something which can hardly be exaggerated—*pace* [American Ambassador] Dr. [Andrew D.] White. They hate us in France, but French hate is a straw fire compared to German. And France has nothing to fear from us while the Vaterland is all on fire with greed, and terror of us. They want the Philippines, the Carolines, and Samoa—they want to get into our markets and keep us out of theirs. They have been flirting and intriguing with Spain ever since the war began & now they are trying to put the Devil into the head of Aguinaldo. . . .

There is to the German mind, something monstrous in the thought that a war should take place anywhere and they not profit by it.[54]

The language of the letter, particularly in the final paragraph, derived almost directly from Cecil Spring Rice.

Hay may well have wanted to keep all the islands by now. Certainly he was moving in that direction. Not only was he angry at Germany, but he had informed the State Department on several occasions that England would not interfere in the destiny of the archipelago. Furthermore, he transmitted copies of a proclamation issued by the Patriotic Junta of the Philippine Islands detailing, so Hay stated, their grievances against the Spanish as well as desired reforms "under the protection of the United States." Yet he never advised the government to keep them. Even when Secretary Day specifically asked for Hay's suggestions, he urged only a strong guarantee of fair treatment for the Filipinos and a prohibition on Spain to transfer any portion of the islands without American approval.[55] Perhaps he was cautious because he was uncertain of McKinley's wishes; perhaps doubts lingered about the burdens of formal imperialism. In any event, his suggested course of action, along lines suggested by Spring Rice, was obviously designed to block German intrusion, in some ways gaining many of the advantages of annexation without the burdens.

One of Hay's reasons for disliking German interference was the fear of commercial competition, an understandable fear given the predominant theories of economic depression. Hay wanted Americans, not Germans, to benefit commercially. The possibilities of commercial exploitation of the Philippines commended themselves to Hay as early as May. On May 16, Hay granted an interview to Frank Karuth, managing director of the London-based firm, Philippines Mineral Syndicate. Karuth informed Hay in great detail of the extensive gold deposits in the islands which Spain had not exploited. In addition to gold, Karuth's firm had found copper ore, silver, zinc, coal, and various gems. Karuth's account, in fact, resembled nothing so closely as the stories of the Brazilian *Paulistas* who returned from the interior with romantic stories of gold and precious gems. "There is no brook that finds its way into the Pacific Ocean, whose sand and gravel do not at least pan the color of gold," the investor told Hay. "Heavy nuggets are sometimes brought down from the Sierra." In addition, labor was extremely cheap and relatively efficient. "The Bicol miners are adept by atavism in their work," Karuth explained, "and so adapt themselves to European methods." On the whole, he concluded, the general conditions for mining were exceptionally favorable.[56]

By implication Karuth advocated American annexation of the Philippines, employing the rationale used by Americans to justify seizure of Indian and Mexican lands: in order to hold title to property one had to demonstrate a capacity to exploit it properly. This the Spaniards (to say nothing of the Filipinos) had failed to do. As Hay explained to Secretary Day when he forwarded Karuth's letter to Washington (indeed, it can be assumed that Hay requested the letter so that he could foward it), "in common with many others, having business connections in the Philippines, he seems most anxious that they shall not fall back, in any contingency, under the rule of Spain, which is incapable, they think, of affording any guarantees of orderly or honest government."[57]

The commercial advantages that might be gained from annexation shaded into larger considerations of Anglo-Saxon rule and national prestige. Both of these goals might be gained in part, Hay seems to have felt, by establishing a colonial empire along the lines of the British model. There is no question that Hay admired not only England but also British imperialism. When the British were engaged in defeating the Dervishes of Sudan, for example, Hay privately congratulated Arthur Balfour on the "great victory" at Atbara, "a victory by which all civilization will profit."[58] Hay made certain that Washington was aware of the British experience, for he forwarded to the State Department a number of pamphlets and newspaper clippings by British authors on the virtues of colonialism, materials which he very favorably commended to the secretary of state. On July 8, for example, Hay forwarded a pamphlet by General Sir Andrew Clarke, whom Hay described as "one of the most eminent of English soldiers and administrators in regard to the Government of the Malay peninsula." Clarke discussed the experiences of a pioneering British imperialist, Sir Stamford Raffles, who was responsible for the earliest British administration in the Malay peninsula, and who, Clarke stated, secured "the road to the Far East."

Clarke defended the imperialism of Raffles on two classic grounds—the benefits which accrued to the heathen, and the benefits which accrued to the imperialists. Like most Anglo-Saxons, Raffles did not feel the natives could govern themselves. Indeed, after Raffles' departure, Clarke related, guerrilla warfare broke out between rival native factions that continued until 1874 when certain Malay chiefs invited British intervention to restore the order which they could not. Hay called this section of the pamphlet to Secretary Day's attention,[59] but, with even more emphasis, he noted the results of British rule since 1874:

The total revenue of 1875 . . . was 409,394 dollars; in 1896 it amounted to 8,434,083.

The value of total imports and exports were in 1876, as far as could be ascertained, a million and a half dollars; in 1896 it just touched fifty millions.

In 1874, beyond an occasional native path or elephant track through the jungle, no road existed; now a network of well graded and macadamised roads traverse these states. In addition railway works have been carried on, and are being rapidly extended, and last year's revenue from these were a little over 300,000 dollars.

Irrigation works have made good progress.

In civil administration the establishment of judicial and police tribunals, school, hospitals, as well as a police station and gaols, all the needs of civilization, have been provided; nor has culture, in the formation of museums and libraries, been wholly neglected.[60]

A few weeks later, Hay sent Secretary Day an article by Benjamin Kidd, famed Anglo-Saxon theorist and imperialist, entitled "The Control of the Tropics." The article, Hay stated, contained "some striking figures in regard to the trade relations existing between the United States, England and tropical countries." The future of Anglo-Saxon commercial nations, Kidd believed, would henceforth be decided in the tropics, and both Britain and the United States had a deep interest in the outcome, for their combined trade with tropical areas amounted to about 44 percent of their total world trade.[61]

All in all, by the time Hay returned to become secretary of state, he was at least inclined toward total annexation of the Philippine Islands. "I fear you are right about the Philippines," he wrote his old mentor, John Bigelow, "and I hope the Lord will be good to us poor devils who have to take care of them."[62]

Although this letter virtually admitted that he now favored annexation, no administration decision had been made, nor had the new secretary of state made his opinion public. He was therefore subjected to increasing pressure to retain the islands. Senator Lodge, never one to waste time, greeted Hay on his return to the United States with a letter asking if he had seen the platform adopted by the New York Republicans, which urged complete retention of the islands. "If you have not seen it look it up," the senator ordered Hay. ". . . Nobody tolerates the idea of giving back to Spain anything."[63]

As the peace commissioners organized themselves in Paris, pressure continued for complete annexation. The commissioners were divided on the question, but the parade of witnesses before them provided no testimony favoring the return of the islands to Spain and precious little supporting independence or a protectorate.[64] One of those to testify was John Foreman, British author of a well-known book on the Philippine islands.[65] Like Frank Karuth, Foreman had spent several years in the Philippines engaged in business, and, like Karuth, he painted a picture of easily exploitable wealth with a minimum of problems from unruly natives who were not, of course, capable of governing themselves. Not only did Foreman's testimony reach Hay through the commission's official report, but from London Henry White strongly urged Hay to consider Foreman's advice that the United States retain the islands.[66]

Shortly after Foreman's testimony, Admiral Dewey reported to the secretary of the navy on the deteriorating condition in the Philippines. "General anarchy prevails without the limits of the city and bay of Manila," he cabled, noting reports of "inhuman cruelty" in some islands. "The natives appear unable to govern," he concluded. Secretary of the Navy Long showed Dewey's cable to Hay, who sent it on to the peace commissioners for their consideration. The same day, Stanford Newel, American ambassador at The Hague, reported that the Dutch government preferred that either England or the United States take the Philippines if they were not to remain Spanish. Two days later, Whitelaw Reid, one of the commissioners, pleaded with Hay in a personal letter not to divide the Philippines. "Have you considered that there is hardly one of those islands from which you cannot shoot across to another!"[67] he pointed out.

Despite such pressure, Hay prudently refrained from committing himself publicly until the president decided, although in private he probably agreed with those who were urging total annexation. Late in October the peace commissioners finally forced the president to act. Making his decision apparently without Hay's advice, McKinley ordered the American peace commissioners to demand cession of the entire archipelago.[68]

As was the case with the declaration of war against Spain, McKinley's decision resolved whatever doubts may have lingered in Hay's mind. Following up the president's order to the peace negotiators, Hay urged total retention. The element of ambiguity that characterized Hay's thought before McKinley's decision, and his immediate acquiescence thereafter, may indicate that it was Hay and not McKinley whose backbone resembled a chocolate eclair.

Indeed, Hay, in his telegram to the peace commissioners, noted the essentially negative character of the annexation decision. "Greater difficulties and more serious complications, administrative and international," he stated, "would follow any other course."[69]

It was more likely, however, that Hay fully agreed with the president's decision and for positive reasons. He was not adverse to criticizing (politely) the president's ideas, as he did, for example, regarding American policy in China. But in this case there was no hint of criticism, and Hay's official note to the commissioners ordering total retention was followed by a private telegram to Day stating that the Cabinet was fully behind the policy. Further, when a division appeared among the commissioners, Hay strongly reiterated his position, both officially and personally.[70]

As if to emphasize his solidarity with the administration's position, Hay wrote to White, "there has been no vacillation, no divided council from beginning to end. We have stood by our first propositions and shall stand upon them to the end." Indeed, Hay remained so immovable that a certain undertone of criticism developed among some of the commissioners. "You can explain our good will" to the Spaniards, Commissioner George Gray remarked at one point in the negotiations to John Bassett Moore, one of the American legal advisers, "but say that Col. Hay is firm."[71]

Hay also struck out at the anti-imperialist outcry, a move emphasizing further his total agreement with Mc-Kinley's decision. Writing late in November to General William M. Osborne, for example, about "Andrew Carnegie and Erving Winslow, and some of our Boston cranks," Hay stated exultantly, "the war and the peace will be two more titles of fame and honor to McKinley." The same day, he wrote to Reid about the "wild and frantic attack now going on in the press against the whole Philippine transaction. Andrew Carnegie really seems off his head...," Hay continued. "He says the administration will fall in irretrievable ruin the moment the administration shoots down one insurgent Filipino. He does not seem to reflect that the Government is in a somewhat robust condition even after shooting down several American citizens in his interest at Homestead."[72]

There was, in sum, very little about the decision with which Hay might disagree, philosophically or practically. In the months preceding the Spanish-American War, during the war itself, and in the weeks in which a final decision was made on the Philippines, Hay demonstrated lines of thought similar to those which may have contributed to his desire to annex Hawaii in 1893. His belief in the beneficent effects of capitalism, both commercial and investment, contributed to his desire to retain the islands. Furthermore, Hay felt that the Filipinos were incapable of self-government, that the United States had a duty to protect them since Spain had demonstrated a horrifying incapacity to govern its possessions, and that the Germans should be stopped in their Pacific ambitions. His concern for America's prestige, his hope that the nation would begin to act like the great power it was—including the acquisition of a colonial empire—was evident in a number of ways. All in all, the progress of civilization demanded an increased American effort on the international scene.

Similar considerations found expression as Hay considered a problem almost totally new in American history—the governance of a large number of non-European people thousands of miles from the mainland. The most immediate problem concerned the Filipino rebels led by Emilio Aguinaldo. After initially cooperating with American forces to throw out the Spanish, the rebels turned against the United States when it became apparent that independence was not in the cards. Indeed, even before ratifications of the Treaty of Paris were exchanged, Alvey Adee opined to Hay.that he favored "immediate coercive action against Aguinaldo as a disturber of *our* peace."[73]

Hay's reaction to the rebels exemplified in particular his racial presuppositions, his belief in upholding legitimate authority, and his concern with America's image in the world, all of which led him to conclude that the rebellion must be utterly crushed. Henry Adams foresaw the quagmire. "Of course we can thrash the Philippines and kill them by the hundred thousand," he wrote with some exaggeration, "but it will cost us in one season at least fifty thousand men, fifty millions of money, and indefinite loss of reputation."[74] But, as with many things, Hay did not agree with Adams. Not only were the natives totally incapable of handling their own affairs, he had personally disliked Aguinaldo ever since the summer of 1898 when Spring Rice intimated that he was something of a German puppet. Hay thought of this Filipino patriot much as he did of his other devils—Mormon leaders, labor agitators, agrarian radicals, William Jennings Bryan—as misguided, insincere, venal, and without much support among the general populace. He therefore expected a short military campaign.

The advice Hay received made such a misevaluation understandable. Both military and civilian leaders from America and Europe who testified before the peace commission consistently underestimated the military effectiveness of the rebels and minimized the popular support that they enjoyed. Nor did reports from the Philippines suggest that there was anything wrong with military repression. Throughout April, 1899, the Schurman Commission, appointed by the president to investigate conditions in the islands, sent a number of optimistic dispatches which lent support to Hay's preconceptions. Recent military victories, the commission first reported, "have had good effect everywhere. . . . Populations feeling secure would doubtless declare for the United States." Furthermore, desertions were high among the insurgents and ammunition supplies were low. A subsequent cable asserted that the insurgents were "fed on silly lies, with leaders ambitious of power and money. . . . All witnesses assert Filipinos in general incapable of self-government." At the end of April the commissioners urged a continuation of hostilities until the insurgents indicated a desire to surrender. Eighty to 90 percent of the people opposed the insurgents, it was felt, while the rebels themselves had already degenerated "into disorganized marauding bands."[75] With such reports at hand, Hay exclaimed to the president in terms hauntingly similar to those issued from Vietnam at a later date, "the news from Manila is splendid. We can see light at last."[76]

Ludicrous as Hay's optimism appears in retrospect, it was not completely without foundation. While Aguinaldo certainly did enjoy the support of the masses (a fact even some Americans admitted), a significant minority of well-educated, wealthy, and conservative *ilustrados* resented this upstart, and some frankly urged the Americans to put down the rebellion and rule the islands.[77] There was a genuine split among the Filipinos (although both the Schurman Commission and Hay placed entirely too much faith in the conservatives' estimates of the situation). Furthermore, the rebels had not done very well militarily, and when, on April 4, the Schurman Commission issued a vaguely conciliatory proclamation promising limited self-government, rebel solidarity broke, and the leaders expressed interest in pursuing further a negotiated settlement. At the end of April, Apolonari Mabini, a rebel leader usually opposed to compromise, even admitted to the commission that the rebel force felt "itself weak before the advance of American troops, whose valor it admires." Colonel Manuel Arguelles, representing Aguinaldo, expressed similar feelings.[78]

It appears that the rebels were genuinely willing to negotiate. They hoped for independence but, admitting that this was not possible in view of America's determination to remain in control, were willing to consider autonomous status with the United States retaining hegemony, not unlike Canada's position within the British empire. They asked, in return, a three-month cessation of hostilities so they could ascertain the state of Filipino opinión. Mabini gave the commissioners fair warning should the United States prove inflexible. "We confess ourselves weak," he wrote, "but we still possess resources, above all the unfaltering resolution to prolong the war for an indefinite space of time, if the undertaking to dominate us by force is persisted in."[79]

The United States, believing that the rebels were nearly crushed, continued its military operations. But Secretary Hay did authorize the Philippine Commission to propose a specific form of government for the rebels to consider. The rhetoric accompanying Hay's plan was somewhat encouraging to the insurgents, advocating "at an early day . . . the largest measure of local self govt. consistent with peace and good order." It was clear, however, that Hay considered "the largest measure of local self govt." to be miniscule, at least for the time being.[80]

The commission communicated Hay's plan to the rebels on May 22 and spent several hours discussing the ramifications with them. The emissaries again asked for a suspension of hostilities in order to communicate with their people, but since such a suspension was a "military affair" the commission refused to discuss it.[81] In addition to disliking the commission's attitude on the suspension question, the insurgents were skeptical about America's ability and willingness to carry out any agreements arrived at. Spain, they contended, made promises only to break them. To this contention, Schurman replied haughtily, "the United States is not Spain," and Charles Denby suggested that if they would only "study and reflect on American institutions and American history, . . . they would find answers to their doubts."[82]

After the rebels retired to consider the situation, Jacob Schurman also turned his thoughts toward a final settlement. Schurman had no aversion to the use of force against the Filipinos, and in many ways his views were as tough as those of General Otis or Secretary Hay. He shared most of their prejudices and had urged military pressure. But, unlike many people connected with policy-making in the islands, Schurman believed that the stated American policy of "force and conciliation" meant what it implied—that conciliation was an equal part of the policy. The other commissioners, the military, and the administration in Washington (at this time) paid mostly lip service to this portion of the stated policy. Schurman now decided that since the rebels seriously wanted peace, the time had arrived for a bold act of conciliation. The insurgents, he cabled secretly and at length to Hay, were "exceedingly skeptical of our intentions" and cited the sad case of the American Indians as evidence. The commission, he pointed out, had urged reconciliation as the evidence of American good will and by so doing had succeeded in bringing to power moderate elements among the rebels. A continuation of the war, he went on, would only increase the power of those who wished to continue killing Americans. "The United States is in a false position," he stated. "Henceforth continuation of fighting tends to make Filipinos consider us as conquerors rather than to liberate. Campaign closing has secured us all moral effects possible by force. . . . Conciliation as necessary as force whether we consider present situation or future government. . . . Believe magnanimity our safest, cheapest and best policy."[83]

Hay's hatred of Aguinaldo and his insistence that the rebels be utterly crushed for resisting the beneficent and legitimate authority of the United States caused him cavalierly to dismiss Schurman's courageous cable. "Here is a long disquisition from Dr. Schurman," Hay remarked snidely to the president. "If he had given the money this cable cost to Aguinaldo, he might have ended the war." Hay's reply to Schurman was tart. "There is no excuse for further resistance by the Filipinos," he cabled, "and if it continues the President will send all the force necessary to suppress insurrection and establish the authority of the United States in the Islands."[84]

Although Schurman had openly stated his views knowing that the other commissioners were opposed to them, he was not inclined to pursue his course, particularly after Assistant Secretary of State David J. Hill sent him a personal telegram urging a united front since the country strongly favored "energetic military action."[85] Shortly thereafter, Schurman left to visit the southern islands; he then returned to the United States.

The rebels resumed military operations, and a chance for peace was lost. Hay saw no course except continued military pressure. Theodore Roosevelt, having urged Hay to send "ample forces" to the islands, found both McKinley and Hay satisfied "as to the outcome in the Philippines during the next dry season."[86] Aguinaldo's public statement that the Democrats were on his side was not likely to lessen the secretary's determination, and, at the end of the summer, Hay cabled Denby that the administration's immediate goal was "to establish our authority and restore order and peace in the Archipelago by prompt and energetic military operation."[87]

As the guerrilla war dragged on, Hay continued to emphasize the value of upholding America's authority in the islands, lest national prestige shrink. In September, he wrote to the chairman of the executive committee of the Republican party of Ohio, a letter that was soon printed and widely circulated as a campaign document. Hay chided the Democrats for criticizing the outcome of the Spanish-American war. They could not convince the people, he wrote, that "we are the worse off, because our flag has gained great honor, our possessions have been extended, our position in the world increased, and our opportunity for work and usefulness widened, through the fortunes of war and the valor of our soldiers and sailors." By fortune, he continued, the Philippines were left to America, and America would not fail in her mission. "It is not permitted us to shirk the vast responsibilities thus imposed upon us," he stated, "without exhibiting a nerveless pusillanimity which would bring upon us not only the scorn of the world, but what is far worse, our own self-contempt." The anti-imperialists (especially those who were Democrats), he went on, did a disservice to the nation's honor. "All other countries have bid us Godspeed in the Philippines," he exclaimed, "and it was left to a man in Cincinnati the other day to wish that 'Otis and his army might be swept into the sea.' . . . There are, thank God, many Democrats in Ohio who do not desire the humiliation of their country or the dishonor of their flag."[88]

William A. Croffut, secretary of the Anti-Expansionist League in Washington, read Hay's letter. Incensed, he wrote to the *Washington Post,* neatly dissecting Hay's contentions. Lest Hay overlook his letter, Croffut sent him a clipping. Aptly appealing "from John the politician to John the poet," Croffut waded into American policy in the Philippines. "The poor Filipinos, with our help, have rescued their lands from the Spanish oppressors," he wrote. "Why should we slaughter them now?"[89] Hay, however, could not understand such reasoning. He saw no reason to stop oppressing a small group of selfish revolutionaries who refused to acknowledge America's beneficent suzerainty. He would have treated disorderly labor agitators in the same way. Thus he replied to Croffut, "I cannot for the life of me see any contradiction between desiring liberty and peace here and desiring to establish them in the Philippines."[90]

The emphasis on duty and authority had deep domestic roots, stretching back to Lincoln and rekindled in a different form by the labor troubles of the 1870's and 1880's. But the means of governing the Philippines also had European, and particularly English, antecedents. Where indeed was one to learn how to be an imperialist if not from the English, by all odds the most successful? America's experiences with the Indians offered little guidance, for there were relatively few Indians in a vast country; besides, white men soon outnumbered them. Alaska had little in common with the Philippines. Hay's own experiences drew him naturally toward the British. Not only had he developed a strong sense of Anglo-Saxonism, but, well before his ambassadorship, many of his best friends were British, including such well-known imperialists as Rudyard Kipling and Joseph Chamberlain. During the war Hay relied on a British diplomat, Cecil Spring Rice, for advice, and he also sent Secretary Day information on British colonial experiences. For advice on the commercial possibilities of the Philippines, Hay had listened to a British entrepreneur, Frank Karuth, while the American commissioners in Paris interviewed other British authorities, such as John Foreman.

The British colonial experience appears to have impressed Secretary Hay quite directly. For example, he for-

warded to the Schurman Commission a personal letter from
Judge George S. Batcheller, an American living in Egypt,
who thought Hay might find "models of instruction" in
the British experience in India. Hay also sent the commissioners an unpublished article by an Englishman, T. H.
Haynes, entitled, "The United States and The Sooloo Islands." The commissioners found this article very useful
and employed many of the Haynes' suggestions when they
attempted to arrange a modus vivendi with the Sultan of
Sulu.[91]

More significantly, Hay's proposed plan of government
for the Philippines (which the Schurman Commission
suggested to the insurgents in May, 1899) was strikingly
similar to one urged by his English friend James Bryce.
Bryce opposed annexation, but since the United States had
decided otherwise, he concluded that he should provide
"suggestions drawn from British experience as to the best
way of managing a semi-civilized tropical colony," and he
soon prepared an article on colonial administration for
Century magazine. Richard Watson Gilder, the anti-imperialist editor of the publication, and a friend of Hay, advised the secretary of Bryce's forthcoming article and sent
him the advance sheets. Hay read the article "with great
interest," said that he was in agreement with Bryce's suggestions, and thanked Gilder for sending it.[92]

Bryce's article, printed in March, considered in some
detail the problems posed by the Philippines. Due to the
mixture of races, languages, and religions, Bryce immediately ruled out institutions suitable for Anglo-Saxon culture. The few Spaniards, he wrote, were "scarcely fit" for
them, while the Chinese and most Malays were "obviously
unfit." Britain, Bryce concluded, would send a governor
with colonial experience who would be given far-reaching
power, limited only by general guidelines furnished by the
home government. After a time, an advisory council would
be established, composed of the chief officials and a few
of the natives—"for example, one or two of the resident
British, American, and German merchants. . . , one or two
Spaniards, possibly a Chinese merchant, probably one or
two of the most intelligent and influential natives." With

time the council might evolve into a "partly representative body." Hay's plan, proposed shortly thereafter, implicitly followed Bryce's suggestions.[93]

Hay's tacit reliance on the British imperial model greatly angered William A. Croffut, who lambasted Hay's denial of an Anglo-American alliance:

What need of a certified "alliance" between those who are hunting in couples? What need of an alliance, when England, whose merciless pillage in India has for generations been the abhorrence of mankind, is eagerly offering to teach this public how to become an empire? When the eagle is fixing its unstained beak in the vitals of an Asiatic people struggling to be free, and the lion is closing its jaws on the peaceful and happy republic of South Africa? What need of an "alliance" between two burglars looting separate banks? Is there not likely to be a tacit understanding even if they have never been introduced?[94]

If Croffut's language was sensational, his main contention was essentially correct. Indeed, the "two burglars" in this case were not only well acquainted, but the elder thief had actually instructed the younger in the arts of the profession.

Hay never changed his views of the propriety of American action in the Philippine Islands. The new possessions provided opportunities for American trade and investment which in turn helped enlighten the natives. The United States provided benevolent and efficient government for the Filipinos, Hay felt, and allowed them what little participation they could handle. Over a very long period, perhaps they could, as Bryce suggested, assume a larger and larger share of the government. To crush the rebels was therefore an act both of self-interest to the United States and of kindness to the Filipinos.

If Hay had been a reluctant imperialist as late as early 1898, he was soon converted to the expansionist gospel. Seldom given to the hyperbole that characterized Spring Rice, Reid, Roosevelt, and other outspoken expansionists, Hay nevertheless accepted the basic tenets of the creed. In May, 1904, for example, Hay traced with pride the expansionist history of the United States since the Louisiana Purchase, an expansion for which the "Unseen

Director of the Drama" was held responsible. It was clear that Hay thought the American course in the 1890's was part of "a cosmic tendency" against which no man could prevail.[95] During the presidential campaign in the autumn of 1904, Hay was more explicit and severely blasted the Democratic stand in favor of freeing the Philippines. To do so, Hay told the enthusiastic, overflow crowd in Madison Square Garden, "would cover us with indelible discredit, which would be an abdication of our position in the Pacific, the surrender of our commercial prestige in the Far East, a base treachery and betrayal of the loyal and intelligent Filipinos who have trusted us, and a direct invitation to intestine war and foreign intervention."[96] The rhetoric was overblown; the sentiments were essentially sincere.

The extent to which China lay behind Hay's enthusiasm for the acquisition of the Philippines is murky. But, once the islands were obtained, Hay was quick to acknowledge that they could and should be used as a base for the China trade. When problems developed in China, Hay was thankful for the proximity of America's new possessions. "The new and strange ever excite fear, and the courage and prescience which accept them always arouse criticism and attack," Hay wrote in July, 1900, while suggesting some remarks for inclusion in one of McKinley's speeches.

Yet a great departure and a new policy were never more justified than those undertaken by you. On the possession of the Philippines rests that admirable diplomacy which warned all nations that American trade was not to be shut out of China. It is to Manila that we owe the abilities to send our troops and ships in defense of our ministers, our missionaries, our consuls, and our merchants in China, instead of being compelled to leave our citizens to the casual protection of other powers, as would have been unavoidable had we flung the Philippines away. . . . It is to Manila, again, to our fleet in the bay and our army on the land, that we shall owe our power, when these scenes of blood in China are closed, to exact reparation, to enforce stern justice, and to insist in the final settlement, upon an open door to all that vast market of our fast growing commerce. Events coming with terrible rapidity, have been swift witnesses to the wisdom of our action in the East.[97]

VI

Hay and China

The acquisition of the Philippine Islands heightened America's century-old fascination with the fabulous Orient, a land of mystery and trade. As the author (or more accurately, as the promulgator) of the Open Door notes of 1899 and 1900, John Hay's name has long been linked to America's China policy.

Although it was widely assumed at the time that Asian matters dictated Hay's selection as secretary of state, some historians have asserted that Hay was generally ignorant of the Far East until at least the middle of 1898.[1] But in fact, Hay's service on the *New York Tribune* in the 1870's led him to write a few editorials on Far Eastern questions, in which he commented on the progressiveness of Japan and the stupidity of the Grant administration in appointing incompetent diplomats. Much of Hay's information on Asian affairs certainly came from Edward H. House, a long-time *Tribune* reporter who, after 1870, spent much of his time in Japan. As a sometime professor, reporter, and editor in Japan, House acquired considerable empathy for the Japanese and at one time became so critical of Western treatment of his adopted homeland that the American minister demanded his ouster.[2]

An occasional correspondence continued between Hay and House during the quarter-century following Hay's resignation from the *Tribune*; then, in 1897, the House sent Hay an eloquent and lengthy appeal urging him to espouse an active and intelligent policy toward the Orient. House's letter so impressed the newly appointed ambassador that

143

he took it personally to President McKinley and then sent it on to his future adviser on Asian affairs, William W. Rockhill.[3]

If Hay was thus aware of Far Eastern questions well before he entered the McKinley administration, his knowledge was second-hand and his concern largely traditional. Hay thought China important for geopolitical and cultural reasons. But ever since the *Empress of China* sailed for Canton in 1783, the primary American interest had been commercial gain, and Hay did not disagree. He did not say so in so many words, but the severe depression of the middle 1890's almost certainly deepened his interest, for it was widely believed that additional foreign markets, especially in Asia with its teeming millions, could provide a safeguard against future economic gluts at home. "We are keenly alive to the importance of safeguarding our great commercial interests in that empire,"[4] he wrote to editor Paul Dana.

If Hay's concern was mostly traditional, his tactics were flexible. He told Dana he could not state American policy "with any exactness" and did not want his hands tied "for future eventualities." Flexibility was in order, for beginning in 1897, several European powers had carved out spheres of influence in China. The United States had always felt its interests best served by an independent and open China. All the Americans needed, it was said, was "a fair field and no favor" with the government generally remaining aloof. But the spheres of influence posed a potential threat to the United States for American trade and influence might be frozen out of areas controlled by European powers. Consequently, Hay was willing to experiment.

Clearly annoyed with the creation of the spheres, Hay immediately upgraded the government's interest and involvement in Chinese developments. He tried to shore up American treaty rights, insisting that China honor her commitments to the letter, despite the newly created spheres and China's general weakness. American rights, Hay instructed the American minister, Edwin Conger,

were not to be waived "merely because the Chinese authorities may feel unequal to the task of securing them."
And when Conger later tried to arrange a compromise with
the Chinese government involving the rights of American
missionaries, he was promptly and severely chastised.[5]

As a part of this new assertiveness, Hay kept a watchful
eye on any development that might endanger American
commerce, whether it be a new set of Chinese regulations
affecting inland navigation, the threatened recall of a
Chinese consul in San Francisco who had greatly pleased
that city's commercial circles, or Chinese favoritism of
non-American businesses. "You will do what you can to
see that your fellow citizens have a fair and equal chance
with others," Hay instructed Conger.[6] Direct diplomatic
support for specific American firms symbolized most dramatically the government's changed attitude, and within
a few months after Hay became secretary of state the State
Department had exerted its direct influence on behalf of
the American Asiatic Association, the Pepperell Manufac-
turing Company and other firms engaged in the export of
textiles, the American Trading Company, and, most
dramatically of all, the American China Development
Company, which was negotiating to build the Canton-
Hankow railway and also to secure extensive mining concessions in Hunan province. The State Department's efforts on behalf of the Development Company created considerable consternation among the Chinese, and a worried
Wu Ting-fang called at the State Department. The answer
he received could hardly have assuaged his misgivings,
and Hay continued to promote the interests of the
company.[7]

Under the new circumstances, Hay was even tempted
to create American outposts on the Chinese mainland, a
policy that flew in the face of America's traditional insistence that China's national integrity be maintained. Hay
considered such possibilities in November, 1898, March,
1899, and, most seriously of all, in July, 1900, when it was
proposed to construct an American outpost at Samsah Bay
in Fukien. The fact that such proposals received serious

consideration demonstrates Hay's flexibility. Yet none of the proposals was consummated; the most serious took place at the height of the Boxer rebellion; and they must finally be judged relatively insignificant. In no case did Hay initiate such a proposal, and he never advocated a genuine sphere of influence for the United States to compare with those of the European powers.

A more serious challenge to the traditional policy of the United States arose from those who argued that Hay should acquiesce in the establishment of the spheres and work within that context to secure an open door as protection for American rights. Like the proposals to create American lodgments, acceptance of the spheres would have meant an abandonment of America's traditional insistence on China's integrity. In terms of tactics, it implied a less aggressive defense of American treaty rights, premised as they were on an independent China. Great Britain had, however, followed such a policy since January, 1898, and even Rockhill argued that since the spheres existed, the best the United States could do realistically was to work for an open door within the spheres. The spheres, he wrote to Hay in a note explaining his proposal for the first Open Door note of September, 1899, *"are an accomplished fact,* this cannot be too much insisted upon."[8] Concern for China's national integrity had nearly dropped from sight.

Others, however, urged Hay not to give in so easily. Lord Charles Beresford, a British businessman, author, adventurer, and friend of Hay, urged the secretary of state to support both the open door and the integrity of China, while another English acquaintance wrote that "to couple the two—'open door' & 'sphere' . . . will lead to failure."[9] Even Rockhill did not like the spheres or recognize their legality. In the same note in which he pressed for *de facto* recognition of the spheres, he admitted that the United States would suffer a perhaps fatal blow to her interests if they were legitimatized. Thus, while Rockhill admitted the necessity of recognizing the spheres for the present, he wanted them stopped and in time rolled back.

These questions came to a head during the summer

of 1899 when Rockhill and Alfred Hippisley (an English friend of Rockhill employed by the Chinese Imperial Customs Service) urged Hay to state formally American policy and try to get other powers with interests in China to adhere to the American statement. The result was the first Open Door note of September 6, 1899, originally sent to Britain, Germany, and Russia, and later to three lesser powers. The notes to Russia and Germany did not attack the spheres per se but, as Rockhill had argued in his memorandum, asked them to ensure an open door within their own spheres. Hay's note to England, however, revealed that China's integrity still concerned him, for in it he explicitly refused to recognize the spheres as legal entities. Thus, while the notes marked a realistic accommodation with the events of the previous two years (and as such constituted a partial retreat from America's traditional position), the ultimate objective of securing China's integrity still remained.[10]

Hay put considerable effort into getting favorable responses from the great powers. He even told the American ambassador to Russia (before he knew how Russia would respond) that the United States would assume that Russia's response would be favorable. When the answers came in, it must have been clear to the secretary of state that none was an unambiguous endorsement of either the open door principle or the maintenance of China's integrity. Indeed, the Russian response can be viewed as a rejection of the American position. Hay, however, blandly announced in March, 1900, that the acceptances were "final and definitive" and urged his friends in the press to support his achievement. "I hope you will not let the [Philadelphia *Public*] *Ledger* get wrong on our Open Door matter," he wrote to L. Clarke Davis, father of novelist Richard Harding Davis. ". . . We have done a great thing for ourselves and the commerce of the world and I should be sorry—independent of any personal consideration—to have it misrepresented."[11] The Open Door notes were well received in the United States, and for a time Hay enjoyed considerable popularity. "Hay has had some sunshine to make up for the failure of his Canal Treaty,"[12] wrote Henry Adams, referring to the Senate's emasculation of the first Hay-Pauncefote Treaty and Britain's consequent refusal to ratify it.

The sunshine of March went under a cloud in June when Chinese traditionalists (known as Boxers) challenged Western penetration of the empire. China seemed in anarchy, and it was feared, even assumed, that the Western diplomats in Peking had perished. Beyond the immediate tragedy, Hay's China policy hung in the balance, for if the Western powers chose this opportunity to dismember China, either with direct intervention or with demands for excessive reparations, China might totally collapse, and American interests would suffer in the downfall. The pressure on Hay became so severe that, combined with a hot Washington summer, it drove him toward physical collapse.

On July 3 he responded. After extensive discussions with John Bassett Moore and others, Hay issued the so-called second Open Door note (it was really a circular stating America's position) in which he announced that the policy of the United States was to "preserve Chinese territorial and administrative entity, protect all rights guaranteed to friendly powers by treaty and international law, and safeguard for the world the principle of equal and impartial trade with all parts of the Chinese empire."[13] If the first Open Door note had been a muffled attack on the spheres, the second note was an open assault on them. Historians have noted that this circular, with its clear thrusts at the spheres, represented a substantial broadening of the first notes which stressed attainment of the open door within the spheres.[14] But the second note actually followed logically from the underlying assumptions of the earlier documents.

The future of American trade was uppermost in Hay's mind as the disturbing events in China unfolded. Yet, in the case of China, Hay's thought did not move on a single track. The preservation of Anglo-Saxon vitality, coupled with a geopolitical fear of Germany and Russia, were also elements of moment. Brooks Adams was the first to analyze Hay's policy in these terms, while Edward H. House was only one of Hay's friends who spoke in apocalyptic terms of the consequences for the race if Anglo-Saxons were found wanting in the China scramble. Hay himself warned of a Russian, French, and German conspiracy to exclude the Anglo-Saxon powers from the Far East, and until well after the Boxer rebellion he usually equated English and American interests and policies.[15] Because the two countries' policies were quite distinct, Hay's blindness in this regard can only be explained by his broad vision of a world dominated by Anglo-Saxon civilization and his fear of the alternative. Compared to such a vision, the differences in China policies probably seemed trivial.

In any event, from the beginning, Hay desired a joint policy with England in the Far East. An alliance was his dream, though he knew it was not possible. Before he became secretary of state, he twice urged Washington to forge a cooperative policy (he even appears to have offered his services to the British government to enlist American support),[16] but McKinley was not then interested. As ambassador, Hay did not again press his point of view on the administration. And even as secretary of state he pursued a very careful, even excessively cautious course in this matter, believing that the public and the Senate would never countenance joint action, to say nothing of an open alliance. Consequently, he felt constrained to ignore possible opportunities for a joint approach and at one point reluctantly declined Pauncefote's direct inquiry.[17]

But in Hay's own mind, the public was stupidly short-sighted. Ideally, Hay would have acted with Great Britain to ensure Anglo-American markets and, more broadly, to preserve Anglo-American vitality and dominance. When the Boxer rebellion broke out he was therefore discouraged to find Britain suffering military defeat in South Africa. "It is a portentous fact, altogether deplorable in my opinion," Hay wrote, "for their influence on the whole made for peace and civilization. If Russia and Germany arrange things, the balance is lost for ages."[18]

Only five days earlier he had felt compelled to warn Edwin Conger, "there must be no alliances." But his innermost feelings were revealed in a letter to John W. Foster. "On one side there is a great danger, on the other a great opportunity," he began.

I think I see both the danger and the opportunity. It is enough to turn the hair gray not to be allowed to avoid the one and embrace the other. But what can be done in the present diseased state of the public mind? There is such a mad-dog hatred of England prevalent among newspapers and politicians, that anything we should now do in China to take care of our imperilled interests, would be set down to "subservience to Great Britain." France is Russia's harlot—to her own grievous damage. Germany we could probably get on our side by sufficient concessions and perhaps with England, Germany and Japan we might manage to save our skins. But such a proceeding would make all our fools throw fits in the market place—and the fools are numerous.

. . . Cassini has gone to Europe: Cambon was to have sailed last week but has stayed over for a few days: Holleben is absolutely without initiative and in mortal terror of his Kaiser: Pauncefote has apparently no power to act, nor even to talk. And even if he had, every Senator I see says, "For God's sake don't let it appear we have any understanding with England." How can I make bricks without straw? That we should be compelled to refuse the assistance of the greatest power in the world, *in carrying out our policy*, because all Irishmen are Democrats and some Germans are fools—is enough to drive a man mad.[19]

Only with the signing of the Anglo-German Treaty of October, 1900 (and then only after some reflection) did Hay concede that Britain's policy was, in some important respects, at odds with his own, for the agreement was closely tied to the spheres of influences concept and even hedged on the open door. "My heart is heavy about John Bull,"[20] he lamented to Adams.

If the shortsightedness of the public, the stupidity of the Senate, and the gullibility of the English prevented a joint Anglo-American policy in the Orient, Hay could at least attempt to take the lead unilaterally and act in all the ways a great power should (with the notable exception of being unable to form alliances). This had always been one of his objectives, evident in many phases of his diplomacy, and the circular of July 3, 1900, had spoken bravely of holding "to the uttermost accountability" those who wronged American citizens.

Sending American troops to China during the Boxer rebellion to relieve the beseiged legation in Peking gave the United States an unprecedented opportunity to back its diplomacy with force. Henry White saw the possibilities most clearly, writing, "I am very glad to see that we are . . . acting generally as a great power with our vast commercial interest should." Hay, too, realized the advantages of the American military presence. "The talk of the papers about 'our preeminent moral position' giving us the authority to dictate to the world is mere flapdoodle," he wrote to Adee. Proud of America's leadership, Hay even claimed that the powers were now treating the United States "as a Central Hello office."[21]

Because he was exhilarated by the forcefulness his diplomacy possessed when backed by military might, Hay strongly (if politely) resisted President McKinley's efforts to withdraw the troops once the immediate emergency was past. For a time he succeeded. His plan, he wrote to Reid, was "to do everything we can for the integrity and reform of China, and to hold on like grim death to the Open Door."[22]

In fact, the American presence in Peking may have toned down the vengeful demands of European powers for Chinese blood and money in the conference following the Boxer rebellion. Hay thought so, in any event (though, according to Rockhill, he continued until his death to be very much disturbed by the size of the indemnity wrenched from China, even by the United States).[23] But the dangers Germany and Russia posed to China, and hence to American interests and Anglo-Saxon vitality, did not cease with the Boxer settlement. Germany had made the most vindictive demands during the conference, but Hay knew that Russia posed the most serious threat in the foreseeable future. From January, 1901, until the outbreak of the Russo-Japanese War in 1904, ominous hints appeared that

Russia was forcing a treaty on China that would effectively
keep the United States and other powers out of Manchuria.
In the meantime, Russian troops remained. If true, the
outlook for Hay's policy of insisting on both the open door
and China's integrity would be bleak indeed. Given the
discouraging fact that no American troops could be used
to back up American demands (the troops used during the
Boxer rebellion had been withdrawn), Hay occasionally
confessed his weakness. He told the Russian ambassador
that American concern extended only to the open door, not
to the integrity of China. Nor could he promise the Chinese
more than moral support. More significantly, he felt bound
to discourage pointed Japanese inquiries about possible
material support in the event of a clash with the Russians
in Manchuria. "I thought it proper not to leave him [the
Japanese ambassador] with any illusions," Hay wrote in
September, 1903, "and told him plainly we could not take
part in any use of force in that region. . . . And it was a
hard thing to say." He added prophetically, "I believe those
little people will fight if they are crowded too far." The
traditional rhetoric continued to appear from time to time,
however.[24]

The reports of shadowy Chinese-Russian negotiations
were, in fact, true, although Russia continually denied
them. "Dealing with a government with whom mendacity
is a science is an extremely difficult and delicate matter,"
Hay wrote to President Roosevelt. "We are not charged
with the cure of the Russian soul," he concluded wryly,
"and we may let them go to the devil at their own sweet
will." Russia's lying led to an interesting exchange of
letters between Hay and Roosevelt, in which each talked
fancifully about going to "extremes" in the matter. Hay
knew, however, that America's position was almost entirely
a moral one, that troops would not be sent, and that in
the end the Chinese would be forced to come to terms with
the Russians—"the open hand will not be so convincing
to the poor devils of chinks as the raised club," as Hay
colorfully put it.[25]

Hay nevertheless bent every effort to have a Sino-

American commercial treaty signed which would, on paper at least, undermine Russia's privileged position in Manchuria. Such a treaty was finally signed on October 8, 1903, giving the United States the right to trade in the Manchurian cities of Mukden and Antung. Even then, however, China (under Russian pressure) had signed only after Hay agreed not to set a time for the opening of the ports or to include a provision for foreign settlement. Hay was right; American moral posturing was not as effective as Russian armed might. In the end, even this weak treaty was never consummated for shortly after it was signed the Russo-Japanese War broke out. The treaty was not ratified, and American merchants never did achieve the glittering markets and enticing investment opportunities which Hay projected when presenting the treaty to Congress.[26]

Hay and his advisers had been the architects of America's Far Eastern policy ever since 1898. Even Roosevelt, who tended to be his own secretary of state, more or less left Chinese matters to Hay.[27] With the onset of the Russo-Japanese War, Roosevelt exerted more personal control. But while the president concerned himself more directly than he had in the past, he continued to consult Hay on a regular basis. Hay did not cease to concern himself with Asian matters, nor was his influence nil; his diary entries for the years 1904–1905 indicate a continuing close relationship with the president.

Without detailing American policy during the war (a story related so superbly elsewhere),[28] it is clear that Hay's thoughts on the Far East remained unchanged in their essentials. To be sure, the war, fought in Manchuria and Korea, made the Open Door policy and the territorial and administrative integrity of China nothing more than a theory. But Hay insisted on retaining the theory for future use while, in a practical vein, localizing the conflict for the present so as to minimize the immediate threat to China and American policy. Thus, when the conflict appeared imminent he took a German proposal calling for the great powers to induce the belligerents to respect China's "neutrality" and boldly transformed it into a circular calling for the maintenance of the "administrative entity of China."[29] Soon, the major powers agreed to support the terms of the circular, and even Russia responded in a vaguely positive way which Hay promptly accepted as completely satisfactory,[30] much as he had pronounced the ambiguous responses to the first Open Door note as "final and definitive" acceptances.

Nearly a year later, Hay made his last major contribution to American policy. On January 5, 1905, the German government, fearful of French intentions, urged the United States to issue another circular note, this one to ask the powers once again to adhere to the policy of the open door and to maintain China's integrity. Hay and Roosevelt both agreed to take action on the German initiative (partly to "nail the matter down" with the Kaiser). On January 13, this third Open Door note went to the powers who accepted it within a matter of days. "Our policy," Hay wrote in his diary, "is not to demand any territorial advantage and to do what we can to keep China entire."[31]

Throughout the war Hay kept a watchful eye on both belligerents vis à vis China. Occasionally Japanese actions distressed him, as, for example, when Japan violated Chinese neutrality in seizing the Russian destroyer *Ryeshitelui*.[32] But privately Hay and Roosevelt were convinced that the Japanese posed less of a threat to American interests than did the Russians. Past dealings with the Russians had taught Hay to be extremely skeptical of that country's intentions.

Russia and her ambassador were often tactless in their dealings with the United States, which Hay recorded humorously from time to time. Early in the war, for example, Cassini called on the secretary of state and "talked for an hour about American unfriendliness. I told him that the Japs were clever," Hay wrote, "they talked of our friendliness."[33] On another occasion he told Cassini that the Russian attitude reminded him "of a man who should get into a quarrel on the street and then go home and beat his wife."[34] Hay's abilities to maintain friendships were nowhere more evident than in his dealings with the Russian ambassador. Privately, Hay disliked both Russia and her petulant ambassador yet he maintained tolerably good relations with Cassini.

The Japanese, for their part, were quick to exploit Russian diplomatic blunders. While Cassini "seemed little affected by the imminence of war," for example, Takahira "talked of the situation with profound emotion, which expressed itself in a moment of tears and sobs as he left me."[35] And whereas Russia continually lied and gave only reluctant, vague, and misleading assurances about the Open Door, Japanese diplomats assured Hay that Japan was "determined to pursue the American policy of the Open Door."[36]

Hay was dead before the war ended, and he played little if any role in bringing about the negotiations which resulted in a well-deserved Nobel Peace Prize for President Roosevelt. From the issuance of the first Open Door note until his death, Hay tried to preserve American policy in China—the Open Door always coupled (at least in theory) with the maintenance of China's territorial and administrative integrity. In the end he failed almost completely. To some extent he moderated German demands on China following the Boxer rebellion, and, in combination with England and Japan, the United States may have delayed Russia's total control of Manchuria. But, in reality, China's territorial and administrative integrity were dead after 1897 with the result that American commercial investments and noncommercial interests were constantly being threatened. Hay was also unable to forge a joint policy with England that would protect both English and American interests and preserve the vitality of Anglo-Saxon civilization. Finally, Hay could not even push the country to act unilaterally as a great power should, as his weak responses to Chinese and Japanese inquiries in the face of Russia's obdurateness in Manchuria showed. It is doubtful, however, if anyone could have achieved Hay's dreams. Hay, like Roosevelt, appears to have been willing to go to war to save American policy. But China was very far away, and senatorial and public opinion would not permit an ener-

getic policy that required American troops. He was left
with an enraged impotence and was forced into a continual
compromise with reality. Hay never lost sight of his ultimate goals, but without public support there was little
prospect of success. Secretary Hay struggled with the limited rhetorical tools he had, while recognizing their fra-
gility. He accomplished more than most men could have
under the circumstances, and some of his tactical moves
approached genius.

Hay's tactical brilliance, however, was matched by the
mediocrity of the end in view. His attempts to extend
American commerce and influence were accompanied by
a disdain for real Chinese integrity. The one constant in
both Hay's thought and action was the position of China
itself, around which the arguments swirled. China was
always an object to be acted upon. Years later, Alfred
Hippisley, who suggested the original Open Door notes
to Rockhill, understood the arrogance of the American
position. "China," he wrote, referring to the Open Door
notes, "regarded the whole proceeding as a national af-
front."[37] If Hay is lauded in moral terms for trying to save
China from rapacious predators, as he was at the time and
has been occasionally since, the praise is misplaced. As
Hay explained to Rockhill during attempts in 1903 to open
Manchuria to American commerce, "we have done the
Chinks a great service, which they don't seem inclined to
recognize. It will never do to let them think they can treat
us as they please & that the only power they need fear
is Russia."[38]

VII

Hay as Anglophile: The Boer War and the Alaska Boundary Dispute to the Modus Vivendi

John Hay's affinity for Anglo-Saxon civilization, and his concomitant belief that its vitality must be maintained, found expression in his outlook and the policy recommendations he made with respect to the Philippine Islands and China. In these matters, however, a complex interaction of motives obscured the cultural aspect of Hay's thought. With respect to the Boer War, on the other hand, Hay's Anglo-Saxonism clearly outranked other considerations; there were too few concrete American interests involved to muddy Hay's perceptions.

Hay was introduced to the South African problem while he was ambassador to England. He not only sent the State Department the British Blue Books dealing with the problem but, of more significance, he developed contacts with Cecil Rhodes, the South African entrepreneur who was the arch-opponent of Transvaal President Paul Kruger. At Hay's request, John Hays Hammond, an American engineer who had recently served as an undercover agent for Rhodes in Johannesburg, arranged a meeting with Rhodes. The Englishman, Hammond wrote, "told Hay the whole story of South Africa as only he could tell it, and Hay was won over to Rhodes and his aspirations."[1]

When Hay returned to Washington as secretary of state, he was able, according to Hammond, "to impress upon the President the true situation in South Africa."[2] Hammond may have exaggerated Rhodes' influence on Hay, but clearly the secretary of state brought to the capital his approval of British efforts to retain control of the Transvaal.

When, late in the summer of 1899, South Africa began to boil, Hay made no secret of his position. Bourke Cockran, a Tammany Hall Democrat of Irish extraction, urged the president to offer mediation. Unlike Hay, Cockran did not believe that an Anglo-American understanding would further civilization. Cordial relations, he contended in a note to the president, only permitted England to carry out "wanton acts of aggression."[3] Hay returned Cockran's letter to the president, noting that he had received urgent appeals of a contrary nature. "Mr. Cockran's logic is especially Irish,"[4] Hay snorted.

Miffed by Cockran's efforts to swing American support toward the Boers, Hay took an extreme position. "As long as I stay here no action shall be taken contrary to my conviction that the one indispensable feature of our foreign policy should be a friendly understanding with England," he wrote to White, regretting only that a genuine alliance remained "an unattainable dream." He therefore desired a smashing British success. "I hope," he continued, "if it comes to blows that England will make quick work of Uncle Paul," adding that he had refused to answer "Bourke Cockran's fool letter to the President."[5]

However, Britain suffered serious setbacks in the early weeks of the war, leading Hay to comment on the "dreadful state of things in South Africa." Because of the British defeats, he continued, "the welkin rings with oratory against her, flavored with a brogue, and the lower breed of politicians begin to join the outcry." British victory, he thought, "would quiet everything considerably." In June he confessed that the administration had had "great trouble" in preventing the Republican convention from resolving to support the Boers.[6]

Hay greatly feared increasing political support for the Boers, for he viewed British control of South Africa as necessary for the spread of civilization, even as the United States was "civilizing" the Philippines. "Sooner or later . . . [British] influence must be dominant there," he wrote, "and the sooner the better."[7] In March, 1900, he found it incredible that no one in the Senate would openly express the opinion held by "most men of sense" that "the fight of England in South Africa is the fight of civilization and progress, and that all our interests are bound up in her success."[8]

Since American economic and political "interests" in the Transvaal were minimal, Hay was clearly thinking in racial-cultural terms. A British victory and the continued existence of the British empire was in America's interest because only then would "civilization and progress" be ensured. Hay seldom defined "civilization," but his correspondents understood him without elaborate exposition. The English-speaking people embodied the virtues he accepted implicitly as superior. The Irish, the Andrew Jackson Offitts, William Jennings Bryans, and Bourke Cockrans of this world, the socialists and Anglophobic Democrats, Germany, and Russia, aimed, as Hay had written in *The Bread-winners,* at "nothing less than the emancipation of the world from its old fashioned decencies."

Most of Hay's actions as secretary of state in the Anglo-Boer conflict reflected his pro-British point of view, even though the United States remained officially neutral. The appointment of Hay's son, Adelbert, as the American consul at Pretoria was not, in itself, an unneutral act. Adelbert comported himself so well, in fact, that Richard Harding Davis, Adelbert's contemporary and a Boer sympathizer, wrote that neither side was certain of his sympathies.[9] But Adelbert did give the appearance of favoritism by traveling to Africa via London, where he visited prominent British officials. And even his genuinely neutral behavior in Africa was a change for the worse from the Boer point of view, for Adelbert replaced an ardent pro-Boer. As Henry White wrote to Hay in October, 1900, "what a mercy it was for our credit that you sent Del out there. I don't imagine he arrived a moment too soon."[10] Furthermore, Hay's letters to his son in the summer and fall of 1900 were increasingly less neutral in tone than earlier letters which had been carefully composed to conform to the official policy. Del would want to return home, Hay suggested in one of them, "after the war is over and the British rule established."[11]

Hay's Anglophilia also showed in his attitude toward Britain's concentration camps. Adelbert's replacement at Pretoria, Consular Agent William Gordon, joined representatives of several states to protest Britain's policy in this regard, while William T. Stead, leader of the British peace movement, asked Hay to intervene and sent him his pamphlet, "Methods of Barbarism," that described the camps in detail.[12] Hay did help forward private relief to the refugees, but, in striking contrast to his attitude to Spain's policy of *reconcentration* in Cuba, Hay had no quarrel with Britain's methods. "The Boer women and children are in the concentration camps simply because their husbands and brothers want them there," he wrote to Lodge, "and as to the war with all its barbarities, it will stop the instant Botha and DeWet wish it to stop."[13] Consular Agent Gordon was fired. "There was nothing of the sort in my son's time,"[14] Hay fumed to Choate.

Hay's thinly disguised pro-British attitude led to protest from some quarters. Boer sympathizers, for example, thought Hay's response to British seizures of American goods bound for South Africa was insufficient. They also charged that he was extremely slow to investigate complaints of alleged British efforts to secure war supplies illegally in the United States. Hay vigorously defended his actions, and his protestations of innocence were essentially accurate, if somewhat shrill.[15]

Hay's critics were on stronger ground in protesting his responses to Boer efforts to obtain American mediation, although one historian has contended that Hay's responses were perfectly correct.[16] Before the outbreak of hostilities Hay rejected a request from President Steyn of the Orange Free State for diplomatic intervention,[17] but with the war's commencement public pressure grew for American action. Hay admitted to Edward Everett Hale that he had received "a great many" letters, petitions, and memorials urging that the government act in accordance with the good-offices provisions of the recently signed Hague Convention. Hay refused to take any initiative, however, claiming that the convention had not yet been ratified and that, in any event, the United States had signed with the understanding that she would not be required to interfere in European quarrels. Furthermore, the Boers were doing well and did not, Hay contended, want mediation.[18]

In fact, the Boers did, and Hay knew it. Not only was there President Steyn's abortive appeal of September, 1899, but Henry White wrote Hay in December of the same year that the Boers were about to send four representatives to the United States to pressure the administration into making a mediation offer. "You are doubtless aware," White added pointedly, "that this country [England] is in no mood for mediation now and means to fight it out and from this point of view—I mean that of the prestige of the empire—they are quite right."[19] The latter argument was more likely to appeal to the secretary of state than that posed by Boer sympathizers.

On March 10, 1900, the South Africans made a positive request for intervention, and a similar request was made to the continental powers.[20] The secretary of state immediately forwarded the request to Britain with an expression of hope that peace might result, and he offered the good offices of the United States to that end.[21] Hay's quick response led one historian to defend Hay's claim that he was neutral,[22] and Hay himself snapped to a critic, "this government was the only Government on the face of the earth that . . . acceded to the request of the Boers."[23]

Despite appearances, however, Hay's action was disingenuous and was, after all, fully in accordance with his pro-British views. Had he not forwarded the message and offered America's good offices, the outcry would have been overwhelming. To oppose the pro-Boer sentiment, as Hay wrote to White, "would defeat our our own purpose. For this reason, I saw there was nothing to be done with the Boer message but to send it on to you with an expression of the President's platonic desire for peace. . . . For the present we seem to have spiked their guns."[24]

Thereafter, criticism dropped markedly. The correspondence with Great Britain was published, and Hay could now reply to critics that the United States had tendered its good offices to bring about peace. His action did not please the South Africans, however, for they had hoped the United States would organize a joint movement for intervention. Hay's prompt offer and the British rejection immediately killed that possibility, a course which Russia, in fact, was attempting to follow. All told, Hay's prompt action was, as John H. Ferguson concludes, "a master stroke" for his policy of cooperation with England.[25]

Despite this setback, a Boer delegation arrived in the United States to press in person for mediation or intervention. They requested two meetings with Hay, an informal one to present their case and clear the air, and a later formal one in which they would present their official credentials. The envoys were under the impression that the State Department had agreed to this arrangement, but the secretary of state treated the first meeting of May 21, 1900, as a formal affair, received the delegates contemptuously, read a prepared rejection of their plea for mediation, ushered them out of the office, and received the British ambassador.[26] "It was a bit discouraging to see our answer lying on the table as we entered and before we had had opportunity to open our mouths,"[27] the Boer leader commented. They were never given an opportunity to present their credentials.

Before they left the United States, the envoys explained to the president that they had not presented their credentials "solely because of the formal statement prepared for and before our meeting with . . . the Secretary of State."[28] Hay suggested angrily that no reply be sent to them. Their letter was, he felt, "disingenuous, not to say untruthful." He insisted that the Boers had had ample opportunity to present their credentials when they met with him.[29]

Clearly there existed a basic misunderstanding about the nature of the meeting. The question is whether the misunderstanding was honest, or whether either Hay or the Boer envoys deliberately misrepresented the nature of the meeting. According to Hay's account (in a letter to the president), General James O'Beirne, an American citizen who acted as a go-between, called to make arrangements. Hay told him that the normal procedure was for envoys to send their credentials to the State Department prior to a personal meeting with the secretary. In subsequent correspondence, Hay maintained, O'Beirne never raised the credentials question. Even the "formal note" of May 19 from the "delegates" of the South African Republic requesting an interview avoided the credentials issue, Hay contended. Nevertheless, he "met them, heard all they had to say, and gave our reply."[30] Hay gave no intimation to the president that he understood the meeting to be anything but formal or that he anticipated a future meeting to receive credentials.

The Boer delegation, on the other hand, did think an informal meeting had been arranged, and the evidence supports their contention. After O'Beirne returned from his meeting with Hay and informed the Boers of the usual procedure, the envoys sent Hay what O'Beirne described as "an informal communication" (the one Hay called a "formal note") asking if Hay "would grant them the honor of a previous interview."[31] The term "previous interview" was ambiguous and might well have led to an inquiry as to its meaning. But O'Beirne clarified the matter in a letter to Hay the same day, in which he explicitly referred to their "informal communication asking to be allowed to call on you as visitors or unofficially ... and then arrange for their subsequent reception with credentials, at such time as would be agreeable to you after furnishing you copies."[32] Hay then arranged the May 21 meeting, and the Boers proceeded on the assumption that the meeting would be informal. Indeed, the morning of the reception O'Beirne wrote to McKinley that Hay had kindly agreed to meet the Boer envoys "informally," while at the meeting itself spokesman Fischer remarked that he hoped "through an *unofficial visit* [to] give some idea of what the object of our visit is."[33]

Hay had either prepared sloppily or he was deliberately misrepresenting the character of the meeting. The former is unlikely, since he had several opportunities to inquire about allusions to an "informal" or "unofficial" meeting or "a previous interview." Furthermore, Adee had prepared for Hay a list of detailed questions he could ask the Boers, which suggests that a good deal of attention had been given to the entire affair. And two days after the event, Hay himself wrote to Choate, "our treatment of the Boer delegates required very serious consideration."[34]

In addition, Hay's account to the president was patently false at one point, for he reported to McKinley that O'Beirne's letter made no reference to the credentials question. On the contrary, O'Beirne had explicitly explained to Hay that the Boers would present credentials at the subsequent, formal meeting. Hay's suspicion that the Boers had no credentials may have been correct, but he gave them no chance to present any. "From beginning to end they made no reference to credentials," Hay wrote incorrectly to McKinley, "and it is now plain that the reason why they did not was that they intended to make an anti-administration campaign through the country, a proceeding which they would have been debarred from taking if they had presented regular diplomatic credentials."[35] If Hay thought this was the Boers' intention, he should have granted them two meetings in order to ascertain the truth. If they had produced credentials he would have been able to forestall their much-publicized cross-country tour.

The British cheered Hay's handling of the Boer delegates. The sociable Henry White reported that at the Duchess of Devonshire's party he encountered "a perfect chorus . . . long continued over your handling of the Boer Envoy matter."[36] British reaction to the incident clearly pleased Hay, who sent a clipping from the popular English newspaper, the London *Daily Mail*, to the president. "It may be worth your reading," he explained. The *Daily Mail* concluded that the American response to the Boer envoys "marks the complete failure of the Boer mission. . . . Thanks to the political sagacity of the President," the editorial concluded, "all these [Boer] efforts have been wasted."[37]

Hay's reaction to the envoys had been extremely emotional. When the Boer delegates arrived at New York a few days prior to their meeting with Hay, two thousand sympathizers met them; when they came to Washington two days later they received boisterous welcomes at the railroad station and the Arlington Hotel. The day before the meeting with Hay an enormous pro-Boer mass meeting in the Grand Opera House was attended by thirty congressmen and senators, and among those addressing the rally was the Irish, Tammany Hall Democrat, Bourke Cockran.[38] All the forces Hay detested—the Irish, the Democrats, representatives of city machines, Anglophobes, anti-administration congressmen—sided with the Boers. Despite the alleged strict neutrality of the government, Hay did what he could in this case to keep American policy distinctly favorable to the British.

Hay had one more opportunity to stifle Boer hopes before the year was out. Learning that President Kruger, then in Holland, had received a number of private invitations to visit the United States, Hay wrote a personal letter to Ambassador Stanford Newel at The Hague, explaining that "a good many thoughtless and some malicious people" had invited Kruger to the United States. He asked Newel to "discreetly and indirectly" discourage any visit. When McKinley heard of the letter he ordered it recalled, no doubt fearing the political consequences if it were published. Hay acceded to McKinley's wish, writing to Newel to "consider it as not written."[39] He had already accomplished his purpose, however, for the ambassador had seen to it that Hay's sentiments reached Kruger's friends.[40]

In other diplomatic endeavors Hay's actions were usually circumspect but in the South African War Hay's pro-English feelings, largely racial and cultural in nature, clearly influenced his action. He was able to express his feelings so directly primarily because so few American interests were involved, and of those directly affected by the war, most benefited from increased British trade.[41] The Boers could appeal only on moral grounds. Not only is morality a weak base for action in international relations, but it had serious flaws in this case, for the South Africans were notoriously repressive of their black and Catholic populations. Joseph C. Hartzell, bishop of the Methodist-Episcopal Church of Africa, for example, spoke to large audiences across the United States condemning Kruger's racist regime.[42] Hay knew that the Boers prohibited Catholics from holding office, having been supplied with a memorandum to that effect, but he resisted the temptation to make this know publicly to the Boers' Irish supporters.[43]

In sum, under Hay's direction, American neutrality was distinctly benevolent to England. In London, Henry White even kept Balfour abreast of anti-Boer actions in the United States.[44] Hay was unapologetically conscious of the service he rendered to Great Britain. In 1903, the mayor of Dunedin, New Zealand, sent Hay a box of precious ornaments that he had intended to present to Adelbert Hay in recognition of his efforts to ameliorate the condition of New Zealander prisoners at Pretoria. Hay gratefully accepted the ornaments, as his son had died shortly after his return from South Africa. "We are grateful that in the short span of life allotted to him," Hay replied in acknowledgment, "he was able to do something to testify to the sentiments of sympathy and friendship which unite all branches of the English-speaking race, however widely separated they may be."[45]

Coincident with the Boer War, the United States became embroiled with Britain over the disputed boundary between Canada and Alaska. Because American interests were directly involved in this matter, Hay's thoughts and actions were far more complex than they were with respect to the South African imbroglio. As secretary of state during most of the Alaskan controversy, Hay could hardly advocate the British point of view, and, in fact, he thought that the American case was the stronger. He wanted this irritant in Anglo-American relations removed, however, and his continued devotion to an Anglo-American rapprochement and his Anglophilia showed in subtle ways. A defender of the American claim, Hay nevertheless retreated step by step in an effort to sustain the steadily improving relations between the United States and Great Britain. Unlike Theodore Roosevelt and other strong nationalists, Hay (who in other situations was equally ardent) considered good Anglo-American relations more important than upholding the American claim in Alaska.

The question of exactly where the boundary lay between Alaska and British Columbia had been a minor irritant in Anglo-American relations ever since the American purchase of Alaska in 1867. It never approached the seriousness of the seal dispute until well into the 1890's, however, largely because neither Canada nor the United States thought its interests were very great in this vast wilderness. Indeed, more than once Congress balked at appropriating funds to survey the area. Only when gold was discovered in the boundary region did both countries begin to harden their positions. Exactly where the boundary lay was difficult to determine because of the vague wording of the Russo-American Treaty of 1824, the Russo-British Treaty of 1825, the Treaty of Cession of 1867 (which continued the vagueness of the previous treaties), and the records of numerous early explorations, Russian ukases, and diplomatic exchanges, all of which seemed to confuse instead of clarify.[46]

When Hay became secretary of state he was well acquainted with the issues at hand since, as ambassador, he had been involved in establishing a joint high commission to deal with several outstanding disputes between the United States and Canada, including the Alaska matter. Unexpectedly, the commission almost immediately bogged down on the boundary question, a situation Secretary Hay attributed to the cantankerous Baron Farrer Herschell, the only Englishman on the commission, while the British blamed John W. Foster, one of the American commissioners. "Lord Herschell complains with oily sobs in his voice that Foster insults him,"[47] Adams observed sardonically.

Because of the deadlock, Hay was willing to submit the matter to binding arbitration if that were the only way to settle the dispute amicably, particularly after Britain flavored the bait considerably by agreeing explicitly to ratify the pending Hay-Pauncefote canal treaty (something Hay deeply desired) in exchange for an arbitration agreement.[48] Ever sensitive to the Senate's distrust of arbitration, however, Hay did not pursue the matter. "The Senate has sat upon the State Department,"[49] thought the sagacious Adams. A little later, Hay did accept a British proposal for arbitration which guaranteed that Dyea and Skagway, two important towns in the disputed Lynn Canal area, would remain in American hands regardless of the arbiter's final decision.

Thus, for the second time Hay accepted the principle of genuine arbitration and opened the possibility that Pyramid Harbor, as well as other areas claimed by the United States, might fall to the Canadians. He even drew an admission from McKinley that the arbitration proposal was "as good as any that we can secure."[50] Just as Hay was about to wire America's acceptance, however, Canada killed the plan by insisting that she be guaranteed Pyramid Harbor in advance, just as the United States was guaranteed Dyea and Skagway. Ambassador Choate strongly remonstrated to Salisbury, while Ambassador Pauncefote, openly angry at Canada's intransigence, admitted that he was "distressed and disappointed . . . at the failure of our efforts in the matter of the Alaskan Boundary."[51]

For a time Canada's action broke Hay's spirit more than it angered him. To Adams he wrote:

I have worked on this miserable Alaska question for six months. Yesterday Choate wired me a proposition agreed on between him, Pauncefote and Salisbury, which I had spent weeks beforehand getting every body here to agree to. I thought I could intone my little *nunc dimittis*—when this morning comes in young Tower [the British chargé] and tells me Canada won't let Salisbury do it! Now the fat is on the fire, and I "don't much care if I ever get to Texas." I grow wanner and wanner day by day.[52]

But if good relations with England were to be maintained, something had to be concluded about Alaska, for Hay was receiving complaints about Canadian encroachments in the disputed region. He proposed a temporary settlement of crucial portions of the disputed area. Since this modus vivendi proposal temporarily gave to Canada a considerable portion of the American claim, Hay's actions represented a genuine concession. A few days later he accepted a British counter-proposal cutting even deeper into the American claim.

Much to Hay's irritation Britain procrastinated and then, without making a final response to Hay's modus vivendi proposal, suggested a final solution permitting Canada to lease a strip of land in Pyramid Harbor. Canada would also be allowed to construct a railroad through American territory, thus giving the Canadians at least indirect access to the sea, a major Canadian objective. Distressed by Britain's stalling, Hay nevertheless accepted the British proposal since it promised a final settlement.

Hay knew he was already on thin ice as far as the Senate was concerned. His willingness to arbitrate much of the boundary, and then his concession to achieve a modus vivendi, had put on edge the strong nationalists who composed the Senate Committee on Foreign Relations. Yet Hay thought the risks were worth taking. "I am so anxious to have the thing settled that I am willing to run considerable risk in the Senate with a treaty, either of delimitation or arbitration,"[53] he admitted to Choate. Eleven days later he confessed receding "step by step till we were cutting into the quick of our border population,"[54] something not unnoticed by the Senate.

Hay's acceptance of the lease idea tipped the delicate balance against him. Senator Davis warned that the Senate would be opposed, and Reid wrote, unkindly, that he was relieved to learn that the lease proposal came from Britain so that the United States was not committed to it. The proposal, the editor commented, was "unpleasantly suggestive of Chinese rather than American methods."[55] Discouraged by these responses, Hay predicted a melancholy future. If the British proposal could not be accepted, he felt, nothing could. Furthermore, the Hay-Pauncefote Treaty could not be ratified. "We shall be left in a state of dull hostility, varied by commercial reprisals," he wrote.

Hay then stated his main fear: "The friendship between the two countries . . . will prove short-lived and derisory."[56]

In spite of the Senate's opposition, Hay threatened to push the matter, particularly after he learned that Foster favored the lease proposal.[57] President McKinley and the Cabinet agreed to support him, but Hay knew that he daré not follow through because of political repercussions for the administration. The ensuing sense of impotence left him enraged and resulted in some of the bitterest letters of his career directed at the senators, particularly Democratic Anglophobes of Irish or German decent. "The Democratic press," he wrote, "evidently thinks there is some political capital to be made by denouncing any arrangement with England and they, in common with a large number of German newspapers, are ready to attack any treaty with England, no matter how advantageous to us, as a hostile act toward Ireland and Germany."[58]

In the meantime, Hay continued to press for a temporary arrangement. After the exchange of many notes, Hay and the British government finally arrived at a modus vivendi on October 20, 1899.[59] The agreement involved more minor American concessions, most notably Hay's willingness to accept the south bank of the Tlehini as one boundary.

Hay anticipated intense criticism. The day the agreement was finalized he wrote to St. Loe Strachey, "I have already had notice served on me by some of our conscript fathers that I have betrayed my country."[60] But Hay was quite willing to ride out the storm if the end result was improved Anglo-American relations. Throughout the negotiations he consistently revealed this primary objective. Although angry at Britain for its procrastination, his wrath was directed more particularly at Canada, for both Choate and White reported on numerous occasions that Pauncefote and Salisbury regretted Canadian bull-headedness.[61]

As time passed, the virtues of the modus vivendi grew in Hay's mind. It was as if, having made several concessions, he felt a psychological need to justify the agreement with unwarranted praise. "I will be hanged if I can see

what people mean when they attack that Alaska agreement,"[62] he wrote, and he even claimed to have bilked the
British.[63]

Hay's strong rhetorical defenses of the agreement led
Tyler Dennett to conclude, "so much for one phase of
Hay's Anglophilism."[64] But, as has been shown, Hay was
not an avid defender of the American claim. He considered
it on its merits considerably stronger than the British case,
but he was quite willing to compromise—and endure the
wrath of many—in order to promote the greater good, as
he viewed it, of Anglo-American friendship. Indeed, had
it not been for public and senatorial opinion, Hay would
have gone even further than he did in order to settle the
matter.

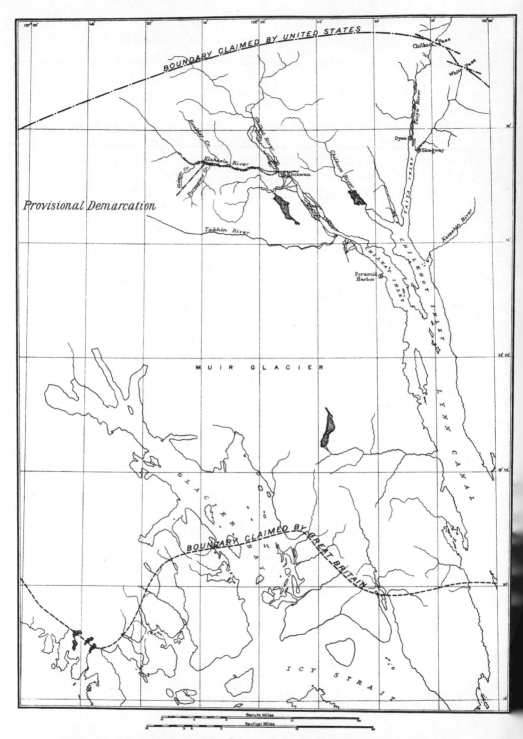

Modus Vivendi agreement, Alaska boundary dispute.
(Reprinted from *Papers Relating to the Foreign Relations
of the United States*, 1899 [Washington, D.C., 1901])

VIII

The Gentleman Diplomat:
Hay and the
Hay-Pauncefote Treaty

Hay's attempt to secure the exclusive right to construct and
control a canal across the Central American isthmus revealed his desire to eliminate yet another irritant in Anglo-
American relations. The canal question also demonstrated
Hay's concern for expanding "civilization," including
American commercial and strategic enterprises. In this
matter, most clearly, Hay emerged as the gentleman diplomat. His anger at the Senate's bad manners, as he viewed
its actions in this instance, was noticeably stronger than
his attacks on that body in other issues and actually led
to two resignation attempts. As John Bassett Moore wrote
a few years after the events, "Mr. Hay's greatest celebrity
to-day rests, no doubt, upon his diplomacy in China, but
I venture to think that in his negotiations with regard to
the canal, his character as a public man underwent the
severest test to which it was ever subjected."[1]

America's dream of a canal across the isthmus of Central America reached back for decades and had found
expression in two early treaties. A treaty with New Granada
(later Colombia), signed in 1846 and approved two years
later, granted American citizens transit rights across the
isthmus equal to those of New Granada's own citizens,
while the Clayton-Bulwer Treaty of 1850 with England
provided for joint Anglo-American control over any future
canal. By the terms of the treaty, the canal would be
unfortified and completely neutral, even in time of war,
and other states were invited to adhere to the treaty. The
treaty with New Granada figured in the American involve-

ment in the Panamanian revolution of 1903, but the Clayton-Bulwer Treaty became an important issue for Hay as early as 1898.

At mid-century, the Clayton-Bulwer Treaty was a fair compromise, but, as the United States increased its strength and began to challenge Europe's position in Latin America, some Americans called for a new treaty that would reflect the nation's growing predominance.[2] The expansionists of the 1890's placed a high priority on a canal, particularly after the Spanish-American War revealed the strategic advantages of a short-cut from East to West.[3]

Hay was not among those who ardently propagandized for a canal in the early 1890's, but, as an admirer of James G. Blaine and a friend of many expansionists, he probably favored one and certainly was not in opposition. Then, in 1898, President McKinley focused Hay's attention on the matter by forwarding to him some documents, including a letter from Senator John T. Morgan, dealing with the canal question. McKinley's initiative prompted Hay to contact former Secretary of State Richard Olney. Hay had heard from an unidentified source, perhaps Senator Morgan, that British Ambassador Pauncefote had once assured Olney that "there would be no objection on the part of England" if the United States desired to abrogate the Clayton-Bulwer Treaty. Olney replied that although Pauncefote's assurances were never so categorical, Britain was willing to amend the treaty so as to give the United States exclusive control, provided only that ships of all nations had equal privileges.[4]

After receiving further assurances from England,[5] Hay asked Pauncefote to draft a revision. Although the British ambassador was a leading authority on international law relating to canals (he had represented Britain at the Suez Canal conference in Paris in 1885), Hay's decision to employ Pauncefote, rather than his own staff, was a mistake. Not only did the decision demonstrate his Anglophilia (would he, for example, have permitted a German or Latin-American expert to undertake a similar task?), but State Department men would probably have been more sensitive to senatorial and public opinion than the British ambassador. In short, Hay might have avoided the bitter exchanges which ensued. On the other hand, Hay thought, with some reason, that there would be no objection to virtually any reasonable treaty which gave the United States control over the canal. This, along with the optimistic reports from London, seemed to assure a quick resolution. "I do not look forward to any protracted negotiations,"[6] Hay casually informed Senator Morgan late in December.

The Pauncefote draft, which Hay accepted with only minor revisions, differed from the Clayton-Bulwer Treaty in only one major respect; it provided that the United States (or a private concern sanctioned by the government) alone could construct, regulate, and manage a ship canal across the isthmus. On January 13, 1899, Hay sent the completed draft treaty to Henry White.

But the optimism that Hay expressed in December had diminished considerably by that date. The Senate, which Hay had seldom respected since Reconstruction days, seemed likely to balk, and he therefore urged White to ask the Foreign Office to consider the treaty as soon as possible. "In the usual reckless manner of our Senate," he explained, "they are discussing the matter with open doors every day, and are getting themselves so balled up with their own eloquences that it is greatly to be feared they will so commit themselves as to consider themselves bound to reject any arrangement that may be made."[7]

Actually, the Senate had been making threatening sounds for several months. As early as June, 1898, Senator Morgan had introduced a bill, without reference to the Clayton-Bulwer Treaty, providing for the construction, ownership, and fortification of a canal by the United States. Hay deplored the actions of those like Morgan, who appeared unconcerned about upholding an international obligation. He did not want to alienate the powerful Democrat, however, for he liked him personally and wanted his support at critical times. Therefore, when he learned in December that Morgan planned to reintroduce his bill, Hay wrote him a typically ingratiating letter stating that he saw "no reason why your work on the canal bill should be checked, on account of any such negotiation [for the revision of the Clayton-Bulwer Treaty]. We are striving for the same object, on parallel lines, and I do not see how we are to interfere with each other." When Morgan's bill convincingly passed the Senate forty-six to six, Hay congratulated the senator for exhibiting "the highest qualities of political generalship, courage, patience and liberality combined with unwearied vigilance and resolution." Hay's flattery paid off when Morgan later fought for adoption of the first Hay-Pauncefote Treaty.[8]

Confrontation with the Senate over the Morgan proposal was avoided because opposition and jealousy in the House of Representatives prevented passage before adjournment in March. Furthermore, England refused to proceed with the draft canal treaty, despite early indications to the contrary, largely because Canada insisted on tying treaty revision to the settlement of issues directly affecting Canadian-American relations. Hay deplored Canada's action, but there was nothing he could do.[9]

Then, in October, after a summer of hard work and harsh words for both the Senate and the Canadian government, Hay managed to secure a modus vivendi in Alaska. Coincidentally the Boer War broke out in earnest, and in December Congressman Hepburn introduced a bill which, like Senator Morgan's, ignored the Clayton-Bulwer Treaty. These three facts made an agreement more likely. The Alaskan modus vivendi temporarily dampened the most outstanding difference with Canada, the Boer War made England sensitive to the need for American friendship, and the Hepburn bill again illustrated the possibility of a bad-mannered abrogation of the Clayton-Bulwer Treaty. As Hay stated to Choate in a long, personal, chatty letter, the Alaska question was "less acute," and the ill-considered Hepburn bill made an arrangement "more imperative than ever." "I think we should be in a most unenviable attitude before the world if that bill should pass in its present form," he continued, a statement indicative of, among other things, his genteel attitudes. He hoped therefore that Britain would agree "so that at least the Administration would have its skirts clear of any complicity in a violent and one-sided abrogation of the Clayton-Bulwer Treaty."[10]

Shortly thereafter, Choate called at the Foreign Office, and Salisbury soon ordered Pauncefote to sign the thirteen-month-old draft treaty. "At this instant," wrote Henry Adams, ". . . Hay is probably signing with Pauncefote an abrogation of the Clayton-Bulwer Treaty! Hay himself actually trembles for fear that he should wake up and find that he dreamt it. . . . He beams with content, and says he is now ready to go." Hay was happy, but he also knew the unpredictability of the Senate and was therefore cautious, writing to Choate that the future lay "with the gods."[11]

As Hay feared, opposition to the treaty soon developed and was, in some cases, almost fanatical. "Hay is about as furious as you can imagine . . . ," Adams wrote. "He regards the Nicaragua matter as personal, and loathes the Senate with a healthy anarchical energy for a gold-bug." Supporting Adams' evaluation, Hay wrote to Everett P. Wheeler that the opposition approached "stupefaction."[12] Hay deplored senatorial perversity, but a press statement calling for the amendment or defeat of the treaty issued by Governor Theodore Roosevelt destroyed Hay's usual impeccable composure. *"Et tu!"* he began a scorching letter to the New York governor.

Cannot you leave a few things to the President and the Senate, who are charged with them by the Constitution? . . .

Do you really think the Clayton-Bulwer Treaty preferable to the one now before the Senate? There is no third issue, except dishonor. Elkins and Pettigrew say 'Dishonor be damned.' I hardly think you will.

Please do not answer this—but think about it awhile.[13]

Roosevelt termed Hay's letter "pathetic" and wondered "what in the world has gotten into John Hay."[14]

"You can imagine to what extent the fat is on the fire!" Adams wrote when he heard of Roosevelt's action. "Poor Cabot! What can he do? If Teddy . . . stabs Hay in the back, he has got to [go] on and tilt with the Major in face. If Hay is beaten on his Treaty, he will resign; if he does not resign, he will certainly hamstring Teddy. Won't it be fun." As Adams implied, Senator Lodge soon had to take a position, and he came out against the treaty in its existing form. "So he has thrown Hay over; declared against his Treaty; alienated the Major, and destroyed all the credit with the administration which he has labored so hard to create," Adams observed, "and probably, within a twelve-month, he will go back on Teddy, and help cut his throat as he is helping to cut Hay's. Everyone sees now that Hay must go out very soon."[15]

The accumulating opposition left Hay outraged. "I have never seen such an exhibition of craven cowardice, ignorance, and prejudice," he wrote to Henry White, adding, ". . . it never entered into my mind that anyone out of a madhouse could have objected to the Canal Convention." Having read in that morning's *New York Tribune* that Andrew Carnegie now opposed the treaty, Hay exploded, "[Carnegie] comes out today in the Tribune saying it will be the death of the Republican Party, if the treaty goes through—the frantic little lunatic."[16]

Unwilling to admit defeat, Hay fought back with pressure and reason. His strongest step for the cause was his decision to enlist the services of John Bassett Moore, an eminent international lawyer. Moore, who had served as legal adviser at the Paris peace conference in 1898, began his research at least by early February, 1900, seeking out precedents in an effort to arrive at America's historical position regarding the neutrality of a canal and its effects on the Monroe Doctrine. Moore reported regularly to Hay.[17] On February 20, he revealed that he had inspired a number of newspaper articles in an effort to correct misleading stories and editorials. However, Moore felt that his efforts, and those of his journalist supporters, amounted only to "patchwork." He wanted instead to write a systematic defense of the treaty. The *New York Mail and Express* had, in fact, offered him "what it evidently considers a large sum" for an editorial series on the treaty. But Moore held off, questioning the paper's influence. Hay, agreeing with Moore, suggested that he might try the *Herald* instead.[18]

Evidently no offer was forthcoming from the *Herald,* but on Sunday, March 4, the prestigious *New York Times* devoted an entire page to Moore's article, "The Interoceanic Canal and the Hay-Pauncefote Treaty." The article was, as Moore intended, a clear, systematic evaluation of the treaty and its precedents. Although purporting to be an objective presentation of both sides, Moore came down hard in favor of those arguments supporting the treaty. Opposition arguments got little space and even less support. Indeed, the introduction stated that the treaty "seems to mark a distinct advance toward the accomplishment of a work which, though long postponed, has been so persistently cherished" and represented "a notable achievement of American diplomacy."[19]

Hay termed Moore's article "splendid—absolutely unanswerable. If there were any reason in the Senate, there would be nothing more to say." He also asked permission to reprint the article for distribution to the Senate Committee on Foreign Relations. In an age when the political elite paid special attention to the newspapers, Moore's article was widely noticed. Indeed, in a follow-up story on Monday, March 5, the *Times* reported that all of the important personages in the senate, including those on the Foreign Relations Committee, had read it.[20]

Moore's article commanded attention, but to opponents of the treaty like Frederick W. Holls it amounted to "feeble special pleading." Something of the depth of feeling that the controversy generated among Anglophobes was apparent in the letters of Holls, a passionate friend of Germany and a prominent representative of German-Americans in the Republican party. Holls was about to travel to Washington, he informed Andrew D. White, to "read the riot act to a sufficient number of Senators to defeat the Treaty *at any cost.* I don't like to openly oppose the administration," he contended, "but this seems to me a *crisis* as important in its way as the silver crisis itself."[21]

Hay knew that Irish and German resentment lay behind much of the opposition to the treaty, and he probably knew of Holls' opposition. But it is unlikely that he knew the lengths to which Holls went to defeat the treaty or of his private contempt for the secretary of state. Proud of his feat, as a member of the American delegation to the recent Hague Conference, of inserting the Monroe Doctrine reservation into the convention adopted by the conference, Holls began his campaign immediately after Pauncefote signed the treaty early in February. In a number of letters, Holls blasted the treaty's neutrality provisions and Hay's failure, as he viewed the secretary's actions, to keep in touch with the public.[22]

Unaware of Holls' attitude, Andrew D. White, the American ambassador to Germany, wrote to him that he deeply regretted the growing opposition to the treaty and particularly that of Roosevelt. He urged Holls to talk to the governor, even suggesting that he show Roosevelt White's letter. White must have been astounded at Holls' reply in which he confessed "very confidentially that Gov. Roosevelt's manifesto was written *in my library* at Yonkers, after a very careful consultation between the Governor, and Messers Albert Shaw, Nicholas Murray Butler, & Asst. Secy of State Hill, all of whom were my guests for the day!! . . . Words fail to express my sense of hopeless incompetence of a Secretary of State who could demand from England just about *one-fifth* what she was ready to grant, and call it a diplomatic victory!" As this letter reveals, the opposition had a man high in the State Department, although there is no evidence that David Jayne Hill attempted to sabotage Hay's policies from within.[23]

On March 9, the Senate Committee on Foreign Relations reported the treaty favorably but with one amendment. Contrary to the impression left by many authors, this so-called Davis amendment did not change the nonfortification clause of the original treaty (Article II, section 7).[24] The amendment stated that "the United States may find it necessary to take for securing, by its own forces, the defense of the United States and the maintenance of public order," but it applied only to the first five sections of Article II; indeed, the committee's report included much testimony against fortifying the canal.[25] The Davis amendment undercut the neutrality provisions, however, by implying that the United States would close the canal to her enemies in time of war, or, indeed, whenever her interests seemed endangered.

Angered by the Davis amendment, coming as it did on top of abuse from both the press and public figures, Hay submitted his resignation. "The action of the Senate indicates views so widely divergent from mine in matters affecting, as I think, the national welfare and honor," he explained to McKinley, "that I fear my power to serve you in business requiring the concurrence of that body is at an end." McKinley, however, refused to accept the resignation, expressing his belief that the malevolent atmosphere would soon "pass away."[26]

The senators, preferring not to commit themselves on such a politically explosive issue before election time, postponed a final vote on the treaty until December, 1900. The intervening months produced nothing to mellow Hay's disgust with the Senate. He viewed ratification of the treaty as a matter of personal and national honor. If the Hepburn or Morgan bills passed without an accompanying agreement with England, the United States would be placed in a position of ignoring and probably abrogating violently a solemn international agreement. To Hay, this was unthinkable. As early as January, 1900, Hay intimated to Ambassador Choate that if this happened, he might resign. After the Davis amendment passed and the Senate delayed further action, the threat of the Hepburn bill increased. Now Hay explicitly threatened to resign if such a measure became law. As he explained in a draft letter to the president (in a paragraph he omitted from the letter he actually sent), "The Government will ... be placed in a position to repudiate and violate a solemn treaty obligation, which England is perfectly ready and willing to release us from. I do not wish to judge any one who holds a different view; but every man must be the guardian of his own honor; and my conscience will not permit me to take part in such an act." The volume and vehemence of these and similar comments suggest considerations of honor, expressed in upholding international agreements, were probably Hay's overriding concerns.[27]

The senator who most disgusted Hay was the floor manager for the treaty, Henry Cabot Lodge. On December 14, 1900, the Senate approved the Davis amendment and, a few days later, with the support of Lodge and the Republican caucus, added two gratuitous amendments formally abrogating the Clayton-Bulwer Treaty and deleting the provision inviting other powers to adhere to the treaty. Hay, appalled at these developments, accused Lodge of not acting "squarely," denounced his insatiable demands for government positions for his friends, and exploded when Lodge contended publicly that a treaty sent to the Senate was not really a treaty but only a "project."[28] A few weeks later he lashed out at the senator's petty political ambition. "He would cut my throat or yours for a favorable notice in the newspaper," he wrote to White. To Henry Watterson, Hay pointed out most explicity his concern for proper behavior as a factor in disliking Lodge's actions on the treaty. Agreeing with those who said that America would eventually do as she pleased in the isthmus, Hay wrote:

Of course, that is just what we are to do—but why say it, when we are going through the motions of ordinary civility? A man don't [sic] say "Please pass the butter"—if you don't I'll take it anyway and slit your dam weazand if you wink.

Yet Mr. Lodge, bred at Harvard, says that is the proper, honest, and honorable way to ask for butter, even when the other side is perfectly willing to pass it along.

Later, Watterson attempted to console Hay with the opinion that one way or another the canal would be built. Hay agreed, but added, "I am sorry that it seems improbable that I can do it my own way, with proper regard to considerations of decency and honor; but I am an old man, and these are old-fashioned ideas."[29]

Although the question of genteel behavior was paramount in Hay's mind, broader considerations were intertwined. The canal, Hay had come to realize, was part of the American dream. "It is disheartening to think that what the country has wanted and striven for, during forty years, and at last has attained without an atom of compensation should be thrown away, through mere spite,"[30] he expostulated to Reid when the Senate's opposition was rising. Beyond this, Hay thought the canal had advantages for "civilization," which, while seldom defined, meant the expansion of Anglo-Saxon and commercial values. He therefore could not understand Britain's initial refusal to sign a treaty that her own ambassador had drafted. "Every intelligent Englishman is ready to admit that the canal ought to be built, [and] that when built it will be to the advantage of the entire civilized world,"[31] he complained to White. After the Senate committee tacked on the Davis amendment, Hay tied together the themes of the American dream and the advantages that a canal would provide. "The thing which is almost intolerable is this," he wrote in a frustrated mood to John J. McCook; "I see the opportunity of great advantages to be gained by timely negotiations, for which all the conditions are wonderfully favorable, advantages which have been the desire and dream of American statesmen for generations, and I can do nothing on account of the Senate."[32]

The theme of Anglo-American friendship was implicit throughout this entire affair, accounting in part for Hay's insistence that an international obligation be honored. Had the Clayton-Bulwer Treaty involved virtually any country other than Britain, Hay would probably not have been so vehement in his criticism of the Senate. But the treaty was with England, and Hay regretted the influence of the Anglophobes in American politics. "It is as much as a man's life is worth here, to speak of England without cursing her," he wrote in May, 1900. "And two years ago she was the only friend we had in the world—and is now, for that matter, if we needed friends."[33]

Despite his disappointment and outrage, Hay, fearing the consequences of inaction, did all he could to induce England to accept the mangled treaty. He cabled Choate, pointing out that the Davis amendment did not affect the nonfortification provisions of the treaty, as was commonly believed. Early in January, 1901, he showed Pauncefote an editorial in Henry Watterson's *Louisville Courier Journal* which pointed out to England the advantages of ratification. He then forwarded the editorial to Ambassador Choate.[34]

Hay's lieutenants in London fully exerted themselves on his behalf. Henry White sent Balfour excerpts from Hay's private letters and saw to it that he read Watterson's editorial, arguing forcefully that the editor's support of the treaty proved that the amendments were not anti-British in nature. Ambassador Choate also used all his persuasive abilities on Lansdowne. But the outlook was not bright. On February 9, newspaper reports indicated that England would not accept the treaty as amended. Without much hope, Hay instructed Adee to prepare ratification papers, just in case. Hay's instincts proved correct, for Lansdowne prepared a rejection on February 22, although he did not inform the Americans for over two weeks, purposely delaying until Congress adjourned.[35]

Some people assumed, along with Frederick W. Holls, that England's action ended efforts at compromise and that the Senate would now proceed without reference to the Clayton-Bulwer Treaty. Theodore Roosevelt suggested unilateral abrogation, and Hay, probably sensing the political climate, again sent in his resignation, though Adams believed his action was only pro forma.[36]

Whether or not Adams was correct, Hay determined to make a final effort to save the country's honor as he perceived it. He began by talking with senators. One undercurrent of complaint during the twenty-seven month debate on the Hay-Pauncefote Treaty was that Hay had not consulted fully with the Senate. For his part, Hay thought that certain senators had reneged on verbal promises to support the treaty as written. For both these reasons, therefore, Hay discussed in general new proposals with Senators Cullom, Frye, Fairbanks, Spooner, Morgan, and others. He went over the new project "word by word" with Senator Foraker, and, most important, he called Lodge to the State Department to discuss Lansdowne's rejection of the amended treaty. He carefully followed up with a request that Lodge state in writing any remarks he had concerning the British rejection "or any suggestions as to a possible arrangment."[37]

Lodge stated his terms in a long and very specific letter in which he also justified unilateral abrogation. Though strict adherence to treaties was both a recognized principle of international law and of American policy, he admitted, so too was the right of a state to abrogate a treaty without the consent of another. Lodge pointed to certain English jurists to substantiate his claim, but he relied especially on a German authority. "I do not know that I can put in a more concise form what I consider the true view of this question than by quoting the language of Prince Bismark [sic],"[38] he wrote.

Lodge's letter irritated Hay, although he thanked the senator for being so explicit, and he concluded, perhaps a bit too hastily, that Lodge thought no arrangement would be acceptable to the Senate which would proceed to ignore the Clayton-Bulwer Treaty—all with Lodge's approval. Hay agreed with Lodge that the American record of adhering to her treaty obligations was excellent, but he was not ready to accept Bismarck as an authority on international morality. "Some of his acts require very ingenious explanation,"[39] he observed wryly.

Hay's conversations with the chairman of the Senate Committee on Foreign Relations hardly boded well, but at least he was fully apprised of the Senate's mood. "Hay will not be so taken aback as he was by the Senate this time,"[40] Adams predicted. Determined to get a treaty in spite of the Senate's objections Hay ordered Adee to proceed with the drafting. Hoping to mollify the Senate, he insisted that, insofar as possible, the new treaty include language that the Senate had previously approved, even if it made the syntax less than ideal.[41]

By April 25 the new project was complete; on April 27, Hay sent it to Choate. He explained the changes—an American adoption of the canal's neutrality instead of a joint guarantee, omission of the nonfortification pledge, a separate article stating that the new convention superseded the Clayton-Bulwer Treaty, deletion of the provisions inviting the adherence of other states—in terms of the Senate's attitude. But he was not pleased. "Nobody loses by it except ourselves,"[42] he wrote Choate. Hay hated to present the new draft to England, but it was preferable to the dishonorable course which he feared would otherwise result.

During the months following the completion of the new project, Hay walked a tightrope. He had to persuade England to accept a convention no more favorable than the amended treaty it had just rejected, and, at the same time, he had to keep the project sufficiently nationalistic to satisfy two-thirds of the Senate. In the end Hay proved capable of both.

The struggle was not easy, however, and Hay continued to be extremely suspicious of the Senate, the press, and the people. When, in July, the Associated Press published an optimistic interview with Lansdowne, for example, Hay thought it "caused all our blackguards to open up on me again, taking it for granted that I have sold out to England." Nor was he certain that his efforts to cultivate the Senate would pay off. "Three years of struggle with unreason, the spite and the narrow minded greed of votes which form the mental equipment of some of our Senators have left me no room for optimism," he complained to Choate. He even apologized to Pauncefote for always having to keep the Senate's attitude in mind.[43]

In October, Hay learned that Congressman Hepburn intended to reintroduce his canal bill regardless of whether England agreed to Hay's new treaty proposal or not. "He says a treaty is unnecessary, because the Clayton-Bulwer Convention never really existed; but adds that it may be as well to have a treaty to satisfy the superstitutiously conscientious. Which shows a degree of intelligence almost human, and a distinct glimmer of moral sense,"[44] Hay wrote sarcastically to President Roosevelt, apparently forgetting that Roosevelt himself had once advocated abrogation.

Still hoping for a successful conclusion, Hay continued his consultations with important senators, despite the risks he knew were involved. The most important senator to convince, of course, was Lodge. Although Hay had consulted extensively with Lodge in April, they were far from agreed, as Hay's rather sarcastic correspondence with Lodge indicated. Hay knew how destructive the senator from Massachusetts could be when in opposition, and he therefore went to some lengths to assuage him. When Lodge traveled to England in September, Hay, through Assistant Secretary of State Hill, instructed Choate to show him all the papers surrounding the negotiations. "I think it will be very wise to do so," Choate replied, heartily agreeing. Henry White also engaged his many social talents to woo the senator. Soon President Roosevelt could write to Hay that Lodge would support the treaty, while from London Choate reported that the senator was "not merely satisfied, but highly enthusiastic about the Treaty."[45]

Lodge had, in fact, turned strongly in favor of the new project. He even wrote to Roosevelt, rather ironically, that "*all* questions of patronage must be kept in abeyance and must wait until the English treaty . . . is out of the way," a position that Hay would have gone to great lengths to attain the previous year when Lodge was trying strenuously to obtain the Italian embassy for a friend. When Choate returned for a brief visit in November, he found Hay "much pleased" with the treatment accorded Lodge in England. "In fact," Choate wrote, "the President . . . said to me in New Haven that Lodge came home regarding it as his treaty (Please never breathe this to a soul!)." And Hay, in figuring the senatorial arithmetic, was now relying on Lodge to swing votes for the treaty.[46]

When the treaty was finally approved in December, 1901 (England approved on November 28), Hay praised Lodge's efforts. "Cabot, who felt himself particularly responsible for the wreck of the last one, put his effort into promoting this one," he wrote. Together with Roosevelt's "extremely zealous" efforts "in rounding up the bunch of doubtful Senators," the second Hay-Pauncefote Treaty "went through with no opposition, except from the irreclaimable cranks. Seventy-two to six was near enough unanimity."[47]

Roosevelt later claimed that he "got the treaty in right shape only by securing the correction of all of the original faults."[48] Taken literally, Roosevelt's claim was incorrect. Hay and the members of the State Department staff composed the treaty finally accepted. Choate and White worked very hard and efficiently in London, and Pauncefote returned to England in September, before Roosevelt became president, to persuade the British government to accept the draft. Britain's decision to accept it was, of course, crucial to its success. This momentous (and ultimately shrewd) decision was apparently designed to retain America's friendship, even though it meant Britain's virtual retirement from the Western hemisphere south of Canada.

Hay's efforts also deserve attention, for despite his personal dislike of the new proposal, it was drawn up and negotiated at his direction. He chose to use the Senate's own language whenever possible, attempting only to put it in an order less offensive to Britain. He wooed the Senate, his efforts with Lodge being particularly successful despite their past clashes. "Theodore was very funny about Cabot," Hay wrote to his wife. "He says 'Cabot thinks he made the *Treaty.*' I said 'I wanted him to think so.' "[49]

On the other hand, Henry Adams' description that Hay, "with infinite effort ... achieved the astonishing diplomatic feat of inducing the Senate, with only six negative votes, to permit Great Britain to renounce, without equivalent, treaty rights which she had for fifty years defended tooth and nail,"[50] is colorful but exaggerated. Hay's ability to impress on Pauncefote and, in turn, the Foreign Office that he could offer nothing better than the second treaty was a significant factor in getting it signed and approved. But the fact that he had to hand Pauncefote a hard-line project incorporating the essence of the Senate amendments was due not to Hay but to Lodge and other Senators. Since Roosevelt's views corresponded so closely with Lodge's in this instance, Roosevelt's boast was not entirely without foundation, at least figuratively, since he was a leader of the opposition. Nor was Lodge's belief, that he made the treaty, entirely incorrect. The treaty was signed and approved in its final form because of Hay's tact and persuasive abilities, which, in turn, were so necessary only because of the firmness of Lodge, Roosevelt, and others.

The positions of both sides had merit. Hay wanted to further the Anglo-American rapprochement and hoped that by behaving honorably the United States could quicken that happy day. The fact that John Bassett Moore, a careful and meticulous scholar, was an enthusiastic supporter of Hay's diplomacy in this instance, makes the secretary of state's position even more creditable. Hay's disgust with the Senate was understandable from his point of view.

In retrospect, however, Roosevelt and Lodge, Hill and Holls, were probably more farsighted. Although recklessly nationalistic, they saw the pitfalls of a completely neutral canal in the Western hemisphere.

IX

Hay and Roosevelt

Theodore Roosevelt's disagreement with Hay's handling of the canal treaty revealed differences both of substance and of style. Hay, the gentleman diplomat, disliked Roosevelt's impetuosity while Roosevelt sometimes thought Hay was a weak man. On at least three occasions shortly after Hay's death, Roosevelt recalled how he had been forced to take over the work of the State Department. "What I did'n't [sic] do myself was'n't [sic] done at all,"[1] he wrote to William Howard Taft.

During Roosevelt's first term the differences occasionally came to the surface. The rocky road to a final settlement of the Alaska boundary dispute illustrated them well. Although he had remained silent at the time, Roosevelt thought Hay gave away too much in the modus vivendi of 1899. The United States yielded, he wrote, "what there really was no necessity in law or morals for yielding."[2]

The second phase of the Alaska problem opened in April, 1901, a few months before Roosevelt became president, when Hay submitted to Britain's ambassador a plan for settlement similar to that the American commissioners had advanced in 1898 and 1899. Britain strenuously pressed the Canadians to agree, but they refused to consider Hay's terms.[3] By delaying, Canada sacrificed whatever chance existed for conciliatory action; for in September Theodore Roosevelt unexpectedly became president of the United States.

Because they were now in close contact, the differences between Hay and Roosevelt became more sharply defined in the later stages of the dispute. Hay knew, or should have known, that the new president would consent to nothing resembling arbitration. Roosevelt had told Hay as much in the summer of 1899, and, at that time, the secretary of state had had to explain that his proposal for a six-man commission (divided equally between Americans and Britons) was not arbitration in the usual sense.[4] (He did not point out that previously he had agreed to Pauncefote's suggestions for a five-man arbitral tribunal).

Evidently Hay's explanation was not convincing, for when, in March, 1902, Hay sent the president a sketch of a tribunal along the lines he had proposed in 1899, Roosevelt reacted quickly and unfavorably to Hay's initiative, feeling that the American claim was so clear as to be non-negotiable. Pauncefote, calling on the secretary of state, found Hay "quite despondent" at being unable to settle the matter. He even intimated to the British ambassador the source of the opposition without directly mentioning the president. Hay's indiscretion does not reflect favorably upon his sense of professionalism and lends some credence to Roosevelt's later contention that his secretary of state could not be trusted where England was concerned.[5]

Whether or not to submit the dispute to a joint body of any kind thus became a point of major disagreement between Roosevelt and Hay, illustrating their different perceptions and temperaments. The British-manufactured globe in the Cabinet room marked the boundary along the line of the American claim, Roosevelt pointed out, and the Canadians had no more right to the territory than the United States had to New Brunswick. Having vented his wrath, however, the president, in July, 1902, did agree in principle to a six-man tribunal, but only to delineate the American claim with precision. The American commissioners would be instructed to yield no territory whatever.[6]

Still, Roosevelt's action did represent a concession of sorts, for he had previously refused Hay's entreaties for any kind of tribunal. Nor does it appear, as Charles Campbell suggests, that Roosevelt meant the tribunal to have advisory powers only; on the contrary, it was to have full power to draw a final line, although the American commissioners were not to accept anything less than the American claim.[7]

The matter was not further explored immediately, perhaps because Hay considered Roosevelt's attitude unnecessarily harsh, perhaps because he felt the Senate would not agree to such an arrangement in an election year.[8] But Roosevelt expressed considerable interest in establishing a tribunal after the elections and, once the British had pressured the ever-reluctant Canadians into going along, Hay and Ambassador Michael Herbert signed a treaty on January 24, 1903. The Hay-Herbert Treaty provided for a tribunal consisting of "six impartial jurists of repute," each of whom would pledge to decide the issues "according to his true judgment."[9]

Hay was happy with the treaty, pointing out that it was substantially the same as the solution he had proposed three years earlier, only to have the British reject it. Now, with the president and Senator Lodge firmly behind it, the treaty sailed through the Senate.[10]

Roosevelt's next maneuver, however, was not calculated to please Hay. After receiving refusals from some, perhaps all, of the Supreme Court justices (after what must have been only pro forma invitations), the president appointed Senator Lodge, Secretary Root, and former Senator George Turner to serve on the commission.[11] The appointments created a storm of protest. White reported that Chamberlain was angered and said that Roosevelt's action made it necessary to make two of the British commissioners Canadians. Canadian Prime Minister Laurier personally protested to Hay that the American appointees could not "with any fairness be styled 'impartial jurists.'" Henry Adams caught the situation best, writing, "Laurier kicks hard against Cabot. He kicks also at Root and Turner, but I feel that Cabot is the real pill. Whenever Canada raises a bristle, Theodore roars like a Texas steer, and ramps round the ring screaming for instant war, and ordering a million men instantly to arms."[12]

Hay defended the appointments. But he knew that Roosevelt's action had negated most of what he hoped to obtain from the arrangement. Had the president appointed men with less widely known views on the subject, Canada could have saved face if it chose. Now that was impossible, and any settlement would create bitterness. He could "well appreciate" English objections, he wrote, particularly objections to Lodge. Senator Lodge was clever and forceful, Hay admitted, "but the infirmity of his mind and character is that he never sees but one subject at a time, and just at present it is the acceptability of his son-in-law to the voters of Gloucester."[13]

The British outcry had no apparent.effect on Roosevelt, for, in March, 1903, when the English asked for a little additional time to prepare their case, Roosevelt refused despite pleas from Ambassador Choate. Again, Hay loyally defended the president's actions, but he clearly felt it was foolish to take actions that would alienate the British and, in particular, Lord Alverstone, who was the only uncommitted "judge" on the tribunal—and Alverstone had told Choate emphatically that the English needed more time.[14]

Something of the depth of Hay's feeling that Alverstone must be handled with kid gloves was evident in his attempt to have Ambassador Choate appointed as the American counsel. Hay first made the offer in February, but Choate twice refused. Even then, Hay pressed the matter, causing the ambassador to compose an impassioned plea not to be appointed. Choate was a competent lawyer, thoroughly familiar with the case and technically an excellent choice for the position. He felt, however, that to argue the American case would seriously undermine the close and confidential lines of communication he had established with the British government. White strongly supported Choate's plea.[15]

Because Choate's reason for refusal was so clearly valid, it seems strange that Hay should write to White that Choate's decision was "a disappointment which I shall never get over." Hay's disappointment was so profoundly genuine because he felt that, beyond Choate's acknowledged fitness for the position, as a gentleman, Choate might possibly offset the damage done by Lodge's nomination. Alverstone, Hay reminded Choate, was the only open-minded commissioner. "If the case were presented to him, with all the facts arranged in order, with all the legal principles lucidly set forth, with tact, with adroitness, with courtesy, and the general knowledge of human nature and especial knowledge of the English character which you alone of all our great American lawyers possess," Hay wrote, "I should consider the result absolutely certain." Choate—and Hay—knew the English, Hay thought. Roosevelt evidently did not. "As it is, we can only hope for the best," he concluded.[16]

Subsequent British requests for a delay deepened the split between Roosevelt and Hay, particularly after the president wrote a strong letter to Hay threatening to "run the line ourselves" if no agreement were reached.[17] Hay did not like the tone of Roosevelt's communication. "I have a vehement letter from the President—started by one from Lodge—protesting against any delay in the Alaska tribunal," he began a letter to John W. Foster. He was particularly angry because he thought Lodge's motives were purely personal and political. "And Lodge!" Hay closed his letter, "when I think of his being put to personal inconvenience, I am moved almost to tears." His reply to Roosevelt was more decorous, but his disagreement was apparent. The British were not acting in bad faith, he pointed out, for the treaty did provide for delays under certain conditions. "We shall be as hard on them as is decent—perhaps rather more so," he concluded.[18]

The newspapers correctly guessed the divergent desires of the president and his secretary of state, even suggesting that Hay wanted to resign. Hay publicly denied the rumors, telling reporters that "there was not a shade of difference" between himself and the president. Roosevelt, in turn, thanked Hay and urged him not to worry about "the newspapers and other swine who delight to invent tales about our relations." Hay was, Roosevelt insisted, a "really great Secretary of State." Hay thanked the president "a thousand times" for his letter. "It is a comfort to work for a President who besides being a lot of other things, happened to be born a gentleman." Perhaps Hay termed Roosevelt a gentleman because he hoped the president would act like one.[19]

The catch was that the rumors were true. Roosevelt did not always act like a gentleman, and his refusal to give Canada a chance to retreat decently angered Hay. Only ten days after this exchange of letters, Hay offered to resign. His ostensible reason, and perhaps to some extent the real reason, was to make way for Elihu Root. Root, it appeared, was about to resign as secretary of war, and Hay professed to believe that he might be persuaded to remain in the Cabinet as secretary of state. At the very least, however, the Alaska question made Hay's move easier. "You are more independent of your Cabinet than most Presidents," he wrote. Perhaps Hay was attempting to pressure the president into a more flexible position on the matter of delay, for on the same day that he offered to resign he wrote an indiscreet letter to Foster stating that the United States could "perfectly afford to be easy with" England when she asked for delays.[20]

Roosevelt reflected on Hay's letter for six days, then asked him to remain. If, in fact, Hay was attempting to pressure the president, Roosevelt called his bluff. Thereafter Hay resigned himself to following a tough line. "*We must get the verdict,*" he wrote to Foster, evidently fearing the consequences of no decision.[21]

The tribunal met, as scheduled, on September 3 and completed its labors on October 20. The final award gave to the United States the essence of its claim, though Roosevelt had to cede two small islands in the Portland Canal at the southern end of the disputed area.

Technically the tribunal was beyond the reach of the governments involved. But in fact, the United States, Canada, and England were all involved in efforts to influence the outcome which, in effect, meant attempting to influence Lord Alverstone. Hay, knowing that this would be the last chance for a peaceful settlement and deploring the consequent effect of failure on Anglo-American relations, kept Henry White aware of Roosevelt's belligerent attitude. White, in turn, kept Balfour abreast, most notably when he spent a weekend at Balfour's estate during which he "left no doubt upon his mind as to the importance of a settlement nor as to the result of a failure to agree." Although the prime minister never told White what, if anything, he did, his confidential secretary met twice with Alverstone before the verdict.[22]

The American victory truly exhilarated Hay, and he claimed credit:

> I have a right to feel gratified, because at first I was the only one who believed such a result possible. I persuaded McKinley, and Pauncefote, and Herbert to adopt the plan and then the hardest of all, I got Theodore to accede to it. . . . I believed our case was so clear and so strong that any English lawyer would see it, and I had confidence in their honor and honesty. . . .
>
> It is one of the most important transactions of my life, and few more important have been accomplished by our State Department.

Furthermore, Roosevelt told Hay that "nobody living could have done the work" as well as he, while the secretary himself allowed that the completeness of the victory was "something amazing."[23]

Hay correctly claimed credit for the idea of a tribunal, although he had been willing, on occasion, to accept genuine arbitration. That the settlement was of great significance was also true, for it removed the last, and most dangerous, significant point of conflict between the United States and Great Britain in the Western hemisphere. As Lansdowne put it in a letter to Lodge, he hoped Canada would some day see "how advantageous to both countries it is that this rock of offense should have been removed from our path."[24] One of Hay's dreams was a de facto Anglo-American alliance; he had a right to be pleased.

Hay's other claims were more tenuous. The weakest was his contention that the American case was so self-evidently strong that he could rely on the impartial decision of a British judge. But Alverstone's judgment was clearly political and not judicial, a point which the disgruntled Canadians noted. It is not entirely certain that, left to his own judgment, Alverstone would have accepted the American claim, particularly in light of America's bad manners.

What would have happened had Hay had complete power over the matter? Almost certainly Canadian pride would have been preserved. Hay was willing to sacrifice more territory than the president in order to gain the main American contention as to where the line should run. Indeed, he confessed to his wife that in order to gain the inlets for America, he would have been willing to lose a fairly large area north of the Klehini and Chilkat rivers, an area that the commissioners won. Hay would have further smoothed relations with Canada by appointing a more neutral commission. When Hay reviewed the history of the dispute after the verdict was announced, he wrote, "and then came the naming of the Commissioners—which I won't talk about." Hay thought that, in addition to himself, Foster, Choate, White, and Don M. Dickinson (an American counsel) were responsible for the victory; he pointedly omitted reference to the commissioners or, indeed, to the president.[25]

As it was, the two Canadian commissioners refused to sign the award and issued an angry statement condemning the tribunal. Prime Minister Laurier complained in parliament about America's "grasping . . . national actions."[26] .In the final analysis, Roosevelt's truculence did not set back the Anglo-American rapprochement and, from a nationalistic point of view, the president gained territory that probably belonged of right to the United States. Nevertheless, adoption of Hay's methods would have smoothed the road to Anglo-American understanding.

The final phases of the Alaska boundary dispute, like the debate over the Hay-Pauncefote Treaty, demonstrated the differences between the secretary of state and the president. Roosevelt's later contention that their views on foreign affairs "coincided absolutely" was poppycock.[27] Their varying styles and perceptions, combined with Hay's increasing physical disability, strained their relationship.

The disagreements can easily be blown out of proportion, however. By and large, Hay's reaction to Roosevelt's personality was one more of amusement and even admiration than of scorn. Adams thought Hay viewed the unpredictable Roosevelt from the vantage of a "benevolent and amused uncle," a judgment Hay substantiated when he told a friend, "the President is all right, provided you can restrain him for the first fifteen minutes after he has conceived a new idea." Only a few months before his death, Hay recorded his amused but altogether favorable reaction to Roosevelt's method of drafting an important state paper. "It was a curious sight," Hay began his account of the president's effort to grapple with the Santo Domingo crisis.

I have often seen it, and it never ceases to surprise me. He storms up and down the room dictating in a loud and oratorical tone, often stopping, recasting a sentence, striking out and filling in, hospitable to every suggestion, not in the least disturbed by interruption, holding on stoutly to his purpose, and producing finally, out of these most unpromising conditions, a clear and logical statement, which he could not improve, with solitude and leisure at his command.[28]

In fact, the two men enjoyed a genuine friendship. In an excellent magazine article written shortly after Hay's death, one of Hay's acquaintances observed that "there was a close and intimate friendship" between Hay and Roosevelt despite admitted differences in lifestyles. "Roosevelt's bouyant, almost boyish, high spirits and rapid-fire comment upon men and matters and Hay's quiet, incisive, dry humor and facility for making pertinent quotations from the whole range of literature . . . gave unalloyed pleasure to both," he wrote. The article was perceptive, for prominent among Roosevelt's private tributes to Hay were those dealing with his conversational and writing abilities. "No one in America can quite fill the gap he makes, because of his extraordinary literary and personal charm as well as his abilities as a public man," Roosevelt wrote in a representative letter. This was, in fact, the quality Roosevelt most remembered about Hay, for he made remarkably similar remarks in 1909 and 1916.[29]

Nor were Roosevelt's compliments without merit. Hay's letters seldom included deep philosophical reflections, but they had—as this one, addressed to the president shortly after the German emperor presented Roosevelt with a medal honoring his China policy—a light and amusing touch:

Count Quadt has been hovering around the State Department in ever narrowing circles for three days, and at last swooped upon me this afternoon, saying that the Foreign Office and even the Palace, Unter den Linden, was in a state of intense anxiety to know how you had received His Majesty's Chinese medal, conferred only upon the greatest sovereigns. As I had not been authorized by you to express your emotions, I had to sail by dead reckoning, and, considering the vast intrinsic value of the souvenir—I should say at least thirty-five cents—and its wonderful artistic merit, representing the German eagle eviscerating the Black Dragon, and its historical accuracy, which gives the world to understand that Germany was it, and the rest of the universe nowhere, I took the responsibility of saying to Count Quadt that the President could not have received the medal with anything but emotions of pleasure commensurate with the high appreciation he entertains for the Emperor's majesty, and that a formal acknowledgment would be made in due course. He asked me if he was at liberty to say something like this to his Government, and I said he was at liberty to say whatever the spirit moved him to utter.

I gave thanks to "whatever powers there be" that I was able to allow him to leave the room without quoting *"quantula sapienta!"*[30]

Hay also managed to congratulate the president in glowing terms after virtually every major speech he made. And, shortly before Roosevelt's second inauguration, Hay gave him, as he had McKinley, a ring containing a few strands of Abraham Lincoln's hair, cut the night he died. Roosevelt, touched by Hay's thoughtfulness, proudly mentioned to George Trevelyan that he wore the ring at the inauguration.[31]

For his part, Roosevelt attempted to keep their personal relations amicable even when they disagreed on policy or method. He insisted on a first name relationship (an apparently unprecedented familiarity), pooh-poohed age differences, referred favorably to his secretary of state in his speeches, stopped over every Sunday after church to chat, gave him the impression that Cabot Lodge was not to be taken too seriously, and reassured him when he half-heartedly attempted to resign.

Even in the midst of the Alaska issue, their most serious disagreement during Roosevelt's presidency, their personal relations were not much damaged. In the spring of 1903, Roosevelt traveled to the West for political and sentimental reasons. When he returned, he dined with Hay and enchanted him and Secretary of the Navy Moody with his account of the trip. Hay prevailed upon Roosevelt to write down his remembrances. What emerged was a letter of approximately 8,000 words, constituting, in effect, a short story of the wild west. Hay received the letter at his summer home in New Hampshire. He and his family found it delightful. He would bind it in leather, he said, to be bequeathed to his children. "But it will not lack companionship in a case which holds the Second Inaugural and the Gettysburg Address." Such were the exchanges between the two men in the midst of the Alaska boundary dispute, some three weeks after Hay offered to resign, as well as during the events leading to the Panama revolution, which Hay is alleged to have detested.[32]

Frequent rumors of disagreement, as well as genuine differences between the two men during Roosevelt's presidency, never threatened a real break. Those who disliked Roosevelt were most likely to see serious differences where only minor ones existed. Roosevelt knew this would happen. "Hay was a really great man, and the more credit is given him the more I am delighted, while the result at the last election showed how futile it was for . . . my enemies to try to draw the distinction between what Hay did and what I did," he wrote shortly after Hay's death. ". . . The same people who, not because they cared for Hay, but because they hated me, insisted that everything of which they approved in the management of the State Department was due to him will now make exactly the same claim in reference to Root and will hope thereby to damage or irritate me."[33]

Roosevelt himself, however, was partly responsible for the later stories of serious differences. In 1908 or 1909, he read through the three volumes of Hay's *Letters and Extracts from his Diary* that Henry Adams and Mrs. Hay had edited and printed privately. Although none of the printed letters contained anything directly damaging to Roosevelt, some of Hay's statements and exaggerated claims riled him. Roosevelt thought that Hay's sharp comments about the Senate, for example, reflected adversely on the president's diplomatic appointments. "To villify in unmeasured terms, utterly without discrimination . . . [the Senate]," Roosevelt wrote, ". . . was to occupy a position both foolish and mischievous."[34]

The president disliked Hay's account of the Alaska boundary dispute and especially his claim to most of the credit. In general, Roosevelt recalled, Hay could not be trusted where England was concerned. Had Hay not, in truth, referred to the prime minister's office as "the most important official post known to modern history"—and while he was secretary of state, too! That, Roosevelt stormed, "was worse than foolish." Hay was likewise "foolishly distrustful of the Germans," Roosevelt thought; and to completely denigrate Hay's significance, Roosevelt claimed his secretary of state had almost nothing to do with any of the important diplomatic developments.[35]

Roosevelt was partly correct. In important respects Hay was a weak man, and his Anglophilia sometimes led to indiscretions. But Roosevelt also exaggerated—his own account of the Alaska matter, for example, contained many more substantive errors than Hay's. In any event, his criticism appeared after Hay's death. If he harbored similar feelings when Hay was alive, Roosevelt hid them well.

Roosevelt's criticisms were not likely to result in good family relations, and, in fact, the Wadsworth and Whitney families, into which Hay's children married, were not on speaking terms with the Roosevelts in later years. When Tyler Dennett showed the Wadsworths a draft chapter of his biography of Hay that was critical of Roosevelt, he found them "almost hysterically pleased. They had long held a similar conclusion." Dennett himself, taking up Hay's defense, wrote to Allan Nevins, "when I am finished with T.R. you will be impressed with Pringle's magnanimity. T.R.'s relations with Hay presents one of the least creditable chapters, perhaps the least creditable, in T.R.['s] life. It is appalling."[36] Such were the results of exaggerated differences.

The fact is that on most matters of policy the two agreed. Their differences about how to conduct Anglo-American relations were balanced by their agreement on other matters. Hay had few qualms about the "splendid little war" of 1898, the brutal suppression of the Philippine insurrection, America's nationalistic treatment of China, the increase of the army and navy, or the seizure of Panama. He might object to the high-handed treatment accorded England, but not Spain, Colombia, or China.

Rumors of a split were rife, however, particularly with respect to the administration's action in Panama in 1903. Henry Watterson, for example, appears to have assumed that Hay disapproved of the president's action, for while the editor's disaffection with Roosevelt reached a nadir over these events, he remained a close friend and admirer of Hay.[37]

William R. Thayer long ago contended that Hay and Roosevelt had no differences with respect to Panama, but Thayer was a friend and partisan of Roosevelt and, indeed, derived some of his material from the former president. On the other hand, John Bassett Moore, certainly no especial defender of Roosevelt's actions, agreed, writing that "some of those who had spoken the praises of Mr. Hay wished to believe that he was not in sympathy with the President's course in the recognition of the republic of Panama, but of such a variance not the slightest evidence has ever been produced."[38]

Very little evidence has since been produced, despite much speculation. But there is just enough deviousness and two-facedness to some of Hay's writing to make such speculation tantalizing. The question of which route Hay favored for the canal, for example, demonstrates this quality.

Throughout most of the 1890's most observers assumed the canal would be constructed in Nicaragua. The Panama lobby was late in getting established and for several years could do nothing more than delay a final decision in favor of Nicaragua. One of the early backers of the Panama route was the venerable John Bigelow, who had looked ancient when he was Hay's superior in Spain in the late 1860's. Bigelow was a close friend of the French canal zealot Philippe Bunau-Varilla. At the end of 1898, after a summer of rising pressure for immediate construction of a canal, Bigelow wrote to Hay asking that the president not commit himself to the Nicaragua route. Although McKinley did explicitly refer to the construction of a Nicaraguan canal in his annual message of December 5, Bigelow's letter may have been one reason for the subsequent consideration of the Panama route. Bunau-Varilla, with the advantage of hindsight, thought it had that effect.[39]

Hay spent the next years doing his best to remove the objectionable features of the Clayton-Bulwer Treaty of 1850 which prohibited unilateral construction of any canal. In 1901, when Hay was in the depths of despair over the matter, Bigelow reminded him of his 1898 letter and sent him one of Bunau-Varilla's pamphlets championing the Panama route. The Frenchman, he claimed, knew more than any other man in America about the canal question. A month later, Bigelow sent Hay a ten-page typewritten letter suggesting that the United States permit Bunau-Varilla to enlist the aid of a French company to build the canal under American auspicies. Although Bigelow did not receive an immediate answer (having written only days before Hay left on a Western tour with the president), he sent Bunau-Varilla a squib from the *New York Evening Post* which he speculatively regarded as an "installment of Mr. Hay's answer to my letter."[40]

The *Post* reported that "Secretary Hay, who at one time could hardly listen to the Panama scheme with patience, now inclines to the belief that it may be the better route after all." Although Bigelow warned Bunau-Varilla that

Hay could not yet express himself on the matter, Hay soon replied very cordially to a letter from Bunau-Varilla himself, whom he had never met. He praised Bunau-Varilla's "clarity of vision and lucidity of expression," adding that he could see "how much is to be said on that side of the question. Thus far there seems to be a nine-tenths majority of Congress that absolutely declines to look at the question through uncolored glasses." Presumably he referred to the Panama route, for nine-tenths of Congress at that time favored Nicaragua. If Hay had not committed himself to the Panama route, he certainly did not spring to the defense of Nicaragua.[41]

On the other hand, throughout 1901 and 1902, Hay fairly showered Senator Morgan, a leader of the Nicaraguan faction, with friendly, almost obsequious, letters in order to retain his good will during the Hay-Pauncefote negotiations. Hay did not tie himself to Nicaragua, but he did tell Morgan that the senator was "approaching the realization of the great enterprise which has so long occupied your thoughts and your endeavors."[42] Senator Morgan might be excused if he thought Hay was in his corner.

The route question suggests why controversy swirled about Hay's beliefs. In fact, one man left an interview with the secretary of state convinced that he privately wanted no canal at all,[43] a most unlikely possibility.

There is scant reason to doubt that Hay supported Roosevelt's actions in the Panama revolution in November, 1903, and the immediate American recognition of the new government of Panama, although the same tendencies displayed in the route question make an absolute judgment difficult. Indeed, Hay once commented to Adams that Roosevelt was trying "to steal Panama," a remark suggesting to some, like Ernest Samuels, that Hay questioned the administration's action and perhaps hated the whole idea. In a somewhat similar vein, Dennett concluded that Hay appeared to welcome the revolution only because he knew that Roosevelt would seize Panama anyway. The revolutionary government at least provided some semblance of legality to American efforts to secure rights across the isthmus.[44]

Such fragments as do exist to support this conclusion are overshadowed by other evidence. Years later, when William R. Thayer persisted in questioning the morality of the administration's action in the Panama case, despite his generous praise of President Roosevelt generally, Roosevelt explained that Colombia was not a civilized country to be dealt with in traditional ways. "To talk of Colombia as a responsible power to be dealt with as we would deal with Holland or Belgium or Switzerland or Denmark is a mere absurdity," he wrote when Thayer published his opinions. "The analogy is with a group of Sicilian or Calabrian bandits. . . . You could no more make an agreement with them than you could nail currant jelly to a wall—and the failure to nail currant jelly to a wall is not due to the nail; it is due to the currant jelly."[45] Hay probably agreed. Nothing in his background suggested that Colombia, or any other non-Anglo-Saxon nation, deserved much respect.

The Spooner Act of 1902 directed the administration to seek first an arrangement with Colombia, and the resulting Hay-Herrán Treaty signed on January 27, 1903, ceded to the United States a strip of land six miles wide across the Panama isthmus. The Senate quickly approved the document, but Colombia hesitated, causing the State Department to express its discontent in threatening language. When it became evident that Colombia would not ratify the treaty, Hay favored exploring the Nicaraguan alternative, a course of action prescribed by the Spooner Act if negotiations with Colombia failed. But when Roosevelt replied that he was tempted to intervene directly in Panama, despite the fact that such a move would clearly violate the will of Congress, Hay offered no resistance. The suggestion that the United States government deliberately violate its own laws would, in other circumstances, have offended greatly Hay's sense of law and order. He would have resigned had the government begun a canal in violation of the Clayton-Bulwer Treaty.[46]

But in this case, Hay replied with only the slightest suggestion of restraint. Although the United States could perhaps justify such intervention under the Treaty of 1846 with New Granada, Hay stated, the legality of such a move "might not greatly impress the jack-rabbit mind." Furthermore, such a move would probably result in war, although it "would, of course, be brief and inexpensive," a remark reminiscent of his famous "splendid little war" opinion in 1898. "Those greedy little anthropoids are alarmed at what they have done," he added, but there was no need for immediate American action. "The Jack Rabbits are in a great funk," he wrote the next day.[47]

Thereafter Hay's thought turned to the serious possibility of an insurrection on the isthmus, a possibility from which he did not shrink or recoil. Those "poor creatures," he wrote, ". . . have had their spree. . . , but now Blue Monday has come." Hay suggested no precipitous action be taken. But the caution was only tactical. "Our intervention should not be at hap-hazard," he wrote. And, in fact, his counsel to await developments was advantageous to the plotters of revolution.[48]

From the middle of September until the actual revolution in November, references to Panamanian affairs rather suspiciously cease in Hay's still extant letters. But the secretary of state appears to have taken a close interest in isthmian affairs. J. Gabriel Duque, the owner of the *Panama Star and Herald* and a leader in the Panama independence movement, kept Hay abreast of developments, apparently at the latter's request. Duque sent at least eight letters to Hay. If the secretary of state did not answer Duque's communications, he read them and forwarded a copy of at least the first one to President Roosevelt.[49] In addition, Bunau-Varilla called on Hay and received the distinct impression that he would welcome revolution. As he left, Hay gave the revolutionary a copy of Richard Harding Davis' novel *Captain Macklin*, the story of a West Point cadet who left the academy to become a soldier of fortune in Central America. Bunau-Varilla chose to interpret Hay's gift symbolically. *Captain Macklin*, he thought, was "the password."[50]

Bunau-Varilla's account of the interview may well be

embellished or it may be dismissed as merely another good example of Hay's ability to mesmerize his acquaintances rather than be taken as an accurate reflection of Hay's views. Indeed, Bunau-Varilla cherished Hay's memory, he wrote, with "an almost religious admiration." Years later, when he wrote a propagandistic book accusing the Germans of attempting to impede construction of the Panama canal, Bunau-Varilla dedicated it to five men, among them, John Hay.[51]

There is, however, little reason to question the essence of Bunau-Varilla's recollection for Hay never expressed regret for any American actions once the revolution occurred on November 3, including the precipitate recognition of the new regime. As he wrote to historian James Ford Rhodes, "I had no hesitation as to the proper course to take and have had no doubt of the propriety of it since." The question was one of order and race. The United States had to decide whether to seize the railroads and keep the transit open, Hay went on, or to "stand back and let these gentlemen cut each other's throats for an indefinite time, and destroy whatever remnant of our property and interests we had there."[52]

The most decisive evidence of Hay's genuine feelings appeared in two letters to his wife. On November 30 he stated that he felt sorry for the Colombians who had lost Panama forever. "But they ought to have thought of that six months ago," he added. ". . . They never will learn that to make an omelette you must break eggs, and the eggs once broken, they can never be mended again." Three days later he became irritated over a personal business matter involving a lease. "I am half inclined to tell him he can't have it—teach him a lesson like that the poor Colombians learned to their sorrow," he wrote his wife. The "poor Colombians," those "creatures," the "greedy little anthropoids," had behaved as shortsightedly as non-Anglo-Saxons could be expected to. They deserved their fate, and they must not stand in the way of advancing civilization. "Do we want to sneak out of the Isthmus of Panama," Hay asked rhetorically during the campaign of 1904, vigorously attacking the critics, "acknowledge we have no right there, and basely surrender the hope and the dream of centuries?" Hay thought not.[53]

As Tyler Dennett observed, Hay should have resigned in 1903. With the settlement of the Alaska boundary dispute, virtually all significant differences with Great Britain were resolved. In the Far East, the days of Hay's creativity were largely over, for more and more President Roosevelt assumed control over China diplomacy as, indeed, he did over foreign relations generally. "The consummation of the Peace of Portsmouth," Dennett wrote, referring to the agreement that ended the Russo-Japanese War, "belongs as much to Theodore Roosevelt as the rescue of the Legations at Peking in 1900 belongs to John Hay."[54] Furthermore, Hay's health failed rapidly after 1903, and during the six months preceding his death in July, 1905, he did almost no work as secretary of state.

Still, Hay was something more than a mere figurehead, at least until illness forced him to seek relief in Europe in the spring of 1905. If Roosevelt directed China policy more closely, Hay continued to advise and have his thoughts seriously considered. Indeed, Hay's diary indicates that he remained actively involved in policy formation in many areas. The Perdicaris affair in the summer of 1904 was the most dramatic, if not the most important example.[55] If Hay felt any sense of displacement, he did not reveal it. On the contrary, he found Roosevelt pressuring him to remain in office an additional four years. Some indication of Hay's continuing influence can be seen in November, 1904, when Roosevelt accepted many of Hay's suggestions for changes in the draft of his annual message to Congress. "He accepted my ideas with that singular amiability and open mindedness which forms so striking a contrast with the general idea of his brusque and arbitrary character," Hay wrote. "We then talked a good deal of the coming year's work," he added.[56]

Hay's entire relationship with Roosevelt demonstrated Hay's essential ambiguity. If Roosevelt was the preeminent representative of the new century, Hay had a foot in both the old one and the new. People like Henry Adams and Henry Watterson, themselves more of the nineteenth century, would not have thought it odd if Hay had chosen to resign in 1901. Adams saw him as a genteel capitalist who had mastered the economic and political games of the late nineteenth century, and Watterson thought of him more as a mugwump resisting the ill-mannered impetuosity of the new age.

Adams and Watterson were both, of course, partially correct. As Adams assumed, Hay never rejected the philosophy of *The Bread-winners.* He resisted the social changes that resulted from changing technology and defended nineteenth-century capitalism as a moral system. As ambassador to England and then as secretary of state, Hay did what he could to protect and extend it. Hay's China policy was the clearest expression of his benevolent attitude toward economic expansion, but similar considerations appeared in his attitude toward the annexation of the Philippines, the building of the Panama canal, and the Anglo-American rapprochement.

Watterson was also partially correct in assuming that Hay belonged to a different age than Roosevelt, an age in which a more genteel and less assertive lifestyle prevailed. Hay's hesitation to permit his son to play football in 1893 contrasts nicely with Roosevelt's extraordinarily strenuous life and corroborates in part Roosevelt's later comment that his secretary of state possessed a very ease-loving nature.[57] Hay wanted, as he had written in *The Bread-winners,* to preserve the "old fashioned decencies." In the novel, Hay directed his remarks toward labor unions that threatened, he thought, the moral fiber of the nation. But he sometimes felt that the pushiness of the younger generation was hardly less deplorable, as his undisguised anger at Lodge's and Roosevelt's unmannerly behavior in the Hay-Pauncefote Treaty matter demonstrated.

Moreover, Hay's closest associates tended to be older than Roosevelt and included men like Henry James, whom Roosevelt thought unpatriotic and effete. To some extent Hay shared the forebodings of Adams and James upon

Roosevelt's accession to the presidency in 1901. He was, at the very least, cognizant of the difference in age and lifestyle. "How strange it seems," he whispered to Anna Roosevelt Cowles at McKinley's funeral, "that I should be here in this position with your father's son."[58]

Differences of age and style extended to some areas of foreign policy. As early as 1892, Hay made fun of Roosevelt's teeth-gnashing during the war scare with Chile, and, having more or less supported Roosevelt's bid for a post in the Navy Department in 1897, Hay thought he was daft to go galloping off to war.[59] Very serious differences erupted over the Hay-Pauncefote Treaty and only slightly less critical ones developed in connection with the Alaska boundary dispute. Clearly, Hay was more comfortable in the age of McKinley.

On the other hand, Hay and Roosevelt agreed on fundamental matters more than they disagreed. Although Roosevelt was friendlier toward labor unions than Hay and was willing to discipline large concentrations of capital on occasion, he detested socialism, anarchy, and the Democratic party nearly as much as did his secretary of state. No doubt he applauded Hay's malicious attacks on William Jennings Bryan in 1896.

There was close agreement between them when principles of maintaining order extended to foreign relations. Roosevelt fully approved Hay's efforts utterly to crush the Philippine rebels who refused to submit to the benevolent authority of the United States. Similar considerations were present in the case of Panama.

Common racial views account in part for their agreement in many matters of foreign policy. Hay was more of an Anglophile than the president, and Roosevelt was somewhat more nationalistic than Hay in matters affecting relations with England and Canada, but he too believed that, as a race, Anglo-Saxons were more fit to rule. (Being of Dutch ancestry, however, Roosevelt preferred the looser term "English-speaking peoples.") Part of the reason that Aguinaldo had to be crushed and that the administration could so remorselessly take Panama derived from the racial outlook of major officials in Washington. The same was true, to some degree, in America's China policy and, indeed, this view was implicit in much of both Hay's and Roosevelt's thought and action.

Henry Watterson could have served under McKinley but not under Roosevelt. Hay, on the other hand, although sometimes uncomfortable with Roosevelt's robustness, had little difficulty serving the new president. He wanted to preserve the genteel style he associated with the late nineteenth century, as well as some of its values. But in many ways Hay was not out of step with the new age. How amazed and severely affected Watterson would have been had he known that in October, 1903, Hay wrote to his wife, "by the way poor old Watterson lectured in Pittsburg [*sic*] against the 400 and there was nobody went [*sic*] except a few 'brave ones.' Poor old Henry! how it would amaze him to know that the people he is yelping about never heard of him & never will."[60] Hay belonged to both the nineteenth and the twentieth centuries.

Notes

Throughout these notes, "lbc" is used to indicate that the letter cited is a letterbook press copy.

CHAPTER I

1. "Distich XVIII," *The Complete Poetical Works of John Hay*, Clarence Hay, compiler (Boston and New York, 1917), p. [185]; Copy. John Hay to Whitelaw Reid, February 2, [1897], John Hay Papers, John Hay Library, Brown University (hereafter cited as JHP:BU).

2. William R. Thayer, *The Life and Letters of John Hay*, 2 vols. (Boston and New York, 1916), 2:63; Horace Traubel, *With Walt Whitman in Camden*, 5 vols. (New York, Philadelphia, and Carbondale, 1906–54), 4:32.

3. Hay to Nora Perry, January 2, 1859, Caroline Ticknor, ed., *A Poet in Exile: Early Letters of John Hay* (Boston, 1910), p. 24; Brooks Adams, "John Hay," *McClure's Magazine* 19 (June, 1902): 177.

4. Hay to Walt Whitman, July 22, [1876], in Traubel, *With Walt Whitman*, 2:26. See also ibid., p. 480 and 4:32.

5. Ibid., 3:91. Thayer also correctly assessed Hay, writing that Hay felt uncomfortable with "poor painters, writers, poets, sculptors and journalists [who] forgot their poverty. He mixed with them, but he was never wholly of them." Thayer, *John Hay*, 1:329–30.

6. Thayer, *John Hay*, 1:387. Howells was not at home when Hay called, but they met later the same year.

7. William Dean Howells to Hay, Christmas Day, 1877, Mildred Howells, ed., *Life in Letters of William Dean Howells*, 2 vols. (Garden City, New York, 1928), 1:245; Hay to Howells, March 26, 1882, in Thayer, *John Hay*, 1:406.

8. Thayer mentions Twain twice. Tyler Dennett, *John Hay: From Poetry to Politics* (Port Washington, N.Y., 1963 [originally published in 1933]) mentions him five times, all in passing references. Twain was, of course, Samuel L. Clemens.

9. Howells, ed., *Letters of Howells*, 1:214; Samuel L. Clemens, *Mark Twain's Autobiography* with an introduction by Albert Bigelow Paine, 2 vols. (New York and London, 1924), 2:118, 133; Hay to Mark Twain, January 14, 1871, Mark Twain Papers, University of California at Berkeley Library (hereafter cited as MTP:UC); Twain to Mary Fairbanks, February 25, [1874], Dixon Wecter, ed., *Mark Twain to Mrs. Fairbanks* (San Marino, California, 1949), pp. 182–83.

10. Twain to Howells, May 18, 1880, Henry Nash Smith and William M. Gibson, eds., *Mark Twain-Howells Letters: The Correspondence of Samuel L. Clemens and William Dean Howells 1872–1910*, 2 vols. (Cambridge, Mass., 1960), 1:308–309; Hay to Howells, May 24, 1880, in Thayer, *John Hay*, 1:439.

11. For a complete discussion of Hay's close friendship with Henry James see George Monteiro, *Henry James and John Hay: The Record of a Friendship* (Providence, R.I., 1965). His close relationship with Henry Adams is so well known as to exclude extended comment in this work.

12. Newspaper clippings, n.d., Adams Family Papers, Massachusetts Historical Society (hereafter cited as AFP:MHS).

13. Hay to Henry Adams, April 15, [1887], ibid.; Hay to C[lara] S. H[ay], July 19, 1896, Clara S. Hay, ed., *Letters of John Hay and Extracts from his Diary*, 3 vols. (Washington, D.C., 1908), 3:55.

14. Elihu Root, *Address by Elihu Root at the Dedication of the John Hay Library, Brown University, November 11, 1910* (New York, 1910), p. 3; James Ford Rhodes, *The McKinley and Roosevelt Administrations 1897–1909* (New York, 1922), pp. 120–25; Rhodes to Clara S. Hay, February 15, 1907, John Hay Papers, Manuscript Division, Library of Congress (hereafter cited as JHP:LC); Hay to Theodore Roosevelt, November 16, 1904, copied in Hay's diary, November 16, 1904, JHP:LC.

15. Rhodes, *McKinley and Roosevelt Administrations*, p. 122; A. S. Chapman, "The Boyhood of John Hay," *Century* 56 (July, 1909): 446; Clara S. Hay to Richard Watson Gilder,

July 9, 1909, Richard Watson Gilder Papers, Manuscript Division, New York Public Library (hereafter cited as RWGP:NYPL); James B. Angell, "Address," in Brown University, ed., *The Dedication of the John Hay Library, Brown University, Providence, Rhode Island (November 11, 1910)* (Providence, R.I., 1911), pp. 31–32.

16.　　Hay to Sarah Helen Whitman, n.d., in Thayer, *John Hay*, 1:45. One such despairing poem is "In the Mist," which Hay sent to his friend Hannah Angell in 1858. See [Amy A. C. Montague, ed.] *A College Friendship: A Series of Letters from John Hay to Hannah Angell* (Boston, 1910), pp. 21–26.

17.　　Hay to Angell, [October 20, 1858] [Montague, ed.], *A College Friendship*, p. 34.

18.　　Howells to Hay, March 22, 1871, Howells, ed., *Letters of Howells*, 1:161–62; review of *Castilian Days, Atlantic Monthly* 28 (November, 1871): 636–38. The quotation is on p. 638.

19.　　Hay to Twain, January 9, 1871, MTP:UC.

20.　　Monteiro, *Henry James and John Hay*, p. 43. For Hay's account of this incident see his diary, January 7, 1905, JHP:LC.

21.　　Traubel, *With Walt Whitman*, 4:32; Alvey A. Adee to Hay, February 28, 1878, and November 13, 1881, JHP:BU; Isaac Marcosson, *Before I Forget: A Pilgrimage to the Past* (New York, 1959), pp. 80–81. In a previous work, *Adventures in Interviewing* (London and New York, 1920), Marcosson also praised Hay in glowing terms (pp. 48–49).

22.　　Hay to Howells, December 31, 1881, William Dean Howells Papers, Houghton Library, Harvard University (hereafter cited as WDHP:HU); ibid., October 26, 1879.

23.　　Hay to Twain, December 15, 1874, MTP:UC; Twain to Howells, December 18, [1874], Smith and Gibson, eds., *Twain-Howells Letters*, 1:56; Clemens, *Autobiography*, 1:233–34.

24.　　John DeLancey Ferguson, *Mark Twain: Man and Legend* (Indianapolis and New York, 1943), p. 185.

25.　　Twain to Charles Orr, July 30, 1906, Bernard DeVoto, ed., *Mark Twain in Eruption: Hitherto Unpublished Pages About Men and Events by Mark Twain* (New York and London, 1940), p. 205.

26.   Hay to Twain, July 16, [1880], MTP:UC; Hay to Twain, August 16, 1880, Smith and Gibson, eds., *Twain-Howells Letters*, 1:271n. The possibility that Howells suggested that Twain send *1601* to Hay is discussed in ibid., pp. 271n–72n. For Hay's involvement in the publication of *1601*, see De-Voto, ed., *Twain in Eruption*, p. 204. Hay's copy of *1601* is now in the Rare Book Room of the Library of Congress.

27.   T. Edgar Pemberton, *The Life of Bret Harte* (New York, 1903), p. 221. For an example of Hay's critical comments see Hay to Bret Harte, n.d., ibid., pp. 238–39.

28.   Harte to Hay, February 11, 1880, JHP:BU; [Hay to Clara S. Hay], March 2, 1880, ibid.; Harte to Anna Harte, March 18, 1880, Geoffrey Bret Harte, ed., *The Letters of Bret Harte* (Boston and New York, 1926), p. 169. In the meantime, Clarence King, who was also attempting to aid Harte, wrote that if he received the new post, he would "owe it chiefly to Hay, who has never lost an opportunity to work for you." (Clarence King to Harte, [March, 1880], quoted in Harte to Anna Harte, March 18, 1880, Harte, ed., *Letters of Harte*, p. 170.)

29.   Hay to Harte, received March 21, 1881, different portions printed in Pemberton, *Bret Harte*, p. 222, and by Harte in a letter to his wife, April 22, 1881, Harte, ed., *Letters of Harte*, p. 194.

30.   Harte to Anna Harte, February 28, 1882, Harte, ed., *Letters of Harte*, p. 205; ibid., June 15, 1884, p. 251; Harte to Hay, June 25, 1885, JHP:BU; Harte to Hay, November 22, 1888, JHP:BU; James G. Blaine to Hay, November 22, 1888, JHP:BU.

31.   When Harte died in 1902, Hay wrote a brief reminiscence of Harte for publication in Harte's journal, the *Overland Monthly*. "Reminiscences of Bret Harte," *Overland Monthly* 40 (September, 1902): [230]–231.

32.   Hay, diary entry, January 12, 1905, JHP:LC.

33.   Richard Watson Gilder to Hay, October 17, 1900, JHP:BU; ibid., August 22, 1904.

34.   Ibid., February 7, 1900; ibid., April 3, 1900.

35.   Hay to Howells, February 26, 1897, Howells, ed., *Letters of Howells*, 1:240.

36.   Hay to Howells, September 16, 1884, WDHP:HU.

37.   Justin Kaplan, *Mr. Clemens and Mark Twain: A Biography* (New York, 1966), p. 69; Twain to Howells, October

27, 1879, Smith and Gibson, eds., *Twain-Howells Letters*, 1:277; Hay to Twain, April 14, [1885], JHP:LC.

38.   Twain to Joseph Twichell, November 4, 1904, Albert Bigelow Paine, ed., *Mark Twain's Letters*, 2 vols. (New York and London, 1917), 2:761–62.

39.   Louis J. Budd, *Mark Twain: Social Philosopher* (Bloomington, Ind., 1962), p. 177. The inscription is dated February 4, 1901, quoted in William M. Gibson, "Mark Twain and Howells: Anti-Imperialists," *The New England Quarterly* 20 (December, 1947): 462–63. Hay to Howells, March 31, 1902, WDHP:HU.

40.   Budd, *Mark Twain*, p. 180; Twain to Hay, February 27, 1900, JHP:LC; Twain to Hay, n.d., in Albert Bigelow Paine, *Mark Twain: A Biography* (New York and London, 1912), pp. 1249–50. The letter reads as follows:

"Dear & honored Sir,—I never hear any one speak of you & your long roll of illustrious services in other than terms of pride & praise—& out of the heart. I think I am right in believing you to be the only man in the civil service of the country the cleanness of whose motives is never questioned by any citizen, & whose acts proceed always upon a broad & high plane, never by accident or pressure of circumstance upon a narrow or low one. There are majorities that are proud of more than one of the nation's great servants, but I believe, & I think I know, that you are the only one of whom the entire nation is proud. Proud & thankful.

"Name & address are lacking here, & for a purpose: to leave you no chance to make my words a burden to you and a reproach to me, who would lighten your burdens if I could, not add to them."

41.   Statement to the press in Paine, *Mark Twain*, p. 1249; Samuel L. Clemens, "John Hay and the Ballads," *Harper's Weekly* 49 (October 21, 1905):1530.

42.   Howells to Hay, October 14, 1898; April 2, 1902; December 1, 1904; all in JHP:BU; William Dean Howells, "John Hay in Literature," *North American Review* 181 (September, 1905): [343]–351.

43.   Andrew Carnegie to Reid, July 6, 1905, Whitelaw Reid Papers, Manuscript Division, Library of Congress (hereafter cited as WRP:LC); Andrew Carnegie, *Autobiography of Andrew Carnegie* (Boston and New York, 1920), pp. 358, 361; Louis M. Hacker, *The World of Andrew Carnegie*

1865–1901 (Philadelphia and New York, 1968), pp. 363–64.

44.   [Hay to Clara S. Hay], June 2, [1884], JHP:BU; Hay to Adams, July 20, [1887], AFP:MHS; Hay to Carnegie, August 22, 1898, Andrew Carnegie Papers, Manuscript Division, Library of Congress (hereafter cited as ACP:LC). When Carnegie returned this letter to Mrs. Hay in 1907 for inclusion in the printed edition of Hay's letters, he wrote on the letter, "Referring to the Phillipines[*sic*] the acquisition of which Sec'y Hay deplored but alas how to get rid of them was the question.

"Mr. Hay was the great statesman here & had he been at Prest. McKinley's side, I think we never would have been burdened with them."

Carnegie also circled and underlined the following passage of Hay's letter: "I have read with keenest interest your letter in the *North American.* I am not allowed to say, in my present fix, *how much I* agree with you."

45.   Carnegie to Hay, November 24, 1898, ACP:LC; see also ibid., November 24, 1898, December 27, 1898, December 29, 1898, and August 7, 1899.

46.   Carnegie to Reid, December 1, 1899, WRP:LC.

47.   Copy, Hay to William M. Osborne, November 19, 1898, Tyler Dennett Papers, Manuscript Division, Library of Congress (hereafter cited as TDP:LC); Hay to Reid, November 29, 1898, JHP:LC.

48.   See Hay to Carnegie, December 10, 1901, and March 7, 1902, ACP:LC; see also, Carnegie, *Autobiography,* pp. 260, 361; Hay, diary entry, December 10, 1904, JHP:LC; Brown University, ed., *The Life and Works of John Hay 1838–1905: A Commemorative Catalogue of the Exhibition Shown at the John Hay Library of Brown University in Honor of the Centennial of his Graduation at the Commencement of 1858* (Providence, R.I., 1961), p.ix; Carnegie, *Autobiography,* p. 275; James B. Angell, "Address," in Brown University, ed., *Dedication of the John Hay Library,* p. 27.

49.   Ethan Allen to William L. Stone, September 26, 1896, TDP:LC.

50.   Reid to Hay, February 19, 1881, JHP:BU.

51.   Reid to Hay, August 21, 1881, ibid.

52.   Hay to Reid, September 4, 1881, WRP:LC; Reid to Hay, September 25, 1881, JHP:BU, printed in George Monteiro, "A Note on the Mark Twain-Whitelaw Reid Relationship,"

The Emerson Society Quarterly 19 (2nd quarter, 1960): 20.

53.   Quoted in Dennett, *John Hay*, p. 173.

54.   Memorandum, signed by Hay, enclosed in Hay to Reid, October 14, 1889, WRP:LC. In his covering letter Hay assured Reid that he could incorporate the account into his autobiography "with a certainty that it is true." Dennett does not mention this memorandum.

55.   William R. Thayer asserts that Reid's "unremitted pre-sentation of his claims when any office was in sight" cooled Hay's friendship as early as 1892. There is, however, vir-tually no evidence that this was true until 1896. (Thayer, *John Hay* 2: 133.)

56.   Hay to Samuel Mather, February 25, 1897, ibid., 2:155; Hay to Reid, November 14, [1896], JHP:BU. George Wash-burne Smalley, American correspondent of the London *Times*, wrote at the time that he was fully aware "of the mag-nanimity which led you [Hay] to put it [the English mission] aside in R's favor." (Smalley to Hay, February 17, 1897, JHP:BU.)

57.   Hay to Reid, December 10, 1896, WRP:LC.

58.   Telegram, Hay to William McKinley, December 26, [1896], William McKinley Papers, Manuscript Division, Li-brary of Congress (hereafter cited as WMcKP:LC); type-script, [December 26, 1896], ibid.

59.   Hay to Reid, January 22, 1897, WRP:LC

60.   Copy, Hay to [Reid], February 2, [1897], JHP:BU. The copy is in Hay's handwriting. Hay to McKinley, February 2, 1897, WMcKP:LC; Reid to Hay, February 8, 1897, WRP:LC, lbc; Hay to McKinley, February 13, 1897, WMcKP:LC.

There is no question that Hay was consciously seeking the English mission. There is in the Hay papers at Brown University a draft letter to the president, undated, but prob-ably written in February, 1897, although conceivably it could have been written as early as December, 1896, putting forth Hay's claims:

I have thought for some days of asking permission to come and talk with you, but have finally concluded that it will take less of your time if I write.

It is perhaps by this time evident to you that you cannot put Whitelaw Reid in the Cabinet or give him an Embassy without more serious embarrassment than it will be wise for you to incur at the outset of your administration. In that case, and only, I have a word to say about myself.

There has been so much talk about my being sent to England that I presume you may have given some consideration to the matter. I have received over a hundred newspaper articles from every part of the country and from Europe all cordially approving the idea. A large number of prominent people have spoken to me about it & have offered to speak to you. I have declined all their offers, because I shrink from worrying you.

I do not think it is altogether selfishness and vanity which has brought me to think that perhaps you might do worse than select me.

1. My appointment would please a good many people & so far as I know would offend nobody. Any appointment from New York would rouse bitterness in some quarter. If Reid can't get it, he would rather have me go, than any one else.

2. I should not hold the office very long. It would be at your disposal in some critical time when it might serve a useful purpose.

3. As I have no claim on the place, and as it is really above my merits and deservings, I think I would be more grateful than any one else would be, and would do as much to show my gratitude.

I beg you will excuse my suggesting that it would be desirable to decide the matter as soon as you can. This will be the fullest year London has ever known. Already it is difficult to find a house suitable for an Embassy—before June it will be impossible, until next season. . . .

I am sure I need not say that whatever may be your decision I shall accept it with cordial acquiescence. If it shall not seem expedient to appoint me, I shall not question either your judgment, or your friendship. I know the burden of care and perplexity which rests upon you. If I thought this letter would add to it in the least I would destroy it. But I cannot help feeling that perhaps you can do this with some relief or advantage to yourself. If this is not so, do not give the matter a moment's thought.

Perhaps the best way to dispose of this letter will be to send it back to me in the enclosed envelope. I do not want it to be filed. You need not answer it. I will understand your silence. There will be no embarrassment between us. (Draft, Hay to McKinley, n.d., JHP:BU.)

61.   Reid to Hay, February 8, 1897, WRP:LC, lbc.

62.   "Draft No. One," [McKinley to Reid, February 15, 1897], JHP:BU; also in WMcKP:LC, where it is misfiled as December, 1896. Hay to McKinley, February 16, 1897, WMcKP:LC; "Draft No. Two,"[McKinley to Reid, February 16, 1897], JHP:BU, and also in WMcKP:LC, where it is misfiled as December 26, 1896.

63.   Draft letter, McKinley to Reid, [February 18, 1897], WMcKP:LC. Hay made a copy of the McKinley draft which is in JHP:BU.

64.   Telegram, Hay to McKinley, February 19, 1897, WMcKP:LC; Hay to McKinley, February 19, [1897], ibid.; telegram, Hay to Reid, February 20, 1897, JHP:BU. McKinley's actual letter to Reid was considerably shorter than the draft he showed to Hay. Most significantly, he omitted any mention of Hay's name and also failed to mention the possibility of a future appointment as he had in the draft. (McKinley to Reid, February 19, 1897, WMcKP:LC.)

65.   Reid to Hay, March 27, 1897, WRP:LC. Reid's reply to McKinley was gracious, although a note of sarcasm lay just beneath the surface when he discussed the state of his health. (Reid to McKinley, March 3, 1897, WMcKP:LC.) Reid lived until 1912; Hay died in 1905; McKinley was assassinated in 1901, but the autopsy revealed that his heart was weak at that time.

66.   Dennett, *John Hay*, pp. 193–94.

67.   Hay to McKinley, July 16, 1897, WMcKP:LC. Two weeks later Hay commented to Henry Adams, "The sight of a worthy human being is comforting to my soul, and I have seen my friend Whitelaw sitting between two princesses at supper every night, a week running—and now I may intone my nunc dimittis. His rapture has aliquid amare that an end must come, but the memory of it will soothe many an hour of ennui at Ophir Farm." Ophir Farm was Reid's New York estate. [Hay to Adams], July 25, 1897, Henry Adams Papers, Massachusetts Historical Society (hereafter cited as HAP:MHS).

68.   Hay to Clara S. Hay, September 18, 1898, JHP:LC; Hay to Henry White, November 21, 1898, Henry White Papers, Manuscript Division, Library of Congress (hereafter cited as HWhP:LC).

69.   Adams to Elizabeth Cameron, Christmas, 1898, Worthington C. Ford, ed., *Letters of Henry Adams*, 2 vols. (Boston and New York, 1930–38), 2:190; Reid to Hay, December 31, 1898, WRP:LC. Hay wrote to his sister-in-law about Reid, "I fear he will never forgive me for not having been able

to get him the English Embassy." (Hay to Flora Stone Mather, December 25, 1898, JHP:BU.)

70.   Hay to [Clara S. Hay], October 18, [1901], Wadsworth Family Papers, Manuscript Division, Library of Congress (hereafter cited as WadFP:LC); see also [Hay to Clara S. Hay], December 5, [1901], ibid. Henry White to Henry Cabot Lodge, February 26, 1902, Henry Cabot Lodge Papers, Massachusetts Historical Society (hereafter cited as HCLP:MHS); Joseph H. Choate to Hay, February 26, 1902, JHP:LC.

71.   Hay to Reid, July, 1902, in Royal Cortissoz, *The Life of Whitelaw Reid,* 2 vols. (New York, 1921), 2:283; Hay to [Adams], July 11, 1902, HAP:MHS.

72.   Hay to Reid, January 6, 1905, WRP:LC.

73.   Reid to Hay, November 26, 1896, JHP:BU.

74.   Henry Watterson to Reid, July 25, 1905, WRP:LC.

CHAPTER II

1.   Dennett, *John Hay,* pp. 119, 126–27.

2.   Hay to Hannah Angell, May 5, 1860, in [Montague,] ed., *A College Friendship,* p. 55.

3.   Brown University, ed., *A Commemorative Catalogue,* p. 6; Dennett, *John Hay,* p. 34; Hay to Angell, January 6, 1861, in [Montague,] ed., *A College Friendship,* p. 58.

4.   John Hay, "Ellsworth," *Atlantic Monthly* 8 (July, 1861); 119–24; diary entry, April 30, 1861, in Brown University, ed., *A Commemorative Catalogue,* pp. 9–10; diary entry, September 5, 1862, in Anne Hummell Sherrill, "John Hay: Shield of Union" (Ph.D. dissertation, University of California, Berkeley, 1967), p. 9.

5.   The phrase is Sherrill's, "Political Development: The Republic Makes a Convert—1863–1864," chapter 2 in "John Hay: Shield of Union." After an intensive study of Hay's Civil War writings, Sherrill concludes, "the most significant deficiency of John Hay's resumes of the years 1861 and 1862 is their almost total lack of understanding or interest in purely political matters." Ibid., p. 126.

6.   Hay to John G. Nicolay, August 7, 1863, in Tyler Dennett, ed., *Lincoln and the Civil War in the Diaries and Letters of John Hay* (New York, 1939), p. 76; Hay to Nicolay, November 7, 1864, Hay, ed., *Letters and Diary,* 1:238.

7.   Sherrill, "John Hay: Shield of Union," preface; Hay to William H. Herndon, September 5, 1866 (a facsimile copy

of this letter is in the Historical Society of Pennsylvania and is "reproduced from the Original in the Collection of Lincolniana founded by Wm. H. Herndon Now in the Possession of Gabriel Wells").

8. Hay, *Complete Poetical Works*, pp. 29–34; John Hay, *Castilian Days* (Boston, 1871).

9. Hay, *Complete Poetical Works*, pp. 107–8; *Liberty* 1 (1880): 1, in Hay's scrapbook, JHP:BU.

10. John Hay, "Daybreak in Spain," (manuscript speech), JHP:BU.

11. Ibid.; John Hay, "The Progress of Democracy in Europe," (manuscript speech), JHP:BU; Robert V. Bruce, *1877: Year of Violence* (Chicago, 1959), pp. 226–27.

12. Hay, "Daybreak in Spain"; Hay, "The Progress of Democracy in Europe"; Hay, *Complete Poetical Works*, pp. 3–5, 17–19.

13. Hay to Milton Hay, September 30, 1866, JHP:BU; Hay to Schuyler Colfax, June 24, 1868, ibid.

14. Hay to Clara S. Hay, August 30, 1870, TDP:LC; clipping, "Reform Impossible With Grant," *New York Tribune*, August 24, 1872, Hay's scrapbook, JHP:LC; Hay to Reid, [June, 1872], WRP:LC; Hay to Reid, August 4, [1872], WRP:LC; clipping, "The Syracuse Convention," *New York Tribune*, September 5, 1872, Hay's scrapbook, JHP:LC. Hay revealed that he did not vote for Greeley in a letter to Howells, February 20, 1877, WDHP:HU; Hay to [Daniel Sickles?], June 13, 1873, JHP:BU; Hay to Howells, February 20, 1877, WDHP:HU; Hay to Reid, April, 1876, quoted in Cortissoz, *Life of Reid*, 1:338. Hay dined with Tilden in 1874 and became his friend. (Hay to Samuel J. Tilden, April 3, 1874, Samuel J. Tilden Papers, Manuscript Division, New York Public Library.)

15. Frederic C. Jaher, "Industrialism and the American Aristocrat: A Study of John Hay and His Novel, *The Bread-winners*," *Journal of the Illinois State Historical Society* 65 (Spring, 1972): 69–93.

16. John Hay, *The Bread-winners: A Social Study* (Ridgewood, N.J., 1967 [originally published in 1883]), pp. 19, 171.

17. Ibid., p. 307.

18. Ibid., pp. 19, 6.

19. Hay to John Bigelow, March 12, 1871, JHP:BU; Hay to

Adee, December 14, 1875, ibid.; *Nation* 38 (January 17, 1884): 58.

20.   Among the cultural accoutrements that Alice gained from her French instructor was the development of a beautiful voice. Such voices could be developed by Europeans, Hay implied, but they were "exceptional everywhere in America, and particularly in our lake country, where the late springs develop fine high sopranos, but leave much to be desired in the talking tones of women." (Hay, *The Bread-winners*, p. 94.)

21.   "*The Bread-winners*: A Letter from the Author," *Century* 5 (March, 1884): 794; Hay, *The Bread-winners*, pp. 5–6; Hay to Adams, October 2, 1883, Theodore Frelinghuysen Dwight Papers, Massachusetts Historical Society (hereafter cited as TFDP:MHS).

22.   Hay, *The Bread-winners*, pp. 89–90.

23.   Hay overlooked the fact, however, that Ananias was struck dead not for ordinary lying but for refusing to give up all his worldly possessions to live a communal life in poverty. See *Acts* 5:1–5.

24.   Hay, *The Bread-winners*, pp. 79, 210, 257, 75, 299, 207, 253, 266. The words, "with his head thrown back, his nostrils distended, a picture of brutal impatience" is found in the manuscript novel, p. 280, but was not included in the printed version, p. 253. The unpublished manuscript is in the Houghton Library, Harvard University.

25.   The lascivious nature of the Bread-winners, although evident in the published work (see, for example, p. 107), is most clearly seen in the unpublished manuscript which contains several passages not included in the novel as published. The quotation is found in the printed version, p. 82.

26.   Hay, *The Bread-winners*, p. 307.

27.   *New York Times*, March 9, 1897, p. 6, col. 4; Hay, *The Bread-winners*, p. 168; *Century* 5 (November, 1883): 158; *Century* 5 (March, 1884): 794–96; John Hay, "The Bread-winners: A Social Study," (manuscript novel), pp. 180–81. Compare this with the published version, p. 168.

John G. Sproat, *"The Best Men": Liberal Reformers in the Gilded Age* (New York, 1968), refers to Hay's novel as "perhaps the most graphic anti-union novel in American literature" (p. 219). Louis Hacker arrived at a similar judgment in 1933 when he called the novel "as mean and unwarranted an attack on organized labor as is to be found anywhere in modern letters." "Middle Western Exquisite," *Nation* 137 (November 8, 1933): 545.

28.   Hay, *The Bread-winners,* p. 90.

29.   John Hay, "The Mormon Prophet's Tragedy," *Atlantic Monthly* 24 (December, 1869): 669–78.

30.   Jaher, "Industrialism and the American Aristocrat," p. 78; Hay, "The Progress of Democracy in Europe"; JHP:BU; Hay, "Daybreak in Spain," ibid.

31.   In one of Hay's scrapbooks is a clipping entitled, "John Hay and His 'Jim Bludsoe'," *Albany Evening Times,* n.d., which contends that Hay did receive $1,000,000 when he married. In the margin Hay scribbled "untrue." JHP:LC.

32.   Hay to Adee, November 28, 1874, JHP:LC; Jay Gould to Hay, July 2, 1883, JHP:BU.

33.   This hypothesis may also help explain why Hay disliked mugwump politics and also why he was not noticeably anti-Semitic. See pp. 53–55; 75–81.

34.   John Hay, *Amasa Stone* (New York, 1883); Jaher, "Industrialization and the American Aristocrat," p. 79; Hay to Amasa Stone, July 27, 1877, in Thayer, *John Hay,* 2:3–4; Hay to Stone, July 21, 1877, WadFP:LC; Hay to Stone, August 23, 1877, WadFP:LC.

35.   Ibid.; one critic of the novel, Hay wrote, insisted "on the right of the workman to sell his labor at the best price; yet he knows that trades-unionism is the very negation of that right," (*Century* 5 [November, 1883]: 158.)

36.   Robert Wiebe, *The Search for Order 1877–1920* (New York, 1967), p. 10; Hay, *The Bread-winners,* pp. 78, 109. In the novel the year was obscured as "187-." When Hay chose to defend his book (against the advice of Henry Adams), he admitted that much of the plot came from newspaper accounts of the disturbances of 1877. (*Century* 5 [March, 1884]: 794–96.)

37.   In fact, Hay had a certain admiration for Hamilton. He once urged Henry Adams, who was writing his famous history of the Jefferson and Madison administrations, to "give Hamilton a fairer show for his money." (Hay to Adams, n.d., TFDP:MHS).

38.   Hay, *The Bread-winners,* pp. 246–47. Such criticism of the wealthy has resulted in some misinterpretations of Hay's intent, it seems to me, by both of Hay's biographers. William

R. Thayer writes that Hay did "not deny that Capital has its faults; he paints individual Capitalists in dark colors"; while Tyler Dennett concludes that Hay's novel was "as much as anything a critique of Cleveland society" which included a "sneering denunciation of the wealthy for their indifference to civic duty." (Thayer, *John Hay* 2:14; Dennett, *John Hay*, pp. 104, 117.)

Both authors overlook the main point. Hay did indeed lampoon wealthy philistines like Mr. Temple, but such criticism constituted only a secondary theme in the novel. The main lesson was that all men of wealth, whether cultured aristocrats or philistine business tycoons, must unite to crush revolutionary organizations such as the Brotherhood of Bread-winners. Furthermore, they must remain constantly alert for future threats from below.

Far from piously criticizing the wealthy for a lack of "civic duty" in the manner of a high-school text, Hay appealed openly to class interests. Fear replaced optimism as Hay searched for a better way to entrench the status quo. One reviewer was closer to the truth than Hay's biographers when he criticized the author's unbalanced judgment of labor. The reviewer found no "hint in it of a destructive tendency from the opposite side,—that of excessive monopoly and of the corruption which is frequently one of the results of great wealth." (*Atlantic Monthly* 53 [May, 1884]: 709.)

39.   Hay to Reid, September 24, 1875, WRP:LC; ibid., October 1, 1875; ibid., May 13, 1876.
40.   Ibid., October 25, 1878; ibid.; October 27, 1878.
41.   Newspaper clipping, "Republican League," n.d. (the application for membership was dated March 4, 1879), scrapbook, JHP:LC; newspaper clipping, "Honest Money," n.d. (pencilled *The Cleveland Leader*, July 10, 1879), ibid.
42.   Newspaper clipping, "Honest Money," n.d.
43.   Hay to Reid, August 20, 1879, WRP:LC; newspaper clipping, "An Ohio Idea," *The Cincinnati Gazette*, October 13, 1879, scrapbook, JHP:LC; Hay to Reid, October 15, 1879, WRP:LC.
44.   Hay to Reid, November 3, 1879, WRP:LC; Hay to Stone, December 8, 1879, JHP:BU; Hay to Walter Phelps, December 23, 1879, John Hay Papers, Huntington Library, San Marino, California; Hay to Reid, March 31, 1880, WRP:LC.

45.   As he explained to Richard Watson Gilder, "I have made a little transaction with my civic conscience thus:—I will spend every year as much time and money as I can afford, in politics, and that is all anybody can ask of me. But run for office I never did and never will." (Hay to Gilder, August 5, 1880, Hay, ed., *Letters and Diary*, 2:50.)

46.   Newspaper clipping, Hay to J. W. Carson, July 8, 1880, printed under the headline, "Garfield Clubs," n.d., scrapbook, JHP:LC; John Hay, *The Balance Sheet of the Two Parties* (Cleveland, 1880). Hay's letters and scrapbook indicate that the speech was widely reported and that reaction was very favorable.

47.   Hay to James A. Garfield, October 18, 1880, TDP:LC. Hay was also involved in the famous controversy over Garfield's decision to name W. H. Robertson to direct the New York customshouse, over the violent objections of Senators Roscoe Conkling and Thomas Platt. Hay, a Blaine Half-Breed, detested the Stalwart Conkling and gladly delivered to the president a long message from Whitelaw Reid concerning Robertson's appointment. Reid detailed Conkling's plans to force the president to withdraw the nomination and urged Garfield to stand firm. (Telegram, Reid to Hay, March 27, 1881, JHP:LC.) The following day Hay saw the president alone in his library, presented Reid's telegram, and got Garfield's assurance that he would not withdraw Robertson's name. (Hay to Reid, March 28, 1881, WRP:LC.)

Reid's telegram to Hay was stolen from the wires and published after Garfield's death, causing great excitement and concern among the newspapers. It was thought that the publication was a Stalwart attempt to show that Garfield was unduly influenced by the Half-Breeds. Presumably, following this logic, the new president would feel obligated to move closer to the Stalwarts.

48.   Hay to Howells, October 24, 1880, WDHP:HU; Hay to Adams, January 22, 1883, TFDP:MHS.

49.   Hay to [Adams], January 22, 1883, TFDP:MHS. The following year Hay asked to be removed from the mailing list of the *Civil Service Record* (to which he had not subscribed). (Hay to William V. Kellen, December 5, 1884, H. H. Edes Papers, Massachusetts Historical Society.)

50.   Dennett, *John Hay*, pp. 112n–13n; *Century* 5 (November, 1883): 158.

51.   *Atlantic Monthly* 52 (May, 1884): 708–10.
52.   *Athenaeum*, No. 2932 (January 5, 1884); 16. (Contrast this
       with Thayer's statement, "The English read 'The Bread-
       Winners' with enthusiasm, and their critics gave it unusual
       praise," *John Hay* 2:13.) *Dial* 4 (February, 1884): 259. The
       Dial's reviewer went on to say that *The Bread-winners* was
       "deliberately insulting" to working people. "The author's
       sense of humor may be gratified by presenting low ruffians
       and assassins as types of the working classes," he continued,
       "but in that case his capacity for humor is not a pleasant
       thing to contemplate."
53.   [Henry F. Keenan], *The Money-Makers: A Social Parable*
       (New York, 1885); clipping in WadFP:LC; Dennett, *John
       Hay*, pp. 101–2. Stone's health had been failing for some
       time, leaving him very depressed. Hay, writing from Europe
       in 1882 and 1883, seemed to fear the possibility of suicide
       for he wrote nervously that he and his wife would return
       to Cleveland whenever Stone wished. Furthermore, he made
       a number of references to prominent men who had suffered
       similarly only to recover completely and enjoy long and full
       lives. Stone died in May, 1883.
54.   Gilder to Hay, February 6, 1885, WadFP:LC; D. Appleton
       and Company to Hay, February 9, 1885, ibid.; clipping,
       Vanity Fair, n.d., ibid.
55.   Hay to Gilder, June 30, 1884, RWGP:NYPL.
56.   Hay to Gilder, July 11, 1884, ibid.
57.   Hay to James G. Blaine, November 5, 1884, James G.
       Blaine Papers, Manuscript Division, Library of Congress;
       Hay to Howells, September 16, 1884, WDHP:HU.
58.   Draft letter, Hay to George W. Curtis, November 28, 1887,
       JHP:BU. (It is possible that Hay did not send this letter.)
       Hay to Blaine, December 8, 1887, in David S. Muzzey,
       James G. Blaine: A Political Idol of Other Days (New York,
       1934), p. 367.
59.   Hay to Reid, March 5, 1888, WRP:LC; Hay to John
       Sherman, June 25, 1888, John Sherman Papers, Manuscript
       Division, Library of Congress; Hay to Adams, June 25,
       [1888], AFP:MHS. To Whitelaw Reid, Hay wrote, "Well,
       anything to clean out the White House." (Hay to Reid,
       August 3, 1888, WRP:LC.)
60.   Hay to Benjamin Harrison, October 1, 1888, Benjamin
       Harrison Papers, Manuscript Division, Library of Congress;

Mark Hanna to Hay, October 19, 1888, JHP:BU; Hay to Reid, November 7, 1888, WRP:LC.

61.   Hay to Adams, July 12, [1890], HAP:MHS; ibid., August 6, 1890; ibid., December 12, 1890; ibid., August 29, 1893; ibid., May 28, 1894.

62.   Ibid., October 27, 1894; Hay to Adams, June 27, 1895, Hay, ed., *Letters and Diary*, 2:356.

63.   Hay to Reid, October 12, 1894, WRP:LC.

64.   Hay to Adams, October 24, 1891, HAP:MHS; ibid., December 30, 1890; ibid., January 10, 1891. For similar comments, see Hay to Reid, April 12, 1891, WRP:LC, and Hay to Adams, August 20, 1891, HAP:MHS.

65.   Hay to Reid, October 24, 1891, WRP:LC. (In contrast to the Democratic campaign, Hay felt the Republican one was "perfectly straightforward, honorable, and manly, a direct appeal to reason and conscience.") Hay to Adams, June 16, [1892], HAP:MHS; Hay, untitled manuscript speech, [1892], JHP:LC.

66.   Hay to Adams, March 9, 1893, HAP:MHS; ibid., July 3, [1893], (misdated 1903); Hay to Reid, October 12, [1893], WRP:LC; ibid., March 9, 1894; [Hay to Clara S. Hay], August 5, 1894, WadFP:LC.

67.   Hay to Adams, May 28, 1894, HAP:MHS.

68.   Adams to Elizabeth Cameron, June 20, 1907, Ford, ed., *Letters of Henry Adams*, 2:480; William McKinley to Hay, February 26, 1893, JHP:BU; ibid., November 10, 1894. The amount Hay gave was something less than $5,000. See Gilder to Hay, February 27, 1893, JHP:BU.

69.   Hanna to Hay, March 23, 1895, JHP:BU; McKinley to Hanna, April 13, 1895, WMcKP:LC; McKinley to Hay, April 13, 1895, JHP:BU; McKinley to James A. Gary, April 13, 1895, WMcKP:LC; Hanna to Hay, April 15, 1895, JHP:BU.

70.   Hay to Hanna, December 20, 1895, JHP:BU; Hanna to Hay, January 4, 1896, ibid.; Hay to Hanna, January 27, [1896], WMcKP:LC.

71.   Hay's gifts can be traced in the following letters: Hanna to Hay, October 12, 1895, JHP:BU; ibid., January 4, 1896; ibid, March 5, 1896; ibid, March 27, 189[6]; Hay to McKinley, August 3, 1896, WMcKP:LC.

72.   In fact, one of Hay's acquaintances wrote, "The reference to 'the wandering orator from the muddy and widemouth Platte' is as racy as some of the dialogue in an anonymous

novel called 'The Breadwinners.'" (Clarence Clough Buel to Hay, October 13, 1896, JHP:BU.)

73.   John Hay, *A Platform of Anarchy* (n.p., n.d.).

74.   Hay to Reid, August 31, 1896, WRP:LC; Hay to Adams, September 8, 1896, HAP:MHS.

75.   Unsigned memorandum, probably a press release, November, 1896, JHP:LC; newspaper clipping, Hay to Myron T. Herrick, November 14, 1896, scrapbook, ibid.; Hay to Reid, November 7, 1896, WRP:LC. For Carnegie's unifying efforts, see Joseph F. Wall, *Andrew Carnegie* (New York, 1970), p. 469.

76.   Hay to Henry Cabot Lodge, July 27, 1898, HCLP:MHS; Hay to Charles Dick, September 11, 1899, JHP:LC. (Dick assured Hay that the letter had "unprecedented circulation" in Ohio. Dick to Hay, October 21, 1899, JHP:LC.) Hay, "Fifty Years of the Republican Party," *The Addresses of John Hay* (New York, 1906), p. 290; Hay, diary entry, April 10, 1904, JHP:LC.

77.   Hay to Adelbert Hay, July 1, 1900, JHP:LC, 1bc; Hay to Roosevelt, November 12, 1898, ibid.

78.   Hay to Roosevelt, November 15, 1901, WMcKP:LC; Hay to Roosevelt, September 8, 1903, JHP:LC. Commenting on Roosevelt's address, Hay wrote that he admired the president's "dignity and . . . truthful unreserve" and wondered if the "so-called 'working men' . . . knew the honor you do them when you talk like that—or do they prefer the sickening flattery of the demagogue."

79.   Quoted in John St. Loe Strachey, *The Adventure of Living: A Subjective Autobiography* (London, 1922), p. 419.

CHAPTER III

1.   Thomas F. Gossett, *Race: The History of an Idea in America* (Dallas, 1963), pp. 270–73; John Higham, *Strangers in the Land: Patterns of American Nativism 1860–1925*, 2nd ed. (New York, 1965). George Washburne Smalley, American correspondent for the London *Times*, caught the anti-Semitic flavor of the age in a letter written from the Oriental Hotel in Manhattan Beach, New York. Governor Theodore Roosevelt, Elizabeth Cameron (Henry Adams' confidant), and other luminaries were there, Smalley wrote, "provided they be not Jews. The 'Ebrew Jew is excluded," he ex-

plained, "since there is in America an anti-Semitism which expresses itself in this form of social persecution." (George Washburne Smalley to the Duchess of Sutherland, July 25, 1899, George Washburne Smalley Papers, Manuscript Division, Library of Congress.)

2. Gossett, *Race*, p. 144.

3. Bradford Perkins, *The Great Rapprochement: England and the United States, 1895–1914* (New York, 1968), p. 74. The influence of racist thought on American foreign policy at the turn of the century is noted in most works dealing with American expansionism. See particularly Ruben Francis Weston, *Racism in U.S. Imperialism: The Influence of Racial Assumptions on American Foreign Policy, 1893–1946* (Columbia, S.C., 1972), Julius W. Pratt, *Expansionists of 1898: The Acquisition of Hawaii and the Spanish Islands* (Baltimore, 1935), Howard K. Beale, *Theodore Roosevelt and the Rise of America to World Power* (Baltimore, 1956), and Oscar M. Alfonso, "Taft's Early Views on the Filipinos," *Solidarity* 4 (June, 1969): 52–58. There is also a large literature on general attitudes toward race and ethnicity in the late nineteenth and early twentieth centuries.

4. Hay to Clara S. Hay, February 15, 1880 and February 22, 1880, JHP:BU; David H. Burton, "Theodore Roosevelt's Social Darwinism and Views on Imperialism," *Journal of the History of Ideas* 26 (January–March, 1965): 103–18.

5 Hay, diary entry, April 4, 1904, JHP:LC.

6. Hay, "A History of the Jesuits," manuscript speech, ibid.

7. Hay, "Washington in Wartime," a speech recorded in a newspaper clipping, pencilled date, January 15, 1873, ibid.

8. Hay, *Castilian Days*, p. 75, flyleaf.

9. Thayer, *John Hay*, 1:18; diary entry, September 26, 1862, Dennett, ed., *Lincoln and the Civil War*, p. 50. See also Hay's diary entry for October 23, 1863 in which Hay stated that slavery was "an institution which is as odorously defunct as was Lazarus" (p. 106).

10. Hay to Nicolay, April, 1863, in Thayer, *John Hay*, 1:150; diary entry, July 31, 1863, Dennett, ed., *Lincoln and the Civil War*, p. 74.

11. Diary entry, [February 10, 1867], Dennett, ed., *Lincoln and the Civil War*, p. 270; newspaper clipping, pencilled date, 1873, JHP:LC.

12.　Hay, *Complete Poetical Works*, pp. 10–13. "Banty Tim" was based on fact, for Hay later wrote that Tilmon Joy was actually Major Dorus Bates, whose sister married John G. Nicolay. (Hay to Clinton Scollard, May 22, 1899, JHP:BU.)

13.　Diary entry, August 14, 1863, Dennett, ed., *Lincoln and the Civil War*, p. 81. Hay's treatment of the riots in the biography of Lincoln was similarly vituperative. John G. Nicolay and John Hay, *Abraham Lincoln: A History*, 10 vols. (New York, 1890), 7:17–26. [John Hay], "Two Fenians," enclosed in Hay to Charles Graham Halpine, August 24, 1867, John Hay Papers, Huntington Library, San Marino, Calif.

14.　Hay to Schuyler Colfax, June 24, 1868, JHP:BU.

15.　Hay to Stone, April 8, 1883, WadFP:LC.

16.　Hay, *The Bread-winners*, pp. 74–75, 303, 86. Hay expressed similarly violent sentiments only toward American Indians. He did not write very much about Indians, but he approved the warfare waged against them. The massacre of General Custer's forces prompted Hay to write a commemorative poem. "It is a well-intentioned poem, calculated to make people kill Indians," Hay wrote to Whitelaw Reid, asking him to print the poem anonymously. "I think H. H. [Helen Hunt Jackson] ought to be a Ute prisoner for a week," he added. (Hay to Reid, January 27, 1880, WRP:LC.) The poem, "Miles Keough's Horse," honored the lone survivor of the massacre. *(Complete Poetical Works*, pp. 77–80.) See also Hay's poem "Golyer," one of the Pike County Ballads, *Complete Poetical Works*, pp. 17–20.

17.　Hay, *Castilian Days*, 2nd ed. (Boston, 1890), preface. The deletion of the six chapters in the 1903 edition was explained by the fact that they were "less descriptive than the rest of the book." Ibid., 3rd ed. (Boston, 1903), preface.

18.　Hay to Albert Rhodes, September 25, [1868], JHP:LC; Hay to [Clara S. Hay], October 19, 1903, ibid.

19.　Hay to Henry White, January 20, 1898, HWhP:LC; Hay to Elizabeth Cameron, March 10, 1898, quoted in Ernest Samuels, *Henry Adams: The Major Phase* (Cambridge, Mass., 1964), p. 184.

20.　John Higham, "Anti-Semitism in the Gilded Age," *Mississippi Valley Historical Review* 43 (March, 1957): 573.

21.　Hay to Oscar Straus, October 18, 1899, and May 19, 1900, Oscar Straus Papers, Manuscript Division, Library of Congress (hereafter cited as OSP:LC); Dennett, *John Hay,* p. 396; Hay to Charles S. Wilson, July 17, 1902, in U. S. Department of State, *Papers Relating to the Foreign Relations of the United States, 1902,* pp. 910–14; Hay to Robert S. McCormick, August 11, 1902, ibid., pp. 42–45.

22. Hay to Adee, August 30, 1902, JHP:LC.

23. *New York Times,* November 10, 1902, p. 8, col. 7.

24. Ibid., September 22, 1902, p. 9, col. 1; Dennett, *John Hay,* p. 397; Collector Treat to Theodore Roosevelt, October 17, 1902, JHP:LC.

25. Hay to Adee, August 12, 1902, JHP:LC.

26. Hay to Jacob Schiff, May 20, 1903, ibid.; Dennett, *John Hay,* p. 398. Much of Hay's letter to Schiff is printed in Dennett. Dennett, however, quoted Hay as writing in part, "I feel precisely as you do in regard to it, but you are free to express your feelings and I am not." Actually the letter reads, "I might feel precisely as you do. . . ."

27. Hay to White, May 22, 1903, HWhP:LC; Hay to Roosevelt, July 1, [1903], JHP:LC; Roosevelt to Hay, July 1, 1903, Elting E. Morison, ed., *The Letters of Theodore Roosevelt,* 8 vols. (Cambridge, Mass., 1951–54), 3:508; Hay to Simon Wolf, June 24, 1903, printed in the *New York Times,* June 26, 1903, p. 1, col. 1.

28. Telegram, Chargé Riddle to Hay, July 16, 1903, Theodore Roosevelt Papers, Manuscript Division, Library of Congress (hereafter cited as TRP:LC); Hay to Roosevelt, July 16, 1903, JHP:LC; Hay to Straus, July 17, 1903, OSP:LC.

29. See Hay to Roosevelt, July 1, [1903], JHP:LC; ibid., July 3, 1903; B. F. Barnes to Hay, July 15, 1903, TRP:LC; draft speech, n.d., JHP:LC.

30. Henry Adams to Clara S. Hay, July 10, 1903, HAP:MHS; Hay to Roosevelt, July 16, 1903, JHP:LC.

31. *Unveiling and Consecration of the John Hay Memorial Window at the Temple of the Reform Congregation of Keneseth Israel (Philadelphia, Sunday, December 2, 1906).* (Copy in the Jewish History Room, New York Public Library.) There were also laudatory addresses by Oscar Straus, Elihu Root, and Andrew White. In addition, there were two poems written for the occasion.

32. *Jewish American* [Detroit], June 14, 1907, p. 5. I am indebted to Professor Robert A. Rockaway for this information. *A Memorial Address from the Jews of America and*

Great Britain to Mrs. Clara Hay in Honor of her Deceased Husband John Hay United States Secretary of State, September 20, 1898, to July 1, 1905 (n.p., n.d.). (Copy in the New York Public Library.)

33.   Oscar S. Straus, *The American Spirit* (New York, 1913), pp. 376–78.

34.   Newspaper clipping, "Benevolence," n.d., scrapbook, JHP:LC. Sentiments such as these led one newspaper to comment in praise that there had been many eloquent comments on behalf of the migrating blacks, "but nothing more appealing than the brief speech of Colonel John Hay. . . ." (Newspaper clipping, pencilled *The Cleveland Leader*, ibid.) Howells also praised the speech. (Howells to Hay, May 2, 1879, Howells, ed., *Life in Letters of Howells*, 1:268–69.)

35.   Nicolay and Hay, *Abraham Lincoln*, 1:314, 312; 6:452, 469. It has not been determined who wrote which chapters of the work. The authors' preface states that the biography was "in the fullest sense, and in every part a joint work." (Ibid., 1:xiv.) Both men read and apparently approved the entire manuscript. The style in the chapters dealing with slavery and Negroes appears to be Hay's. Dennett suggests that Hay was the primary author, while Nicolay was primarily a research man. (Dennett, *John Hay*, pp. 137–38.)

36.   "Hay as Philanthropist," *New York Times*, July 5, 1905, p. 7, col. 1. Martha L. Sternberg, *George Miller Sternberg: A Biography* (Chicago, 1920), pp. 254–55, 228–36, 142.

37.   John Hay, untitled manuscript speech, [1892], JHP:LC.

38.   Hay to [Clara S. Hay], October 7 and October 13, [1898], ibid.; Hay to White, November 21, 1898, HWhP:LC; Hay to Adelbert Hay, July 1, 1900, JHP:LC; Hay to Roosevelt, August 2, 1903, JHP:LC.

39.   Dennett, *John Hay*, p. 157. The "Five of Hearts" was a secret group of friends including the Hays, the Henry Adamses, and Clarence King. The group had its own set of teacups and distinctive stationery.

40.   Booker T. Washington to Hay, November 22, 1898, JHP:LC; Hay to Washington, February 5, 1905, Booker T. Washington Papers, Manuscript Division, Library of Congress; clipping, "A Worthy Memorial to a Great President," n.d., TRP:LC. In 1897 the name of the school was shortened to The John Hay Industrial School. Clipping, "John Hay

Industrial School," pencilled *Washington Post,* January 30, 1897, scrapbook, JHP:LC.

41. Hay to George B. Cortelyou, June 10, 1902, TRP:LC.

42. Adams to Hay, June 8, 1882, AFP:MHS. For some of the arrangements Adams made, see Adams to Robert Cunliffe, May 29, 1882, and July 9, 1882, ibid. Adams and Mrs. Adams also instructed the Hays in great detail about protocol. Mrs. Hay, for example, was advised to wear woolens or calico for daytime and long gowns in the evening. (Adams to Hay, May 25, 1882, ibid., and Marian Adams to Clara S. Hay, June 29, 1882, ibid.)

43. Hay to Howells, March 26, [1882], WDHP:HU; Hay to Adams, September 17, 1882, TFDP:MHS.

44. Hay to Stone, February 9, [1883], WadFP:LC; Hay to James R. Lowell, March 18, [1883], John Hay Papers, Houghton Library, Harvard University.

45. Hay to Mrs. Amasa Stone, April 8, 1883, WadFP:LC.

46. Adams to Hay, November 19, 1883, AFP:MHS.

47. Ibid., April 6, 1884; [Hay to Clara S. Hay], May 22, 1884, WadFP:LC; Adams to Cunliffe, January 15, 1887, AFP:MHS; Hay to Adams, May 12, [1887], AFP:MHS.

48. Hay to Adams, August 25, [1887], AFP:MHS.

49. Copy or draft letter, Hay to Sackville West, n.d., JHP:BU; Adams to Elizabeth Cameron, May 2/5, 1889, AFP:MHS. When Hay was mentioned for the London legation, Henry White, the secretary of the legation, wrote to say that such an appointment "would be too delightful for us and your many other friends here, I need hardly say." (White to Hay, December 14, 1888, JHP:BU.)

50. Hay to Adams, June 11, [1888], AFP:MHS.

51. Clara S. Hay to Mrs. Amasa Stone, June 23, 1889, WadFP:LC.

52. The other trip was a whirlwind vacation in 1896 with his daughter, Elizabeth Warder, Henry Adams, and Bay Lodge. The trip was so strenuous that, in Adams' opinion, it nearly killed Hay. (Adams to Rebecca Gilman Rae, July 23, 1896, Harold D. Cater, ed., *Henry Adams and His Friends: A Collection of His Unpublished Letters* [Boston, 1947], p. 375.)

53. Anna Roosevelt to Hay, January 2, 1887, JHP:LC; Rudyard Kipling to Hay, February 16, 1892, JHP:BU; Kipling to Clara S. Hay, April 24, 1907, JHP:BU. For evidence of

additional contacts between Hay and Kipling, see C. E. Carrington, *The Life of Rudyard Kipling* (Garden City, N.Y.), pp. 173, 198, 208, 214, 226.

54. Cecil Spring Rice to Hay, May 7, 1898, JHP:LC; John Hay, "A Partnership in Beneficence," *Addresses*, p. 79; Hay to Henry Cabot Lodge, May 25, 1898, HCLP:MHS; newspaper clipping, London *Times*, September 9, 1898, enclosed in Hay to William R. Day, September 9, 1898, Department of State, Diplomatic Despatches: Great Britain; Hay to Henry White, March 18, 1900, in Allan Nevins, *Henry White: Thirty Years of American Diplomacy* (New York and London, 1930), p. 151; Perkins, *The Great Rapprochement*, pp. 81–82.

CHAPTER IV

1. Clarence King, "John Hay," *Scribners Monthly* 7 (April, 1874): 736.

2. Hay to John Bigelow, April 27, 1868, Dennett, ed., *Lincoln and the Civil War*, p. 290.

3. Hay to John Jay, August 16, 1869, Jay Family Collection, Manuscript Division, Butler Library, Columbia University; Hay to Helen L. Hay, April 14, 1869, TDP:LC; Hay to Bigelow, July 21, 1870, JHP:BU; Hay to Jessie L. Bross, Christmas Eve, 1869, TDP:LC. The themes outlined in this paragraph run very strongly through Hay's correspondence during this period and can also be found in *Castilian Days*.

4. Hay, *Castilian Days* p. 351; Hay to Charles E. Hay, May 6, 1870, TDP:LC. For more on the *Aspinwall* case, see James M. Callahan, *Cuba and International Relations: A Historical Study in American Diplomacy* (Baltimore, 1899), pp. 395, 395n.

5. Hay, *Castilian Days*, p. 402; Hay to Charles Sumner, May 9, 1870, TDP:LC. That Hay's optimism was largely a continuation of the democratic fervor he had developed during the Civil War and in his previous European assignments is clearly seen in the emotional concluding chapter of *Castilian Days*, "Necessity of the Republic."

6. Hay, *Castilian Days*, pp. 256, 366, 369–70, 406. See also pp. 413–14.

7. Ibid., p. 322. Castelar first caught Hay's attention when he delivered an address to the Cortes in June, 1870, in which

he paid tribute to Lincoln and called for the abolition of slavery in Cuba. Hay, who heard the speech, responded with a gracious letter (perhaps of questionable tact from one in his position), in which he referred to the Spaniard as "the greatest orator of our time." (Hay to Castelar, June 22, 1870, TDP:LC.) In later years, Hay wrote a number of flattering letters of this nature as a matter of course or political necessity, but he genuinely admired Castelar and spoke glowingly of him in private letters. See Hay to Mrs. S. Hooper, June 27, 1870, TDP:LC, and Hay to Jessie L. Bross, June 20, 1870, TDP:LC.

8. Hay to Charles E. Hay, July 25, 1870, TDP:LC; Hay to his family, August 10, 1870, ibid. Hay blamed the war on Louis Napoleon of France.

9. Clipping, "The Republic in Spain," *New York Tribune* (penciled date, February 12, 1873), JHP:LC; Adee to Hay, February 15, 1873, JHP:BU. Republican rule replaced that of Amadeo, the Duke of Aosta and son of the Duke of Genoa, who had served an unhappy two years as a constitutional monarch. On Amadeo's accession, Hay had written an anguished poem, "The Surrender of Spain," in which he predicted the monarch's eventual overthrow. (*Complete Poetical Works*, pp. 38–40.)

10. Clipping, "Spanish Affairs," *New York Tribune* (penciled date, March 29, 1873), JHP:LC; clipping, "The War Faction in Spain," *New York Tribune* (penciled date, August or September 10, 1873), ibid. See also newspaper clipping, "Injustice to the Spanish Republic," (penciled date, September 25, 1873), ibid. The monarchists did, in fact, receive outside aid, but, despite their desires, no European state, including England, accorded them even belligerent rights.

11. Newspaper clipping, "The Hopes of the Alfonists," [1875?], ibid.

12. Norman Graebner, *Ideas and Diplomacy: Readings in the Intellectual Tradition of American Foreign Policy* (New York, 1964), p. 268; Hay to Mrs. John Bigelow, February 27, 1868, JHP:BU; J. C. S. Abbott, "The Pope and the Temporal Sovereignty," *Putnam's Magazine* 11 (April, 1868): 463; Hay to William Douglas O'Connor, April 10, [1868], JHP:BU.

13. Hay to Nicolay, January 30, 1870, TDP:LC. See also Hay to Bigelow, July 21, 1870, JHP:BU. For a discussion of

Spanish-American relations during this period, with emphasis on the Cuban problem, see Callahan, *Cuba and International Relations*, pp. 364–452, and French E. Chadwick, *The Relations of the United States and Spain: Diplomacy* (New York, 1909), pp. 287–410. The most recent account of the Cuban revolution is Hugh Thomas, *Cuba: The Pursuit of Freedom* (New York, 1971), pp. 245–70.

14.   Hay to Charles E. Hay, March 10, 1870, TDP:LC; Hay to Edward King, June 18, 1870, ibid.

15.   Clipping, "Spanish Policy in Cuba," *New York Tribune* (pencilled date, November 7, 1873), JHP:LC.

16.   Clipping, "The Massacre of Santiago," *New York Tribune* (pencilled date, November 9, 1873), ibid.

17.   Clipping, "The Massacre of Santiago," ibid.; clipping, "Our Duty in Cuba" (pencilled date, November 14, 1873), ibid. Hay did, however, call for a continuing show of naval force.

18.   Clipping, "The Cuban Meeting," *New York Tribune* (pencilled date, November 18, 1873), ibid.; clipping, "The Peacemakers," *New York Tribune* (pencilled date, December 23, 1873), ibid. Hay gave great editorial praise to Castelar for his constructive role in settling the dispute.

19.   Clipping, "The Spaniards in Cuba," *New York Tribune* (pencilled date, March 24, 1874), ibid.

20.   Hay to William Dean Howells, November 5, 1879, WDHP:HU.

21.   Hay's efforts on behalf of Bret Harte are detailed in chapter 1. He also appointed James Ford Rhodes consul at Rouen. (Hay to Rhodes, August 10, 1880, Allan Nevins Collection, Manuscript Division, Butler Library, Columbia University.)

22.   Hay to Stone, December 8, 1879, JHP:BU; Hay to Albert Rhodes, June 18, [1881], JHP:LC.

23.   Hay to Bigelow, July 21, 1870, JHP:BU; "Hawai," (pencilled date, 1884), Carl Schurz Papers, Manuscript Division, Library of Congress. Hay's manuscript poem is unclear in places, and Tyler Dennett's translation differs slightly from mine. See Dennett, *John Hay*, p. 276.

24.   For Adams' reports on conditions in the Pacific islands, see Adams to Hay, September 15/23, 1890, JHP:BU; Adams to Hay, November 16, 1890, Cater, ed., *Henry Adams and His Friends*, pp. 213–20; and Hay to Adams, December 30, 1890, HAP:MHS. Hay to Reid, May 16, 1893, WRP:LC; Hay

to Adams, January 1, 1894, HAP:MHS.

25. Hay to Reid, May 16, 1893, WRP:LC.

26. Hay's friendship with Spring Rice was especially close; indeed, they were fast friends by tne end of 1887. See Spring Rice to Daisy Spring Rice, December 15, 1887, in Stephen Gwynn, *The Letters and Friendships of Sir Cecil Spring Rice: A Record,* 2 vols. (London, 1929), 1:81.

27. Walter LaFeber, *The New Empire: An Interpretation of American Expansion, 1860–1898* (Ithaca, N.Y., 1963).

28. Roosevelt to Anna Roosevelt Cowles, January 26, 1898, Morison, ed., *Letters of Theodore Roosevelt,* 1:511.

29. Smalley's sentimental Anglophilia is evident in his letters to the Duchess of Sutherland. In one, for example, he expressed his regret at having to return to the United States, adding that his mind turned "slowly to American politics or to anything American except a friend or two." (Smalley to the Duchess of Sutherland, October 12, 1898, George Washburne Smalley Papers, Manuscript Division, Library of Congress.) For Hay's views of English (and French) literature see Hay to Howells, December 31, 1881, WDHP:HU. Hay's low opinions of the Prince of Wales are found in Hay to Stone, January 25, [1883], and April 26, 1883, WadFP:LC. Hay also criticized British politics and diplomacy on occasion. See, for example, Hay to Adams, May 16, [1884], HAP:MHS, and Hay to Reid, February 15, 1896, WRP:LC.

30. Hay to Adams, May 28, 1894, HAP:MHS. (Hay's personal relations with Bayard remained friendly, however.) Hay, *Addresses,* pp. 63–65. Henry White was so furious at the London Society for tactlessly scheduling the banquet after Hay's arrival that he refused to be present. Hay, however, decided to attend, Mrs. Hay explaining that "it might look churlish" if he did not. White to Lodge, April 20, 1897, HCLP:MHS; Clara S. Hay to Mrs. Amasa Stone, May 9, [1897], WadFP:LC.

31. Hay to McKinley, May 9, 1897, WMcKP:LC. White confirmed Hay's account, although he timed Bayard's remarks at a precise forty-seven minutes. (White to Lodge, May 14, 1897, HCLP:MHS.)

32. Hay to Lodge, May 9, 1897, HCLP:MHS.

33. Hay to John Sherman, May 12, 1897, No. 33, U. S. Department of State, Diplomatic Despatches: Great Britain.

34.   Hay to Sherman, September 23, 1897, ibid., No. 123. In December, Hay sent another spate of similarly optimistic dispatches.

35.   For an elaboration of these themes, see Perkins, *The Great Rapprochement.*

36.   Hay to Adams, May 28/June 4, 1897, HAP:MHS; ibid., May 24, 1897; ibid., July 25, 1897. Such matters upset Hay partly because he was simply not used to an eight-hour day. See Clara S. Hay to Mrs. Amasa Stone, April 17, 1897, WadFP:LC.

37.   For an excellent and detailed discussion of the dispute up to McKinley's administration, see Charles C. Tansill, *Canadian American Relations, 1875–1911* (New Haven, Toronto, and London, 1943), pp. 267–352.

38.   See U. S. Department of State, *Papers Relating to the Foreign Relations of the United States, 1897,* pp. 261–80; Hay to Sherman, May 1, 1897, No. 14, U. S. Department of State, Diplomatic Despatches: Great Britain; Sherman to Hay, May 6, 1897, U. S. Department of State, Diplomatic Instructions: Great Britain, 32:32.

39.   Sherman to Hay, May 10, 1897, U. S. Department of State, *Foreign Relations, 1897,* pp. 280–90. In another dispatch Sherman ordered Hay to cable the State Department immediately after he presented the note. (Sherman to Hay, May 10, 1897, U. S. Department of State, Diplomatic Instructions: Great Britain, 32:87).

40.   Telegram, Hay to Sherman, May 20, 1897, U. S. Department of State, Diplomatic Despatches: Great Britain; telegram, Sherman to Hay, May 21, 1897, U. S. Department of State, Diplomatic Instructions: Great Britain, 32:104. "Intention was to present instruction . . . in advance of Foster's arrival," Sherman cabled sharply. "He sailed yesterday. Present instruction at once." Hay took the dispatch to the Foreign Office the next day.

41.   Hay to Adams, May 24, 1897, HAP:MHS; Adams to [Hay], May 25, 1897, ibid.

42.   Telegram, Sherman to Hay, July 1, 1897, U. S. Department of State, Diplomatic Instructions: Great Britain, 32:156–57; Hay to Sherman, July 2, 1897, U. S. Department of State, Diplomatic Despatches: Great Britain.

43.   "England and the Seals," *New York Tribune,* July 14, 1897, p. 2, col. 3. (The following day the *Tribune* editorially supported the American position.) Hay to Sherman, July 16,

1897, No. 70, U. S. Department of State, Diplomatic Despatches: Great Britain. Hay to McKinley, July 16, 1897, WMcKP:LC. In fact, the printed dispatch did have adverse repercussions among British officials. See Wilfred Laurier to John W. Foster, July 16, 1897, John W. Foster Papers, Manuscript Division, Library of Congress (hereafter cited as JWFP:LC).

44. Marquis of Salisbury to Hay, July 28, 1897, U. S. Department of State, *Foreign Relations, 1897*, p. 300; Hay to Salisbury, July 29, 1897, ibid., p. 301.

45. White to J. Addison Porter, August 31, 1897, HWhP:LC, lbc. White went to great lengths to dispel Foster's public claims that he had convinced Britain to negotiate.

46. See the correspondence in U. S. Department of State, *Foreign Relations, 1897*, pp. 303–5; Hay to McKinley, September 25, 1897, JHP:BU.

47. Hay to Sherman, September 25, 1897, U. S. Department of State, *Foreign Relations, 1897*, p. 305; Hay to Foster, October 18, 1897, JWFP:LC; (see also Hay to [Clara S. Hay], October 1, 1897, JHP:LC); Hay to McKinley, October 6, 1897, WMcKP:LC. Henry White, in a letter to Hay, placed the blame squarely on Foster's shoulders. (White to Hay, October 11, 1897, HWhP:LC.)

48. Telegram, Hay to Sherman, December 25, 1897, U. S. Department of State, Diplomatic Despatches: Great Britain; copy, Salisbury to White, February 11, 1898, ibid.

49. John W. Foster, *Diplomatic Memoirs*, 2 vols. (New York and Boston, 1909), 2:189. One outgrowth of the seal dispute further demonstrated Hay's concern with correct manners. The tribunal of 1893 had decided the United States was wrong in hindering the pelagic sealers thus making the American government liable for damages. Congress, however, repeatedly refused to appropriate any money for damages, even after a joint Anglo-American commission agreed on a sum. Hay regretted the commission's action, but he thought the award should be paid. "It seems to me now a debt of honor," he explained to Foster. "The luck is against us and to kick would be discreditable." (Hay to Foster, December 27, 1897, JWFP:LC.) In the midst of war preparations in 1898, Hay prevailed upon Senator Lodge to drop his opposition, and in June, 1898, the full amount was paid. (Hay to Lodge, April 5, 1898, HCLP:MHS.)

CHAPTER V

1.   John A. Garraty, *Henry Cabot Lodge* (New York, 1953), p. 180.

2.   According to Ernest Samuels, Adams' "house was now a hotbed of Cuban intrigue." Not only was Adams' house connected to Hay's, but Adams also expressed his views to Hay in letters from the scene of the revolution. See Ernest Samuels, *Henry Adams: The Major Phase* (Cambridge, Mass., 1964), p. 163, and Cater, ed., *Henry Adams and His Friends*, p. 336 and elsewhere.

    Clarence King published a passionate article in *Forum* magazine, calling for Cuban freedom. See "Shall Cuba Be Free?" *Forum* 20 (September, 1895): 50–65. See also Henry White's correspondence with Henry Cabot Lodge in 1895, HCLP:MHS.

3.   Hay to [Adams], September 3, 1895, HAP:MHS. Adams to Hay, October 28, 1896, Cater, ed., *Henry Adams and His Friends*, p. 393. If Hay replied to Adams the reply is no longer extant, and since the Hay-Adams correspondence during these months appears to be complete, it is quite possible that Hay did not reply, at least not in writing.

4.   Adams to Elizabeth Cameron, February 18, 1898, Ford, ed., *Letters of Henry Adams*, 2:150n.

5.   Hay did send his condolences to the president on February 20. (Hay to McKinley, February 20, 1898, WMcKP:LC.)

6.   Clara S. Hay to Mrs. Amasa Stone, March 4, 1898, WadFP:LC.

7.   Adams to [Cameron ?], March 5, 1898, HAP:MHS.

8.   Clara S. Hay to Mrs. Amasa Stone, March 7, 1898, WadFP:LC.

9.   Roosevelt to Brooks Adams, March 21, 1898, Morison, ed., *Letters of Roosevelt*, 1:797; White to Hay, February 21, 1898, HWhP:LC.

10.   Hay to [Clara S. Hay], March 30, 1898, JHP:LC; ibid., April 2, [1898]. Mrs. Hay was apprehensive about the possible outbreak of war, and when it broke out she attempted to dissuade her son from enlisting. "I would not object if it were our own country that was in danger," she wrote to her mother, "but I do not feel that he ought to sacrifice his life for the benefit of that miserable island of Cuba." (Clara S. Hay to Mrs. Amasa Stone, April 21, [1898], Wad FP:LC.)

11. Roosevelt to Brooks Adams, March 21, 1898, Morison, ed., *Letters of Roosevelt,* I: 798. Pratt, in *Expansionists of 1898,* stresses the pacifism of business. LaFeber, in *The New Empire,* has called into question some of Pratt's long-accepted conclusions in this respect. Hay's attitude, although difficult to define precisely, appears to lend more support to Pratt's thesis than to LaFeber's.

12. Hay to McKinley, February 10, 1898, WMcKP:LC. McKinley's·speech can be found in *Speeches and Addresses of William McKinley from March, 1897, to May 30, 1900* (New York, 1900), pp. 66–67.

13. Hay to Sherman, August 20, 1897, No. 107, U.S. Department of State, Diplomatic Despatches: Great Britain; enclosure, "Cuba As It Is," *Daily Chronicle,* August 20, 1897.

14. Stewart L. Woodford to McKinley, August 10, 1897, WMcKP:LC.

15. Copy, Hay to Herbert W. Bowen, November 23, 1897, JHP:LC. Hay also commented to Bowen, "Cuba seems to me lost to Spain."

16. Hay, "Speech before the American Society in London, Thanksgiving Day Banquet, November 25, 1897," *Addresses,* pp. 68–69. Five days later Hay commented to the Royal Society that his mission was "to do what I can to draw closer the bonds that bind together the two Anglo-Saxon peoples." (*Addresses,* p. 85.)

17. Sherman to Hay, June 30, 1897, U. S. Department of State, Diplomatic Instructions: Great Britain, 32: 155–56.

18. Woodford to McKinley, August 10, 1897, WMcKP:LC.

19. Hay to McKinley, October 6, 1897, ibid.

20. Hay to Sherman, October 15, 1897, No. 143, U. S. Department of State, Diplomatic Despatches: Great Britain; enclosure, clipping from the *Morning Post,* October 15, 1897. See also Hay to Sherman, October 26, 1897, ibid., No. 155.

21. Hay to Sherman, March 26, 1898, ibid., No. 331; enclosure, clipping from the *Daily Chronicle,* March 26, 1898. Within two weeks Hay sent at least five more dispatches containing English expressions of sympathy for the position of the United States. One of them, No. 334, March 29, 1898, included a poem by England's poet laureate (and Hay's personal friend) Alfred Austin which, Hay felt, expressed "the general desire for a closer relationship between the two countries." The poem, "A Voice from the West," voiced strong attachment to America.

22.   Hay is paraphrased in St. Loe Strachey, *The Adventure of Living*, p. 391.

23.   Telegram, Sherman to Hay, April 5, 1898, U. S. Department of State, Diplomatic Instructions: Great Britain, 32:453; Hay to Lodge, April 15, 1898, HCLP:MHS.

24.   Hay to Lodge, April 5, 1898, HCLP:MHS. In his letter Hay asked Lodge to take certain legislative steps that would help improve relations with England, and the senator acceded to Hay's requests. This was perhaps the last time Hay prevailed in a contest with the senator.

25.   Hay, "Speech to the American Society in London, July 4, 1898," *Addresses*, pp. 70–72.

26.   Hay, "A Partnership in Beneficence," April 21, 1898, ibid., pp. 77–80.

27.   Lodge to Hay, April 21, 1898, HCLP:MHS.

28.   Hay to Sherman, April 21, 1898, No. 362, U. S. Department of State, Diplomatic Despatches: Great Britain.

29.   Hay, "A Partnership in Beneficence," *Addresses*, p. 79.

30.   Hay to Lodge, May 25, 1898, HCLP:MHS; newspaper clipping, London *Times*, September 9, 1898, enclosed in Hay to Day, September 9, 1898, No. 517, U. S. Department of State, Diplomatic Despatches: Great Britain.

31.   Hay, "Speech to the American Society in London, July 4, 1898," *Addresses*, p. 73.

32.   Hay, "A Partnership in Beneficence," ibid., p. 77.

33.   Hay, "Speech to the American Society in London, July 4, 1898," ibid., p. 72.

34.   Bertha A. Reuter, *Anglo-American Relations During the Spanish American War* (New York, 1924), p. 157.

35.   Hay to Sherman, April 23, 1898, No. 364, U. S. Department of State, Diplomatic Despatches: Great Britain; Adee to Hay, April 27, 1898, U.S. Department of State, Diplomatic Instructions: Great Britain, 32:474; Hay to Day, May 4, 1898, U. S. Department of State, Diplomatic Despatches: Great Britain.

36.   "The American Ambassador," *Saturday Review* [London] 86 (August 20, 1898): 231; Balfour is quoted in Hay to [Clara S. Hay], August 29, 1898, JHPL:LC; London *Times*, July 3, 1905, p. 10.

37.   Clipping, London *Times*, September 9, 1898, enclosed in Hay to Day, September 9, 1898, No. 517, U. S. Department of State, Diplomatic Despatches: Great Britain.

38.   Henry Adams, *The Education of Henry Adams* (Modern Library edition; New York, 1931), p. 363.

39.   Hay to Arthur James Balfour, August 22, 1898, Arthur

James Balfour Papers, Manuscript Division, British Museum (hereafter cited as AJBP:BM).

40. [Hay to Clara S. Hay], August 29, 1898, JHP:LC.
41. Hay to Sherman, June 17, 1897, U. S. Department of State, No. 61, Diplomatic Despatches: Great Britain; enclosure, clipping, London *Times*, June 17, 1897.
42. Hay to McKinley, June 18, 1897, WMcKP:LC. ·
43. Hay to Clara S. Hay, March 22, 1898, JHP:LC; Cecil Spring Rice to Hay, April 30, 1898, ibid.; Hay to Day, May 3, 1898, U. S. Department of State, Diplomatic Despatches: Great Britain. The State Department sent a copy of Hay's dispatch to the president. Hay to Spring Rice, May 5, 1898, in Gwynn, *Letters and Friendships of Sir Cecil Spring Rice*, 2:247.
44. Spring Rice to Hay, May 7, 1898, JHP:LC.
45. Newspaper clipping, "The Secret of Power" (University of Pennsylvania baccalaureate service, June, 1898), George Dewey Papers, Manuscript Division, Library of Congress.
46. Hay to Day, July 14, 1898, No. 454, U. S. Department of State, Diplomatic Despatches: Great Britain. Hay's Anglophilia had, in fact, blinded him somewhat to German sensibilities. See Lester B. Shipee, "Germany and the Spanish-American War," *American Historical Review* 30 (July, 1925): 762.
47. Pratt, in *Expansionists of 1898*, argues the former thesis, while LaFeber, in *The New Empire*, pp. 360–62, and Thomas J. McCormick, in *China Market: America's Quest for Informal Empire* (Chicago, 1967), pp. 107–8, argue the latter.
48. Adams to [Hay], May 5, 1898, HAP:MHS.
49. Hay to Day, May 10, 1898, No. 386, U. S. Department of State, Diplomatic Despatches: Great Britain. See also, telegrams, Hay to Day, May 8, May 9, and May 10, 1898, ibid.
50. Adams to Hay, May 17, 1898, Ford, ed., *Letters of Henry Adams*, 2:180; Hay to Adams, May 27, 1898, HAP:MHS.
51. Hay to Day, June 17, 1898, No. 434, U. S. Department of State, Diplomatic Despatches: Great Britain; ibid., June 15, 1898, No. 432.
52. Strachey, *The Adventure of Living*, pp. 393-94. For Hay's official response, see Hay to Day, July 18, 1898, No. 460, U.S. Department of State, Diplomatic Despatches: Great Britain.
53. Spring Rice to Hay, July 23, 1898, JHP:LC.
54. Hay to Lodge, July 27, 1898, HCLP:MHS.

55.   Draft dispatch, Hay to Day, July 28, 1898, JHP:LC. In the actual cable, Hay added a final paragraph stating that the British wanted the United States to retain the islands or at least to insist on an option in case Spain later sold them. Balfour, through Spring Rice, had conveyed this information to Hay; it was not in the original draft. See A. Whitney Griswold, *The Far Eastern Policy of the United States* (New York, 1938), p. 19.

56.   Copy, Frank Karuth to Hay, May 17, 1898, enclosed in Hay to Day, May 18, 1898, No. 398, U. S. Department of State, Diplomatic Despatches: Great Britain. Hay also forwarded to Day a pamphlet written by Karuth in 1894 entitled, "A New Centre of Gold Production."

57.   Hay to Day, May 18, 1898, No. 398, ibid. Karuth appears to have been well known at the American embassy. On several occasions he requested American aid to protect the employees of his company who were in the Philippines, requests that were forwarded to the State Department. Karuth continued his correspondence with the embassy after Hay's departure, and he also maintained his acquaintance with Hay. He congratulated Hay when the peace treaty was signed in February, 1899, and informed him of his plans to establish a new corporation in the Philippines. Hay no doubt wished the new enterprise well. See Hay to Day, September 7, 1898, ibid., No. 520; Frank Karuth to Hay, February 8, 1899, JHP:LC.

58.   Hay to Balfour, April 9, 1898, AJBP:BM.

59.   Hay marked these passages with a single line, those quoted below with a double line.

60.   Sir Andrew Clarke, *Sir Stamford Raffles and the Malay States* (an address delivered May 27, 1898, before the Royal Institution of Great Britain). The pamphlet is in JHP:LC. It was transmitted to Washington in Hay to Day, July 8, 1898, No. 447, U. S. Department of State, Diplomatic Despatches: Great Britain, but was removed by the meticulous John Bassett Moore for study. Moore then asked Hay to send another copy, if possible. This suggests that Clarke's pamphlet received rather careful attention in the State Department.

61.   Hay to Day, July 29, 1898, No. 476, U. S. Department of State, Diplomatic Despatches: Great Britain; enclosure, Benjamin Kidd, "The Control of the Tropics," London *Times*, July 29, 1898.

62.   Hay to Bigelow, September 5, 1898, JHP:BU.
63.   Lodge to Hay, September 30, 1898, HCLP:MHS.
64.   See Day to Hay, October 6, 1898, U. S. Department of State, *Foreign Relations, 1898*, pp. 918–22.
65.   John Foreman, *The Philippine Islands* (London, 1899).
66.   Diary entry, October 7, 1898, H. Wayne Morgan, ed., *Making Peace with Spain: The Diary of Whitelaw Reid, September–December, 1898* (Austin, 1965), pp. 63–64; Day to Hay, October 9, 1898, U. S. Department of State, *Foreign Relations, 1898*, pp. 925–26; White to Hay, October 14, 1898, HWhP:LC, Ibc.
67.   Hay to Day, October 14, 1898, U. S. Department of State, *Foreign Relations, 1898*, p. 928; Stanford Newel to Hay, October 14, 1898, JHP:LC; Reid to Hay, October 16, 1898, WRP:LC.
68.   Hay to Day, October 26, 1898, U. S. Department of State, *Foreign Relations, 1898*, p. 935.
69.   Ibid., October 28, 1898, p. 937.
70.   Ibid., personal telegram, p. 938; ibid., telegram, November 13, 1898, pp. 948–49; Hay to Day, November 14, 1898, TDP:LC. In the note dated November 12 Hay contended that the United States had an obligation to the people of the Philippines.
71.   Hay to White, November 21, 1898, HWhP:LC; diary entry, December 5, 1898, Morgan, ed., *Diary of Whitelaw Reid*, p. 193. Commenting on Gray's remark, Reid wrote, "this was only another of several recent instances of dislike on the part of the Senators [toward] the tone of recent dispatches from the State Department."
72.   Hay to William M. Osborne, November 29, 1898, TDP:LC; Hay to Reid, November 29, 1898, JHP:LC, lbc. Hay was, of course, incorrect about the Homestead affair which involved state militia, not federal troops.
73.   Adee to Hay, December 30, 1898, JHP:LC.
74.   Adams to [Cameron ?], January 29, 1898, HAP:MHS.
75.   Telegram, Jacob Schurman to Hay, April 4, 1899, National Archives: Record Group 59, File E739 ("Philippine Commission to the Department of State"), hereafter cited as NA:RG 59, E739; ibid., April 13, 1899; ibid., April 25, 1899. 76.
76.   Hay to McKinley, April 28, 1899, WMcKP:LC.
77.   Peter W. Stanley, "A Nation in the Making: The Philippines and the United States, 1899–1921" (Ph.D. dissertation, Harvard University, 1970), pp. 70–72.

78. Schurman to Hay, April 4, 1899, NA:RG 59, E739; Apolonari Mabini to the Philippine Commission, April 29, 1899, ibid.; telegram, Schurman to Hay, May 4, 1899, ibid. See also Schurman to Hay, May 1, 1899, ibid.

79. Mabini's statement to the Philippine Commission, May 1, 1899, ibid.; Schurman to Hay, May 1, 1899, ibid.; telegram, Schurman to Hay, May 4, 1899, ibid.; Mabini to the Philippine Commission, April 29, 1899, ibid.

80. Draft telegram (in Hay's handwriting), May 5, 1899, National Archives: Record Group 59, File E740 ("Department of State to the Philippine Commission"), hereafter cited as NA:RG 59, E740. See note 93 for Hay's plan.

81. Telegram, Schurman to Hay, May 23, 1899, NA:RG 59, E739.

82. Schurman to Hay, May 1, 1899, ibid.; Charles Denby to Hay, May 30, 1899, National Archives: Record Group 59, File E738 ("Schurman, Denby, and MacArthur to the Department of State").

83. Telegram, Schurman to Hay, June 3, 1899, NA:RG 59, E739.

84. Hay to McKinley, June 3, 1899, WMcKP:LC; telegram, Hay to Schurman, [June 5, 1899], National Archives: Record Group 59, File E743 ("Telegrams from the Department of State to the Philippine Commission").

85. Telegram, David J. Hill to Schurman, June 9, [1899], NA:RG 59, File E743.

86. Roosevelt to Hay, July 1, 1899, TRP:LC; Roosevelt to Anna Roosevelt Cowles, July 12, 1899, Morison, ed., *Letters of Roosevelt*, 2:1033.

87. Denby to Hay, July 17, 1899, NA:RG 59, E739; Hay to Denby, August 30, 1899, NA:RG 59, E740.

88. Hay to Charles Dick, September 11, 1899, JHP:LC.

89. Newspaper clipping, William A. Croffut to the *Washington Post*, n.d., enclosed in Croffut to Hay, September 25, 1899, JHP:LC.

90. Hay to Croffut, September 28, 1899, in H. Wayne Morgan, *America's Road to Empire: The War with Spain and Overseas Expansion* (New York, 1965), p. 112. A few days later Hay told an audience, "this country is worthy the devotion of every youth in it, worthy to live for, fight for, and if God so wills, to die for." (Speech to the citizens of Quincy, Illinois, October 6, 1899, WMcKP:LC.)

91.   George S. Batcheller to Hay, April 3, 1899, enclosed in Hay to Schurman, March 4, 1899, NA:RG 59, E740; John R. MacArthur to Hay, May 5, 1899, NA:RG 59, E739; Denby to Hay, June 21, 1899, NA:RG 59, E739.

92.   James Bryce to White, December 5, 1898, HWhP:LC; Gilder to Hay, January 25, 1899, JHP:BU; Hay to Gilder, January 28, 1899, RWGP:NYPL. Hay professed to "entirely agree with the advice he gives in his private note to you," the advice being a tactical suggestion to establish a secure center from which to extend control in an orderly manner.

93.   James Bryce, "British Experience in the Government of Colonies," *Century* 35 (March, 1899): 718–28. Hay's plan was as follows:

You are authorized to propose that under the military power of the President, pending the action of Congress, government of the Philippines shall consist of a Governor General appointed by the President[,] a cabinet appointed by the Governor General, a general advisory Council selected by the people[,] the qualification of electors to be carefully considered and determined and Governor General to have absolute veto. Judiciary strong and independent: principal judges appointed by the President; in Cabinet and judiciary natives[,] American[,] or both chosen for fitness. (Draft telegram [Hay's handwriting], Hay to Schurman, May 5, 1899, NA:RG 59, E740.)

94.   Newspaper clipping, Croffut to the *Washington Post,* n.d., enclosed in Croffut to Hay, September 25, 1899, JHP:LC.

95.   Hay, *Addresses,* pp. 243–59.

96.   *New York Times,* October 27, 1904, p. 5, col. 2.

97.   "Suggested remarks by John Hay, July 8, 1900," WMcKP:LC.

CHAPTER VI

1.   *New York Times,* August 23, 1898, p. 7, col. 2; ibid., August 10, 1898, p. 6, col. 2; ibid., August 21, 1898, p. 17, col. 1; *Manchester Guardian,* as quoted in the *New York Times,* August 23, 1898, p. 7, col. 2. Two works mentioning Hay's alleged lack of knowledge are George Kennan, *American Diplomacy 1900–1950* (Chicago, 1951), p. 27, and R. G. Neale, *Great Britain and United States Expansion: 1898–1900* (East Lansing, 1966), p. 200.

2.   Clipping, "A Word About Mr. Delong," *New York Tribune* (pencilled date, February 8, 1873), JHP:LC.

3.   Edward H. House to Hay, February 6, 1897, ibid.; Hay to House, March 25, 1897, JHP:BU; Hay to Rockhill, April 10, 1897, William W. Rockhill Papers, Houghton Library, Harvard University (hereafter cited as WWRP:HU).

4.   Hay to Paul Dana, May 18, 1899, JHP:LC, lbc.

5.   Hay to Edwin Conger, March 13, 1899, U. S. Department of State, Record Group 77, Diplomatic Instructions: China 5:653–54. Adee to Conger, August 24, 1899, ibid.: 6:14–16.

6.   Hay to Conger, October 12, 1898, ibid.; 5:608–9; ibid., December 15, 1899, 6:34; ibid., July 15, 1899, p. 6.

7.   See the following instructions from Hay to Conger: April 3, 1899; February 2, 1899; March 14, 1899; April 27, 1899; July 14, 1899; and July 15, 1899; all ibid., vols. 5 and 6. See also Marilyn B. Young, *The Rhetoric of Empire: American China Policy 1895–1901* (Cambridge, Mass., 1968), pp. 110–12. For Wu's fears and Hay's reaction, see Hay to Conger, July 26, 1899, JHP:LC, lbc.

8.   Memorandum, Rockhill to Hay, August 28, 1899, JHP:LC.

9.   Lord Charles Beresford to Hay, November 20, 1898, ibid.; Archibald R. Colquhoun to Hay, January 12, 1899, ibid. Colquhoun mistakenly thought Beresford was among those who wanted to couple the open door and the sphere of influence ideas. Thomas J. McCormick contends that Colquhoun was a "frequent correspondent of Hay's." (*China Market*, p. 137.) There is, however only one Colquhoun letter in the Hay papers and a reference to another one.

10.   Open Door note, Hay to Choate, September 6, 1899, U. S. Department of State, *Foreign Relations, 1899*, pp. 131–33.

11.   Hay to Charlemagne Tower, January 22, 1900, JHP:LC, lbc; Hay to Choate, March 20, 1900, No. 335, U. S. Department of State, Diplomatic Instructions: Great Britain 33:373; Hay to L. Clarke Davis, March 27, 1900, Richard Harding Davis Papers, University of Virginia Library. See also Hay to Herman H. Kohlsaat, March 30, 1900, TDP:LC.

12.   Adams to Elizabeth Cameron, April 2, 1900, Ford, ed., *Letters of Henry Adams*, 2:280–81.

13.   Paul A. Varg, *The Making of a Myth: The United States and China 1897–1912* (East Lansing, 1968), pp. 24–26. Circular to the Powers, July 3, 1900, U. S. Department of State, *Foreign Relations, 1900*, p. 299.

14.   See, for example, Raymond A. Esthus, "The Changing

Concept of the Open Door, 1899–1910," *Mississippi Valley Historical Review* 46 (December, 1959): 435–54; and John K. Fairbank, *The United States and China* (rev. ed.; Cambridge, Mass., 1958), pp. 255–56.

15. Brooks Adams, "John Hay," *McClure's Magazine* 19 (June, 1902); 173–82; House to Hay, February 6, 1897, JHP:LC; Hay to Sherman, March 25, 1898, No. 325, U. S. Department of State, Diplomatic Despatches: Great Britain. See also Hay to Sherman, April 6, 1898, ibid., No. 344.

16. Salisbury to Pauncefote, January 12, 1898, cited in Charles S. Campbell, Jr., *Anglo-American Understanding, 1898–1903* (Baltimore, 1957), pp. 17–18.

17. Telegram, Hay to Conger, December 23, 1898, U. S. Department of State, *Foreign Relations, 1899*, p. 144; Pauncefote to Hay, January 8, 1899, in Dennett, *John Hay*, p. 288.

18. Hay to Adams, June 15, 1900, in Thayer, *John Hay*, 2:232–33.

19. Draft, Hay to Conger, June 10, 1900, WMcKP:LC. This cable was as much for domestic political purposes as it was for Conger's information. Hay to Foster, June 23, 1900, JHP:LC.

20. Hay to Adams, November 21, 1900, in Thayer, *John Hay*, 2:248–49.

21. White to Lodge, June 25, 1900, HCLP:MHS; Hay to Adee, September 14, 1900, JHP:LC. (When, in 1907, Henry Adams considered including this letter in the printed volumes of Hay's letter, Adee suggested that it be suppressed. See Adee to Adams, March 16, 1907, JHP:LC); Hay to Adams, July 8, 1900, Ford, ed., *Letters of Henry Adams*, 2:292–93.

22. Telegram, Hay to McKinley, September 17, 1900, JHP:LC; Hay to Reid, September 1, 1900, WRP:LC.

23. Hay to McKinley, July 18, 1901, WMcKP:LC; Rockhill to Roosevelt July 12, 1905, which included a memorandum dated December 6, 1904, WWRP:HU; Paul A. Varg, *Open Door Diplomat: The Life of W. W. Rockhill* (Urbana, Ill., 1952), pp. 48–49.

24. Hay to Arturo Cassini, April 20, 1901, JHP:LC; memorandum, attached to Rockhill to Hay, January 31, 1902, ibid.; telegrams, Hay to Tower and Hay to Conger, quoted in Hay to Choate, February 3, 1902, U. S. Department of State, Diplomatic Instructions: Great Britain, 34:88–89; memoran-

dum, n.d. [April, 1903 ?], a fragment of which is in JHP:LC, and a complete copy of which is in TDP:LC; Hay to Roosevelt, September 3, 1903, JHP:LC. See also Hay to Adee, September, 1903, JHP:LC.

25.   Hay to Roosevelt, May 4, 1903, JHP:LC, İbc; ibid., July 22, 1903; Roosevelt to Hay, July 18, 1903, TRP:LC; Hay to Roosevelt, July 22, 1903, JHP:LC; Hay to White, May 22, 1903, HWhP:LC.

26.   The text of the treaty is in U. S. Department of State, *Foreign Relations, 1903*, pp. 91–119; Raymond A. Esthus, *Theodore Roosevelt and Japan* (Seattle and London, 1968), p. 13.

27.   John A. S. Grenville and George B. Young, *Politics, Strategy, and American Diplomacy: Studies in Foreign Policy 1873–1917* (New Haven and London, 1966), p. 311.

28.   Esthus, *Roosevelt and Japan*; Eugene P. Trani, *The Treaty of Portsmouth: An Adventure in American Diplomacy* (Lexington, Ky., 1969).

29.   Hay, diary entries, February 7 and February 8, 1904, JHP:LC; Esthus, *Roosevelt and Japan*, pp. 26–27.

30.   Hay, diary entry, February 19, 1904, JHP:LC.

31.   Ibid., January 5, January 9, January 10, January 13, January 18, January 19, January 20, January 23, all 1905. The quotations are from the entry of January 13.

32.   Ibid., August 12, August 13, August 15, August 16, 1904.

33.   Ibid., March 1, 1904.

34.   Ibid., June 3, 1904.

35.   Ibid., February 8, 1904.

36.   Ibid., March 27, 1904.

37.   Alfred Hippisley, Memorandum, "The Open Door in Tyler Dunnett's [*sic*] 'John Hay,'" enclosed in Hippisley to Dunnett [*sic*], August 22, 1935, TDP:LC.

38.   See, for example, Dennett, *John Hay*, p. 323. Hay to Rockhill, July 24, [1903], WWRP:HU.

CHAPTER VII

1.   John Hays Hammond, *The Autobiography of John Hays Hammond*, 2 vols. (New York, 1935), 2:446–47. Hay met Rhodes on at least one other occasion as well, for Mrs. Hay wrote to her mother that they had attended a dinner "for Mr. Cecil Rhodes the South African who is so distin-

guished." (Clara S. Hay to Mrs. Amasa Stone, April 27, [1898], WadFP:LC.)

2.   Hammond, *Autobiography*, 2:447. Montagu White, a Boer leader active in the United States, expressed a similar opinion. "McKinley . . . ," he wrote, "whatever his private sentiments may have been, was entirely influenced by Mr. John Hay in all that concerns the South African War." (Montagu White to Peter Van Vlissingen, October 10, 1901, in John H. Ferguson, *American Diplomacy and the Boer War*, [Philadelphia, 1939], p. 207.)

3.   W. Bourke Cockran to McKinley, August 24, 1899, WMcKP:LC.

4.   Hay to McKinley, September 6, 1899, ibid.

5.   Hay to White, September 24, 1899, JHP:LC, lbc.

6.   Hay to Choate, January 3, 1900, ibid., lbc. Hay to Foster, June 23, 1900, ibid., lbc. See also Hay to White, March 18, 1900, in Nevins, *Henry White*, p. 151.

7.   Hay to White, September 24, 1899, JHP:LC, lbc.

8.   Hay to White, March 18, 1900, in Nevins, *Henry White*, p. 151. See also Hay to Adams, June 15, 1900, in Thayer, *John Hay*, 2:232–33.

9.   Richard Harding Davis to Hay, April 29, [1900], JHP:LC.

10.   Adelbert Hay to Hay, December 22, 1899, ibid.; Choate to Hay, December 22, 1899, ibid.; White to Hay, December 22, 1899, HWhP:LC; White to Hay, December 28, 1899, HWhP:LC, lbc; White to Hay, October 5, 1900, HWhP:LC.

11.   Hay to Adelbert Hay, July 1, 1900, TDP:LC. See also Hay to Adelbert Hay, October 1, 1900, JHP:LC; Hay to Adelbert Hay, October 5, 1900, JHP:LC; and Hay to Adelbert Hay, November 14, 1900, TDP:LC. For earlier letters that are strictly correct in tone, see Hay to Adelbert Hay, February 6, 1900, JHP:LC, lbc, and ibid., March 17, 1900.

12.   William Gordon to Thomas Cridler, July 26, 1901, in Ferguson, *American Diplomacy and the Boer War*, p. 173. William T. Stead to Hay, July 17, 1901, JHP:BU. Adelbert's decision to resign appears to have been a purely personal one without political overtones.

13.   Hay to Lodge, February 19, 1902, HCLP:MHS. For similar sentiments see Hay to Charles M. Walker, March 10, 1902, JHP:LC, lbc. For Hay's private relief efforts, see Roosevelt to Hay, August 20, 1900, TRP:LC, and Hay to Roosevelt, August 23, 1900, TRP:LC.

14.   Hay to Choate, August 13, 1902, Joseph H. Choate Papers,

Manuscript Division, Library of Congress (hereafter cited as JHCP:LC). Choate informed Lansdowne of Hay's attitude on August 27. (Copy, Choate to Lansdowne, August 27, 1902, JHP:LC.) The British government had declared Gordon undesirable. See Choate to Hay, August 2, 1902, JHP:LC.

15. For Hay's protests of British interference with American trade, see telegram, Hay to Choate, December 28, 1899, U. S. Department of State, Diplomatic Instructions: Great Britain, 33:312; ibid., January 2, 1900, pp. 313–14; ibid., January 3, 1900, No. 269, pp. 315–18; Hay to James McMillan, July 3, 1900, JHP:BU. Hay was slower to investigate the charges of Britain's alleged illegal activities in the United States, but his defense was strong. See Hay to McMillan, July 3, 1900, JHP:BU; Ferguson, *American Diplomacy and the Boer War*, pp. 56–64; and a draft press release, June 3, [1902], JHP:LC.

16. Alfred L. P. Dennis, "John Hay," in Samuel F. Bemis, ed., *The American Secretaries of State and Their Diplomacy*, 10 vols., 2nd ed. (New York, 1958), 9:152.

17. Adee to McKinley, September 20, 1899, in Ferguson, *American Diplomacy and the Boer War*, p. 129.

18. Hay to Edward Everett Hale, January 13, 1900, JHP:LC, lbc.

19. White to Hay, December 28, 1899, HWhP:LC, lbc.

20. Adelbert Hay to Hay, March 10, 1900, in Ferguson, *American Diplomacy and the Boer War*, p. 138.

21. Hay to White, March 10, 1900, in ibid., p. 139.

22. Dennis, "John Hay," p. 152.

23. Hay to McMillan, July 3, 1900, JHP:BU.

24. Hay to White, March 18, 1900, in Nevins, *Henry White*, pp. 151–52.

25. Ferguson, *American Diplomacy and the Boer War*, p. 142.

26. Ibid., pp. 147–51.

27. Abraham Fischer, quoted in [Walter ?] Wellman to Hay, n.d., printed in Alfred L. P. Dennis, *Adventures in American Diplomacy* (New York, 1928), p. 133. Hay's rejection of the Boer plea is in WMcKP:LC.

28. Copy, Abraham Fischer, Cornelius Wessels, and A. Daniel Wolmarans to McKinley, June 23, 1900, JHP:LC.

29. Hay to McKinley, June 27, 1900, WMcKP:LC; also in JHP:LC, lbc.

30. Ibid.

31. Boer commissioners (unsigned) to Hay, May 19, 1900, in

Ferguson, *American Diplomacy and the Boer War*, p. 148.

32.   James O'Beirne to Hay, May 29, 1900, ibid.

33.   O'Beirne to McKinley, May 21, 1900, ibid., p. 149. Fischer's remarks are also quoted on p. 149.

34.   Adee to Hay, n.d. [1900], JHP:LC; Hay to Choate, May 31, 1900, JHCP:LC.

35.   Hay to McKinley, June 27, 1900, WMcKP:LC.

36.   White to Hay, May 26, 1900, HWhP:LC. "How exactly the whole thing went off as you foreshadowed that it would!" White exclaimed. See also Choate to Hay, May 22, 1900, JHP:LC.

37.   Hay to McKinley, June 6, 1900, WMcKP:LC; enclosure, clipping, London *Daily Mail*, [May 23, 1900].

38.   Ferguson, *American Diplomacy and the Boer War*, p. 146.

39.   Hay to Stanford Newel, December 3, 1900, in Dennett, *John Hay*, pp. 243–44; Hay to Newel, December 21, 1900, ibid., p. 245; Hay added, however, "I have not changed my opinion in regard to the matter. I still think a journey of President Kruger to this country would be a great inconvenience both to him and to us, and would do no good, and, although I know of no one who differs with me in this opinion, they seem to think that I had better not give you any directions in regard to it."

40.   Ferguson, *American Diplomacy and the Boer War*, pp. 201–2.

41.   Ibid., p. 49. American exports to Great Britain increased $112 million annually during the war.

42.   Hartzell reported regularly to Henry White about the receptions he received, sending him several newspaper clippings as well. HWhP:LC.

43.   Dennett, *John Hay*, pp. 241, 241n.

44.   White to Balfour, August 24, 1900, AJBP:BM.

45.   Hay to R. Chisholm, July 10, 1903, JHP:LC.

46.   For an excellent discussion of the early phases of the Alaska boundary dispute, see Tansill, *Canadian-American Relations*, pp. 121–63.

47.   Hay to White, December 3, 1898, in Thayer, *John Hay*, 2:204; White to Lodge, December 27, 1898, HCLP:MHS; White to Hay, December 30, 1898, HWhP:LC; Adams to [Cameron], January 29, 1899, HAP:MHS.

48.   For Hay's desire for arbitration, see telegram, Hay to White, February 18, 1899, U. S. Department of State, Diplomatic Instructions: Great Britain, 33:94. For Britain's offer

to ratify the treaty, see telegram, White to Hay, February 16, 1899, U. S. Department of State, Diplomatic Despatches: Great Britain, and Hay to Choate, April 28, 1899, JHCP:LC.

49. Adams to [Cameron], March 5, 1899, HAP:MHS.

50. McKinley to Hay, May 14, 1899, WMcKP:LC.

51. Copy, Choate to Salisbury, May 19, 1899, U. S. Department of State, Diplomatic Despatches: Great Britain; Pauncefote to Choate, May 22, 1899, JHCP:LC. Hay saw Pauncefote's indiscreet letter, for Choate enclosed a copy in a private letter. (Private letter, Choate to Hay, May 24, 1899, U. S. Department of State, Diplomatic Despatches: Great Britain.)

52. Hay to Adams, May 18, 1899, HAP:MHS. Hay wrote similar letters to Choate, White, George W. Smalley, and St. Loe Strachey.

53. Hay to Choate, June 15, 1899, JHP:LC, lbc.

54. Ibid., June 26, 1899.

55. Hay to Davis, August 4, 1899, JHP:BU. Reid to Hay, July 26, 1899, WRP:LC. Hay replied curtly to Reid that the lease proposal was "the most favorable arrangement which has ever been proposed." (Hay to Reid, July 31, 1899, WRP:LC.) To McKinley Hay explained that the "ugly letter" from Reid was the result of his severe disappointment at not being named secretary of war. "What a glorious world this would be, if office seeking and the Senate were not," he concluded. (Hay to McKinley, August 4, 1899, WMcKP:LC.)

56. Hay to Davis, August 4, 1899, JHP:BU.

57. Hay to Adee, August 9, 1899, JHP:LC.

58. Hay to Choate, August 18, 1899, JHCP:LC. So much did Hay want the lease proposal accepted that even after he had virtually arranged a modus vivendi several weeks later, he asked Foster to use his influence to convince Senator Davis to reconsider his opposition to the idea. (Hay to Foster, September 26, 1899, JWFP:LC.)

59. Hay to Tower, October 20, 1899, U. S. Department of State, *Foreign Relations, 1899*, pp. 328–29, and Tower to Hay, October 20, 1899, ibid., pp. 329–30. The text of the modus vivendi is in ibid., pp. 330–31.

60. Hay to St. Loe Strachey, October 20, 1899, TDP:LC.

61. For example, White once reported Pauncefote as saying, "the very name of Canada makes . . . [me] sick." (White to Hay, September 13, 1899, HWhP:LC.)

62. Hay to Edwin M. Hood, September 10, [1900 ?], Edwin Milton Hood Papers, Manuscript Division, Library of Congress.

63.   Hay to Perry S. Heath, August 23, 1900, JHP:LC, lbc; Hay to Adee, August 23, 1900, ibid. For other examples of Hay's excessive praise, see Hay to Choate, November 13, 1899, JHCP:LC; Hay to Hanna, August 2, 1900, JHP:LC, lbc; Hay to the chairman of the committee of miners, Porcupine Mining District, Alaska, August 3, 1900, U. S. Department of State, *Foreign Relations, 1899*, p. 331; and Hay to Choate, August 22, 1900, JHCP:LC.

64.   Dennett, *John Hay*, p. 234.

CHAPTER VIII

1.   John Bassett Moore, "Mr. Hay's Work in Diplomacy," *Review of Reviews* 32 (August, 1905); 173.

2.   See, for example, Carnegie to James G. Blaine, May 14, 1882, James G. Blaine Papers, Manuscript Division, Library of Congress.

3.   See, for example, Roosevelt to Anna Roosevelt, May 20, 1894, Morison, ed., *Letters of Roosevelt*, 1:379; and Roosevelt to Lodge, October 27, 1894, ibid., p. 409.

4.   John A. Porter to Hay, November 7, 1898, WMcKP:LC; Hay to Richard Olney, November 14, 1898, TDP:LC; Olney to Hay, November 15, 1898, JHP:LC.

5.   Hay to White, December 7, 1898, No. 976, U. S. Department of State, Diplomatic Despatches: Great Britain, 33:40–42; telegram, White to Hay, December 21, 1898, HWhP:LC. See also ibid., December 23, 1898, lbc, and Balfour to White, December 26, 1898, ibid.

6.   Hay to Morgan, December 27, 1898, TDP:LC.

7.   Hay to White, January 13, 1899, JHP:LC, lbc.

8.   Hay to Morgan, December 27, 1898, TDP:LC; Hay to Morgan, January 21, 1899, John T. Morgan Papers, Manuscript Division, Library of Congress (hereafter cited as JTMP:LC). For an account of the events surrounding the passage of Morgan's canal bill, see Dwight C. Miner, *The Fight for the Panama Route: The Story of the Spooner Act and The Hay-Herrán Treaty* (New York, 1966 [originally published 1940]), pp. 74–116.

9.   White to Hay, January 26, February 11, February 17, February 27, HWhP:LC, lbc. Hay to White, February 14, 1899, JHP:LC, lbc. One authority contends that Britain merely used Canadian grievances as an excuse to prevent doubling

the effectiveness of the American fleet. See A[lexander] E. Campbell, *Great Britain and the United States 1895–1903* (Glasgow, 1960), pp. 52–53.

10.   Hay to Choate, January 15, 1900, JHP:LC, lbc.

11.   Telegram, Choate to Hay, February 3, 1900, ibid.; Adams to Cameron, February 5/6, 1900, Ford, ed., *Letters of Henry Adams*, 2:261–63; Hay to Choate, February 6, 1900, JHP:LC, lbc.

12.   Adams to Cameron, February 12, 1900, Ford, ed., *Letters of Henry Adams*, 2:266; Hay to Everett P. Wheeler, February 12, 1900, JHP:BU.

13.   Hay to [Roosevelt], February 12, 1900, JHP:LC, lbc. Roosevelt's statement read: 'I most earnestly hope that the pending treaty as to the future treatment of the Isthmian canal will not be ratified unless amended so as to provide that the canal, when built, shall be wholly under the control of the United States, alike in peace and war. This seems to me vital, from the standpoint of our sea power, no less than from the standpoint of the Monroe Doctrine." (Morison, ed., *Letters of Roosevelt*, 2:1186n–87n.)

14.   Roosevelt to Nicholas Murray Butler, February 15, 1900, Morison, ed., *Letters of Roosevelt*, 2:1186; Roosevelt to "Dear Will," February 16, 1900, Anna Roosevelt Cowles, ed., *Letters from Theodore Roosevelt to Anna Roosevelt Cowles 1870–1918* (New York and London, 1924), p. 236. Roosevelt's reply to Hay was friendly, although firm. (Roosevelt to Hay, February 18, 1900, in Thayer, *John Hay*, 2:339–41.)

15.   Adams to [Cameron], February 12/13, 1900, HAP:MHS; Adams to [Cameron ?], February 19, 1900, ibid.

16.   Hay to White, February 27, 1900, in Nevins, *Henry White*, pp. 150–51. Nevins replaced Carnegie's name with a dash. Carnegie's position was made known in a letter to an unnamed friend and was printed on the editorial page of the *New York Tribune*, February 27, 1900, p. 6, col. 6. The letter was dated February 26, 1900. It included the following remarks:

The views you expressed about the canal treaty are in accord with my own. I cannot understand how a Republican Administration could abandon the position hitherto held by the party, that the Clayton-Bulwer Treaty had become nonexistent. The proposed treaty, even if defeated, as it surely is to be, will leave serious mischief behind, since it has recognized the Clayton-Bulwer and given it something like life . . . .

I am inclined to agree with you that to adopt the new treaty is to commit political suicide for the forthcoming campaign.

Yours truly, one who has never voted anything but the Republican ticket and who hopes he may never be compelled to do so."

17. See John Bassett Moore to Hay, February 12, 1900, and Hay to Moore, February 14 and February 19, 1900, John Bassett Moore Papers, Manuscript Division, Library of Congress (hereafter cited as JBMP:LC). All of these letters indicated that additional letters, no longer extant, were exchanged.

18. Draft letter, Moore to Hay, February 20, 1900, ibid.; Hay to Moore, February 21, 1900, ibid.

19. John Bassett Moore, "The Interoceanic Canal and the Hay-Pauncefote Treaty," *New York Times,* March 4, 1900, p. 23.

20. Hay to Moore, March 4, 1900, JBMP:LC; *New York Times,* March 5, 1900, p. 3, col. 2

21. Holls to Cushman K. Davis, March 7, 1900, Frederick W. Holls Papers, Manuscript Division, Butler Library, Columbia University, lbc (hereafter cited as FWHP:ColU). See also Holls to Roosevelt, March 7, 1900, ibid., in which he termed Moore's article "the worst and feeblest pleading I have read in a long time." Photocopy, Holls to Andrew D. White, March 3, 1900, Andrew D. White papers, Cornell University Library (hereafter cited as ADWP:CorU).

22. See, for example, Holls to Valentine Chirol, February 7, 1900, FWDP:ColU, lbc, and Holls to St. Loe Strachey, February 7, 1900, ibid., lbc.

23. Andrew D. White to Holls, February 12, 1900, ibid.; photocopy, Holls to White, March 3, 1900, ADWP:C or U.

24. See, for example, Thomas A. Bailey, *A Diplomatic History of the American People,* 7th ed. (New York, 1964), p. 487, which states that "the most serious objection to the Hay-Pauncefote Treaty was the non-fortification clause." See also Campbell, *Anglo-American Understanding,* p. 196, and Miner, *The Fight for the Panama Route,* p. 96.

25. U.S. Senate, "Report of the Senate Committee on Foreign Relations," *Senate Document 268, 56th Congress, 1st session* (serial set 3868).

26. Hay to McKinley, March 13, 1900, JHP:BU; McKinley to Hay, March 13, 1900, in Thayer, *John Hay,* 2:228.

27. Hay to Choate, January 15, 1900, JHP:LC, lbc. Draft letter, Hay to McKinley, September 22, 1900, ibid. The letter Hay actually sent to McKinley, considerably altered from the draft, is dated September 23, 1900. Ibid., lbc.

28. Hay to White, December 23, 1900, ibid.

29. Hay to White, February 10, 1901, HWhP:LC; Hay to Watterson, January 11, 1901, Henry Watterson Papers, Manuscript Division, Library of Congress (hereafter cited as HWP:LC); ibid., March 12, 1901. Henry Adams, recording these exciting events, stated Hay's case more colorfully. Referring to Lodge as "more of a bloodsucker than Platt or Quay or Hanna or Elkins combined . . . whose methods exceed the endurance of a coral reef," Adams wrote, "Hay frets and rages internally and suffers the more because he keeps, or tries to keep, an external impassivity." Foreign relations did not disturb Hay in the least, Adams insisted. "The trouble is, and always has been, and always will be, with the greed and selfishness and jealousy and ambition of senators." (Adams to [Cameron?], February 25, 1901, HAP:MHS.)

30. Hay to Reid, February 7, 1900, WRP:LC.

31. Hay to White, February 14, 1899, JHP:LC, lbc; see also Hay to Choate, January 15, 1900, ibid., lbc.

32. Hay to John J. McCook, April 22, 1900, ibid.; see also Hay to Gilder, April 24, 1900, RWGP:NYPL.

33. Hay to Flora Mather, May 3, 1900, WadFP:LC; see also Hay to Watterson, December 28, 1900, JHP:LC.

34. Telegram, Hay to Choate, December 29, 1900, U.S. Department of State, Diplomatic Instructions: Great Britain, 33:528; Hay to Choate, January 11, 1901, JHCP:LC; see also Hay to St. Loe Strachey, January 30, 1901, JHP:LC, lbc.

35. White to Balfour, January 12, 1901, AJBP:BM; ibid.; January 14, 1901; Hay to White, February 10, 1901, HWhP:LC; Hay to Adee, February 21, 1901, TDP:LC; Campbell, *Great Britain and the United States*, p. 61.

36. Holls to Andrew D. White, March 12, 1901, FWHP:ColU, lbc; Roosevelt to Arthur H. Lee, March 18, 1901, Morison, ed., *Letters of Roosevelt*, 3:19; Hay to McKinley, March 1, 1901, WMcKP:LC; Adams to Cameron, March 11, 1901, Ford, ed., *Letters of Henry Adams*, 2:321.

37. Copy, Hay to Choate, August 5, 1901, JHP:LC; see also Hay to Morgan, April 2, 1901, TDP:LC; Hay to Lodge, March 27, 1901, HCLP:MHS.

38. Copy, Lodge to Hay, March 28, 1901, TRP:LC.

39. Hay to Lodge, March 30, 1901, JHP:LC, lbc. Lodge replied with a long defense of his position, including seventeen typewritten pages of quotations from various authorities on international law justifying unilateral abrogation.

Hay returned Lodge's letter without comment the following day. (Lodge to Hay, April 2, 1901, HCLP:MHS, and Hay to Lodge, April 3, 1901, ibid.)

40.　　Adams to Cameron, April 22, 1901, Ford, ed., *Letters of Henry Adams,* 2:328.

41.　　Adee to Hay, April 8, 1901, JHP:LC; Hay to Choate, August 5, 1901, ibid. In his letter to Choate, Hay revealed his decision to keep the language previously approved. See also Hay to Bigelow, April 3, 1901, JHP:BU.

42.　　Hay to Choate, April 27, 1901, U. S. Department of State, Diplomatic Instructions: Great Britain, 33: attached to p. 296.

43.　　Hay to White, July 26, 1901, TDP:LC; Hay to Choate, August 5, 1901, JHP:LC; draft letter, Hay to Pauncefote, September 2, 1901, JHP:LC.

44.　　Hay to Roosevelt, October 2, 1901, TRP:LC.

45.　　Hay to Morgan, August 22, 1901, JTMP:LC; Hay to Joseph B. Foraker, August 23, 1901, TDP:LC; Choate to Hay, September 25, 1901, JHP:LC; White to Lodge, September 23, 1901, HCLP:MHS; Roosevelt to Hay, September 30, 1901, Morison, ed., *Letters of Roosevelt,* 3:154; Choate to Hay, October 2, 1901, JHP:LC.

46.　　Lodge to Roosevelt, October 17, 1901, Henry Cabot Lodge, ed., *Selections from the Correspondence of Theodore Roosevelt and Henry Cabot Lodge,* 2 vols. (New York, 1925), 1:507; Choate to White, November 11, 1901, HWhP:LC; Hay to White, November 2, 1901, ibid. Lodge did what he could (which was considerable). See Lodge to White, November 21, 1901, HWhP:LC.

47.　　Hay to White, December 26, 1901, JHP:LC, lbc.

48.　　Roosevelt to Lodge, July 11, 1905, Morison, ed., *Letters of Roosevelt,* 4:1271.

49.　　Hay to [Clara S. Hay], _____ 17th, [1901], WadFP:LC.

50.　　Henry Adams, *The Education of Henry Adams* (New York: Modern Library edition, 1961), p. 423.

CHAPTER IX

1.　　Roosevelt to William Howard Taft, July 3, 1905, Morison, ed., *Letters of Roosevelt,* 4:1260.

2.　　Roosevelt to Arthur H. Lee, March 18, 1901, ibid., 3:20.

3.　　Campbell, *Great Britain and the United States,* pp. 104–5.

4.　　Hay to Roosevelt, July 14, 1899, in Dennis, *Adventures in American Diplomacy,* p. 152.

5.   Hay to Roosevelt, March 24, 1902, TRP:LC; Pauncefote to Lansdowne, March 28, 1902, in Campbell, *Great Britain and the United States,* pp. 105–6.

6.   Roosevelt to Hay, July 10, 1902, TRP:LC.

7.   Campbell, *Anglo-American Understanding,* p. 302. Although Roosevelt's concession was in some ways more formal than actual, it nevertheless seems more significant than his later acceptance of the Hay-Herbert Treaty that established the actual tribunal. Historians have heralded this treaty as a significant concession by Roosevelt and have marvelled at his alleged shift in viewpoint from the summer of 1902 to December. Perhaps there was no basic change at all, for when the president consented to an even-numbered tribunal during the summer, he took the step that would eventually solve the problem. In other words, the Hay-Herbert Treaty was merely a logical outgrowth of the earlier concession. Hay recognized the significance of the president's summer concession. See copy, Hay to Clara S. Hay, January 24, 1903, JHP:LC.

8.   Hay to Choate, July 17, 1902, enclosed in Hay to Roosevelt, July 17, 1902, TRP:LC. Hay did not prohibit Choate from continuing to explore a possible agreement with the English.

9.   The text of the Hay-Herbert Treaty is in U. S. Department of State, *Foreign Relations, 1903,* pp. 488–93.

10.   Hay to Shelby Cullom, February 11, 1903, JHP:LC, lbc; Hay to Lodge, February 11, [1903], HCLP:MHS; Hay to Roosevelt, February 7, 1903, TRP:LC.

11.   According to Hay, Roosevelt did ask all of the justices. (See Tansill, *Canadian-American Relations,* p. 231n). But he also told White in an *"Absolutely confidential"* letter that Lodge "insisted upon this appointment to the tribunal." (Hay to White, April 10, 1903, JHP:LC, lbc.) Lodge more or less substantiated this version. See Charles G. Washburne, ed., "Memoir of Henry Cabot Lodge," *Massachusetts Historical Society Proceedings,* (April, 1925), p. 340.

12.   White to Hay, April 1, 1903, HWhP:LC, lbc; Laurier to Hay, February 24, 1903, in Dennett, *John Hay,* p. 358; Adams to Cameron, March 1, 1904, Ford ed., *Letters of Henry Adams,* 2:399

13.   Hay to White, April 10, 1903, JHP:LC, lbc. Chamberlain

expressed Hay's feelings well, telling White, "it would have been so much easier and would have commanded so much influence if we had appointed judges or lawyers who were not connected with the Government or who had not committed themselves publicly against the Canadian claims." (Quoted in White to Hay, April 1, 1903, HWhP:LC, lbc.) Lodge claimed that Hay protested "in the strongest way" to Roosevelt about Lodge's appointment. (Washburne, ed., "Memoir of Lodge," p. 340.)

14.   Choate to Hay, March 25, 1903, JHP:LC.

15.   Hay to Choate, February 17, 1903, JHCP:LC; Choate to Hay, March 6, 1903, JHP:LC; White to Hay, April 1, 1903, HWhP:LC, lbc.

16.   Hay to White, April 10, 1903, JHP:LC; Hay to Choate, April 3, 1903. Hay's expression of eternal disappointment was followed by several disparaging references to Lodge's mental character.

17.   Roosevelt to Hay, June 29, 1903, TRP:LC. The same day the president assured Lodge that he did not intend for the British to "do any shuffling." (Roosevelt to Lodge, June 29, 1903, Lodge, ed., *Correspondence of Roosevelt and Lodge*, 2:37.)

18.   Hay to Foster, July 2, 1903, JWFP:LC; Hay to Roosevelt, July 2, 1903, in Dennett, *John Hay*, 359–60.

19.   Hay to Roosevelt, July 9, 1903, JHP:LC; Roosevelt to Hay, July 11, 1903, TRP:LC; Hay to Roosevelt, July 13, 1903, JHP:LC.

20.   Hay to Roosevelt, July 21, 1903, JHP:LC; Hay to Foster, July 23, 1903, JWFP:LC.

21.   Roosevelt to Hay, July 29, 1903, Morison, ed., *Letters of Roosevelt*, 3:532; Hay to Foster, August 5, 1903, JWFP:LC.

22.   Hay to White, September 20, HWhP:LC; White to Hay, October 20, 1903, HWhP:LC; White to Lodge, October 1, 1903. See also Hay to Roosevelt, September 25, 1903, JHP:LC, in which Hay made it clear he expected his letters would be seen by Balfour.

23.   [Hay to Clara S. Hay], October 18, 1903, JHP:LC; ibid., October 21, 1903. Other self-congratulatory statements are found in Hay to James B. Angell, October 22, 1903, ibid., and Hay to L. Clarke Davis, October 23, 1903, Richard Harding Davis Papers, University of Virginia Library.

24.   Lansdowne to Lodge, October 21, 1903, HCLP:MHS.

25.   [Hay to Clara S. Hay], October 21, 1903, JHP:LC.

26.   Statement of Jette and Aylesworth, October 20, 1903, in Tansill, *Canadian-American Relations*, p. 260n. Laurier is quoted in John W. DaFoe, *Clifford Sifton in Relation to His Times* (Toronto, 1931), p. 211.

27.   Roosevelt, *Autobiography*, p. 385.

28.   Adams to Cameron, January 18, 1902, Ford, ed., *Letters of Henry Adams*, 2:367. Hay is quoted in Helen Nicolay, *Our Capital on the Potomac* (New York and London, 1924), p. 475. Hay, diary entry, February 27, 1905, JHP:LC. Hay's most amusing description of Roosevelt occurred during the campaign of 1900 when Roosevelt, then governor of New York, was attempting to secure the vice-presidential nomination. "Teddy has been here," Hay wrote to Adams. "Have you heard of it? It was more fun than a goat. He came down with a somber resolution throned on his strenuous brow, to let Mc-Kinley and Hanna know, once for all, that he would not be Vice-President and found to his stupefaction that nobody in Washington, except Platt, had ever dreamed of such a thing. He did not even have a chance to launch his nolo episcopari at the Major. That statesman said he did not want him on the ticket—that he would be far more valuable in New York—and Root said, with his frank and murderous smile, 'Of course not—you're not fit for it.' And so he went back, quite eased in his mind, but considerably bruised in *amour-propre*." (Hay to [Adams], June 15, 1900, ibid., lbc.)

29.   Walter Wellman, "John Hay: An American Gentleman," *Review of Reviews* 32 (August, 1905): 168; Roosevelt to George Von Lengerke Meyer, July 7, 1905, Morison, ed., *Letters of Roosevelt*, 4:1263. See also Roosevelt to Lodge, January 28, 1909, ibid., 6:1489–90, and Roosevelt to Thomas H. Warren, June 7, 1916, ibid., 8:1057.

30.   Hay to Roosevelt, November 12, 1901, JHP:LC, lbc.

31.   Roosevelt to Hay, March 3, 1905, JHP:LC; Roosevelt to George O. Trevelyan, March 9, 1905, Morison, ed., *Letters of Roosevelt*, 4:1133. Hay also wrote a speech about Roosevelt which the president regarded highly. See "President Roosevelt," in Hay, *Addresses*, p. 222.

32.   Elting Morison, ed., *Cowboys and Kings: Three Great Letters by Theodore Roosevelt* (Cambridge, Mass., 1954), pp. 1–23; Hay to Roosevelt, August 12, 1903, TRP:LC.

33.   Roosevelt to Albert J. Beveridge, July 11, 1905, Morison, ed., *Letters of Roosevelt*, 4:1269.

34.   Roosevelt to Lodge, January 28, 1909, ibid., 6:1489–98. The quotation is on p. 1491.

35.   Roosevelt to Lodge, January 28, 1909, ibid. The quotation is on p. 1497.

36.   Dennett to Nevins, March 14, 1932, TDP:LC.

37.   Joseph F. Wall, *Henry Watterson: Reconstructed Rebel* (New York, 1956), p. 250.

38.   Thayer's discussion of Panama is in Thayer, *John Hay*, 2:296–331; Moore, "Mr. Hay's Work in Diplomacy," p. 176.

39.   John Bigelow to Philippe Bunau-Varilla, December 1, 1898, in Philippe Bunau-Varilla, *Panama: The Creation, Destruction, and Resurrection* (London, 1913), p. 160. Bigelow's interest in the canal and his connection with Hay are briefly discussed in Margaret Clapp, *Forgotten First Citizen: John Bigelow* (Boston, 1947), pp. 306–15.

40.   Copy, Bigelow to Hay, March 21, 1901, Philippe Bunau-Varilla Papers, Manuscript Division, Library of Congress (hereafter cited as PB-VP:LC); Bigelow to Bunau-Varilla, May 20, 1901, ibid.

41.   "Isthmian Canal Plans," *New York Evening Post*, May 15, 1901, p. 12, col. 1. (The following day the *Post* editorialized on the matter, welcoming what was alleged to be Hay's shifting point of view. May 16, 1901, p. 6, col. 2.) Bigelow to Bunau-Varilla, May 20, 1901, PB-VP:LC; Hay to Bunau-Varilla, June 1 1901, PB-VP:LC. Despite Hay's alleged change of heart, the year 1901 proved disappointing to backers of the Panama route.

42.   Hay to Morgan, April 22, 1902, in Thayer, *John Hay*, 2:300; Hay to Morgan, April 23, 1902, JHP:LC, lbc.

43.   N. T. Bacon to Hay, October 6, 1904, in Dennett, *John Hay*, p. 378. Bacon refers to an interview with Hay in 1903 before the revolution.

44.   Hay to [Adams], July 11, 1902, HAP:MHS; Ernest Samuels, *Henry Adams: The Major Phase* (Cambridge, Mass., 1964), pp. 322–23; Dennett, *John Hay*, p. 380.

45.   Roosevelt to Thayer, July 2, 1915, Morison, ed., *Letters of Roosevelt*, 8:944. Thayer's first published his opinions in "John Hay and the Panama Republic," *Harper's Monthly* 131 (July, 1915): 165–75.

46.   Draft instruction, Hay to Arthur M. Beaupré, [June 9, 1903], JHP:LC. (Roosevelt had instructed Hay to send a strong protest. "Those contemptible little creatures in Bogota ought to understand how much they are jeopardizing

things and imperiling their own future," he explained a few days later. See Roosevelt to Hay, July 14, 1903, TRP:LC.) Hay to Roosevelt, August 16, 1903, TRP:LC; Roosevelt to Hay, August 19, 1903, Morison, ed., *Letters of Roosevelt,* 3:566.

47.   Hay to Roosevelt, August 22, 1903, JHP:LC; ibid., August 23, 1903.

48.   Ibid., September 7, 1903; Hay to Roosevelt, September 13, 1903, TRP:LC.

49.   Copy, J. Gabriel Duque to Hay, September 21, 1903, TRP:LC. The additional letters from Duque to Hay are referred to in Dennis, *Adventures in Diplomacy,* p. 339n.

50.   Bunau-Varilla, *Panama,* pp. 316–19.

51.   Philippe Bunau-Varilla, *The Great Adventure of Panama Wherein are Exposed Its Relations to the Great War and also the Luminous Traces of the German Conspiracies Against France and the United States* (New York and London, 1920), p. [v].

52.   Hay to James Ford Rhodes, December 8, 1903, JHP:LC. See also Hay to Helen Hay Whitney, November 19, 1903, in Thayer, *John Hay,* 2:318, and Hay to Roosevelt, November 20, 1903, JHP:LC.

53.   Hay to [Clara S. Hay], November 30, 1903, WadFP:LC; ibid.; December 2, 1903; *New York Times,* October 27, 1904, p. 5, col. 2.

54.   Dennett, *John Hay,* pp. 430, 407.

55.   For details about the Perdicaris affair, see ibid., pp. 401–2, and Hay's diary entries for May 28, May 31, June 15, June 18, June 22, and June 23, all 1904, JHP:LC.

56.   Hay, diary entries, June 22, October 4, and November 20, 1904, JHP:LC.

57.   Hay to Adelbert Hay, October 24, 1893, JHP:BU; Roosevelt to Lodge, January 28, 1909, Morison, ed., *Letters of Roosevelt,* 6:1490.

58.   Quoted in Anna Roosevelt Cowles, ed., *Letters from Theodore Roosevelt to Anna Roosevelt Cowles 1870–1918* (New York and London, 1924), p. 252.

59.   Hay to Adams, January 6, 1892, HAP:MHS; ibid., May 9, 1898.

60.   Hay to [Clara S. Hay], October 25, 1903, JHP:LC.

Essay on Sources

For a study of Hay's thought, certain official government documents were essential, others were necessary but not in themselves sufficient. Hay's dispatches to the State Department while he was ambassador to England are the most revealing since these were more likely to indicate his personal thinking than his later instructions as secretary of state. Nevertheless, this study has made use of Hay's instructions to Great Britain and to China, especially those which do provide insight into Hay's thinking. In addition, the official correspondence from the Schurman Commission to the State Department and from Hay to the commission was very useful in determining Hay's feelings about the Filipino rebellion. The *Foreign Relations* series is quite complete, particularly for the correspondence regarding the Alaska boundary dispute and China policy.

More important than the govenment documents were the various John Hay manuscript collections, of which the most important is in the manuscript division of the Library of Congress. This collection includes only a few of Hay's letters prior to his appointment as secretary of state in 1898, but three large letterbooks contain press copies of personal and semi-official correspondence after that date. In addition, the Library of Congress collection contains the diary kept by Hay in 1904 and 1905, a fascinating document. One only regrets that Hay did not keep such a diary during his other years in office. Finally, the collection includes a mass of newspaper clippings and scrapbooks, some of which are extremely valuable.

A secondary but still very valuable manuscript collection is in the John Hay Library, Brown University, a collection that owes much to the efforts of Mr. William Easton Louttit, Jr. The Hay letters in this collection tend to be of an earlier date than those in the Library of Congress and include virtually all of Hay's extant correspondence concerning the election campaign of 1896 and his efforts to receive appointment as ambassador to England. The collection also includes a number of significant letters to Hay from William McKinley, Mark Hanna, Henry Adams, Bret Harte, and others. There are also financial records, scrapbooks, and letterbooks of his years in Europe in the 1860's.

Minor collections of Hay materials are in the Houghton Library at Harvard University, the Butler Library at Columbia University, the New York Public Library, and the Henry H. Huntington Library at San Marino, California. The Huntington collection includes Hay's heretofore uncited poem, "Two Fenians."

Published collections of Hay's letters include the three volumes edited by Mrs. Hay and Henry Adams, *Letters of John Hay and Extracts from his Diary* (3 vols.; Washington, D.C., 1908); they are, however, unreliable and difficult to use since Mrs. Hay chose to delete all names. She also omitted portions of letters without indication. A key to the omitted names, a copy of which is in the Hay papers in the Library of Congress, was compiled by Henry Adams and makes the letters more usable. However, the key, which was apparently designed for Adams' own use, is incomplete. Some early letters of Hay are found in Amy A. C. Montague, ed., *A College Friendship: A Series of Letters from John Hay to Hannah Angell* (Boston, 1938); Caroline Ticknor, ed., *A Poet in Exile: Early Letters of John Hay* (Boston, 1910); Brown University, ed., *The Life and Works of John Hay 1838–1905: A Commemorative Catalogue* . . . (Providence, 1961); and Tyler Dennett, ed., *Lincoln and the Civil War in the Diaries and Letters of John Hay* (New York, 1939). Hay's complete correspondence with Henry James appears in George Monteiro, *Henry*

James and John Hay: The Record of a Friendship (Providence, 1965).

William Easton Louttit, Jr., compiled an almost complete bibliography of Hay's published works; the bibliography is appended to Tyler Dennett, *John Hay: From Poetry to Politics* (New York, 1933). Those writings that were of particular value to this study include *The Complete Poetical Works of John Hay* (Boston and New York, 1917), a descriptive title not entirely accurate. Hay's poems appear in several less complete editions as well. *Castilian Days* (Boston, 1871) is available in a number of editions, as well as in *Harper's Magazine*, where it appeared prior to publication in book form. *The Bread-winners: A Social Study* (New York, 1884) is likewise available in a number of editions, including one published in 1967. Hay's tributes to his father and his father-in-law, *Dr. Charles Hay . . .* [New York, 1885], and *Amasa Stone . . .* [New York, 1883], shed some light on Hay's intellectual development in addition to providing information on the family background. Both books are scarce but available in places such as the rare book room of the Library of Congress. John G. Nicolay and John Hay, *Abraham Lincoln: A History* (10 vols.; New York, 1890) was helpful in determining Hay's views of race. "The Mormon Prophet's Tragedy," *Atlantic Monthly* 34 (December, 1869), 669–78, sheds light on the parameters of Hay's democratic enthusiasm.

Most of Hay's "official" speeches while ambassador and secretary of state are included in *The Addresses of John Hay* (New York, 1906). Unfortunately, this volume omits most political speeches and all those made before 1897. Printed copies of two of Hay's most significant political speeches have survived, "The Balance Sheet of the Two Parties" (Cleveland, 1880), and "The Platform of Anarchy" [Cleveland, 1896]. Manuscript versions of other speeches are available in the Hay papers, especially in the collection at Brown University.

A number of other manuscript collections at the Library of Congress contain material on Hay. The Wadsworth Family papers are extremely valuable, for they contain many of Hay's personal letters to his wife and father-in-law, as well as Mrs. Hay's letters to her mother. The Whitelaw Reid collection is also rich, containing hundreds of Hay letters as well as letterbook copies of Reid's letters to Hay. The Henry White papers are equally rewarding; unfortunately White's letterbooks are disintegrating with age. The Joseph Choate papers contain a voluminous correspondence from Hay, particularly when Choate was ambassador to England. Choate's replies are in the Hay papers, and together the record is almost complete.

Also important is the Tyler Dennett collection of material relating to John Hay. This collection consists of typescripts of Hay's letters gathered from various sources. Dennett's own papers are interesting and were of some value for this study.

Somewhat less valuable are the William McKinley and Theodore Roosevelt papers, with the McKinley collection containing more material on Hay than the Roosevelt one. The John Bassett Moore papers are extremely valuable for information regarding the Spanish American War and Hay's efforts to overcome Senate opposition to the first Hay-Pauncefote Treaty. The John W. Foster papers, although well picked over, are useful for studying the seal and Alaska boundary disputes.

The John T. Morgan, Andrew Carnegie, and Henry Watterson papers have only a few items relating to Hay, but some of Hay's letters in these collections, particularly those in the Watterson collection, are among the most interesting in the Library of Congress.

The Massachusetts Historical Society contains a few valuable collections. The Adams Family papers contain some of Hay's correspondence with Henry Adams through 1889; after that date Hay's letters are found in the separate Henry Adams collection. The Theodore Frelinghuysen Dwight papers, previously unused for a study of Hay, contain one file of Hay's letters to Henry Adams from 1880 to 1886. Though of limited usefulness for this study, the letters are intrinsically interesting. The Henry Cabot Lodge papers are somewhat disappointing regarding materials on

Hay, although there are a few valuable letters from Hay. The Lodge-Henry White correspondence is also of interest.

The Houghton Library at Harvard houses the William Dean Howells papers which include a large number of Hay letters. There are also a number of important Hay letters in the William W. Rockhill papers, a collection more widely used than the Howells papers. The Charles W. Eliot papers in the Harvard University Archives contain one folder of Hay letters, all of marginal significance.

The Butler Library at Columbia University contains the Frederick W. Holls papers which reveal a great deal about the anti-Hay forces in the Republican party. The Holls papers show that David Jayne Hill, an assistant secretary of state, was among those who secretly opposed Hay in the Hay-Pauncefote treaty matter. The slim possibility therefore exists that there was an anti-administration conspiracy within the bureaucracy to defeat the treaty. There is also some Hay material in the Jay Family papers and the Allan Nevins collection.

The New York Public Library houses a number of useful collections. Some of them, such as the Henry J. Raymond collection, have materials dealing with Hay during the Civil War. Beyond that, the Richard Watson Gilder papers are the most valuable collection, particularly for ascertaining Hay's views of the mugwumps. The Samuel J. Tilden papers also contain a few Hay letters, and the Silas Weir Mitchell papers include personal letters about Hay's physical condition. There are also two small boxes of newspaper clippings relating to Hay in the rare book room.

The Andrew D. White and the Jacob G. Schurman papers at Cornell University have some material relating to Hay. The Schurman papers include reports to Hay when Schurman was head of a commission investigating conditions in the Philippines. There is very little in the Schurman papers, however, that is not also available in the official, unpublished records of the commission.

The University of Virginia has the Richard Harding Davis papers. There is little, if any, correspondence between Hay and Davis, but there are a few interesting letters from Hay to Davis's father, L. Clarke Davis.

In the Mark Twain papers at the University of California at Berkeley are perhaps eighteen letters from Hay.

The only foreign collection consulted for this study was the Arthur James Balfour collection in the British Museum, London. In addition to the few letters from Hay, there is a very significant correspondence between Balfour and Henry White.

The first attempt at a book length account of Hay was by Lorenzo Sears, *John Hay, Author, Statesman* (New York, 1914). Though deficient and sketchy, Sears' virtually forgotten book is concise and well written. The first major work on Hay was William R. Thayer, *The Life and Letters of John Hay* (2 vols.; Boston and New York, 1916). Thayer's work is largely a collection of letters with interpretative comment interspersed. John Bassett Moore, in "John Hay," *Political Science Quarterly* 32 (March, 1917), 119–25, strongly criticized Thayer's skewed selection of letters and his obvious anti-German bias.

The best biography of Hay is Dennett, *John Hay*, a solid piece of historical work. Dennett is generally sympathetic to his subject. His pro-Hay, anti-Roosevelt feelings are even more evident in his private letters, now in the Library of Congress. The latest lengthy work on Hay, Anne Hummel Sherrill, "John Hay: Shield of Union"(Ph.D. dissertation, University of California, Berkeley, 1967), analyzes Hay's thought primarily during his years with Lincoln. Her study involves an intensive investigation of Hay's Civil War diaries. Sherrill overestimates the influence Lincoln had on Hay, particularly in his later life. Had Sherrill used the Hay collection at Brown University, as she apparently did not, some aspects of her study would have profited. The Lincoln theme is also stressed by Charles W. Moores in "John Hay, the Making of a Great Diplomat," *Putnam's* 6 (June, 1909), 297–308.

In addition to the Moores' article, there are a number of contemporary periodical accounts dealing with Hay. Among the most valuable are Brooks Adams, "John Hay,"

McClure's Magazine 19 (June, 1902), 173–82; Joseph B. Bishop, "A Friendship with John Hay," *Century* 71 (March, 1906), 773–80; and Walter Wellman, "John Hay: An American Gentelman," *Review of Reviews* 32 (August, 1905), 166–71. Hay's boyhood days are described accurately (according to Mrs. Hay) in A. S. Chapman, "The Boyhood of John Hay," *Century* 56 (July, 1909), 444–54.

Hay, the man of letters, is discussed in [Clarence King], "John Hay," *Scribner's Monthly* 7 (April, 1874), 736–39; William Dean Howells, "John Hay in Literature," *North American Review* 81 (September, 1905), 343–51; and George F. Mellen, "John Hay—Littérateur," *Methodist Review* 101 (July, 1918), 547–56. Sister St. Ignatius Ward, *The Poetry of John Hay* (Washington, D.C., 1930), is an undistinguished, unanalytical study of Hay's poems.

Aspects of Hay's interpersonal relationships can be studied in the very large number of memoirs, letter collections, and biographies of individuals who knew Hay. Among the most interesting is James F. Rhodes' sketch of Hay in *The McKinley and Roosevelt Administrations 1897–1909* (New York, 1922), in which Rhodes describes Hay's success in organizing the Vampire Club in Cleveland. Hay's conversational abilities are emphasized in Henry Watterson, *"Marse Henry": An Autobiography* (New York, 1909) and in several of Roosevelt's letters after Hay's death, which can be found in Elting E. Morison, ed., *The Letters of Theodore Roosevelt* (8 vols.; Cambridge, Massachusetts, 1951–54).

Other important works of this nature containing significant information on Hay include Oscar S. Straus, *The American Spirit* (New York, 1913), Shelby Cullom, *Fifty Years of Public Service* . . . (Chicago, 1911), John St. Loe Strachey, *The Adventure of Living: A Subjective Autobiography* (London, 1922), and, covering only the years prior to 1879, John Bigelow's massive *Retrospections of an Active Life* (5 vols.; New York, 1909).

Hay's relationship with the specific individuals considered in some detail in this study must, for the most part, be traced in primary material since Hay's biographers deal very briefly if at all with the relationships. Virtually all information about the Hay-Walt Whitman relationship is in Horace Traubel, *With Walt Whitman in Camden* (5 vols.; New York, Philadelphia, and Carbondale, Illinois, 1906–64), a massive journal of Traubel's conversations with Whitman in 1888 and 1889.

To some extent the Hay-Mark Twain relationship can be traced in the Twain papers at Berkeley and the Hay papers at the Library of Congress. In addition to manuscript collections, Samuel L. Clemens, *Mark Twain's Autobiography* (2 vols.; New York and London, 1924); Bernard DeVoto, ed., *Mark Twain in Eruption: Hitherto Unpublished Pages about Men and Events by Mark Twain* (New York and London, 1940); Albert Bigelow Paine, ed., *Mark Twain's Letters* (2 vols.; New York and London, 1917); and Henry Nash Smith and William M. Gibson, eds., *Mark Twain-Howells Letters: The Correspondence of Samuel L. Clemens and William Dean Howells 1872–1910* (2 vols.; Cambridge, Massachusetts, 1960), all proved useful to this study. Some of Twain's biographers have noted the Hay-Twain relationship, notably Albert Bigelow Paine, *Mark Twain: A Biography* . . . (New York and London, 1912); Louis J. Budd, *Mark Twain: Social Philosopher* (Bloomington, Indiana, 1962); and Justin Kaplan, *Mr. Clemens and Mark Twain: A Biography* (New York, 1966).

A study of the Hay-Bret Harte relationship requires use of the extensive collection of Harte letters in the John Hay papers at Brown University. In addition, the Hay-Harte relationship is mentioned briefly in Thayer, *John Hay* and in more detail in Geoffrey Bret Harte, ed., *The Letters of Bret Harte* (Boston and New York, 1926), and in T. Edgar Pemberton, *The Life of Bret Harte* (New York, 1903). Less useful is George R. Stewart, Jr., *Bret Harte: Argonaut and Exile.* . . (Boston and New York, 1931). "Reminiscences of Bret Harte," *Overland Monthly* 40 (September, 1902), [220]–[239], contains a letter Hay sent to the magazine discussing his memories of Harte.

The Hay-William Dean Howells relationship can be

traced in manuscript material, especially in the Howells papers at Harvard. In addition, a number of Hay's letters to Howells are printed in Hay, ed., *Letters and Diary,* and Thayer, *John Hay.* For Howells' side, Mildred Howells, ed., *Life in Letters of William Dean Howells* (2 vols., Garden City, New York, 1928) is very valuable, as is Smith and Gibson, eds., *Twain-Howells Letters.* Howells' article, "John Hay in Literature," is very useful in determining Hay's extraordinary ability to remain friends with his philosophical opponents.

There is some manuscript material on the Hay-Andrew Carnegie relationship, notably in the Carnegie collections in the Library of Congress and the New York Public Library. Andrew Carnegie, *Autobiography of Andrew Carnegie* (Boston and New York, 1920) is useful in determining Hay's influence over Carnegie. Louis M. Hacker, *The World of Andrew Carnegie: 1865–1901* (Philadelphia and New York, 1968) is somewhat helpful, but all secondary accounts have been superceded by Joseph F. Wall's definitive biography, *Andrew Carnegie* (New York, 1970).

Both Dennett and Thayer examine Hay's relationship with Whitelaw Reid, but both misdate the beginning of Hay's dislike for his long-time associate. On the other hand, Royal Cortissoz in *The Life of Whitelaw Reid* (2 vols.; New York, 1921) appears to have suppressed material that might reflect adversely on either Hay or Reid. Therefore the relationship must be traced in manuscript collections, especially the Hay and Reid papers at the Library of Congress. The Hay papers at Brown are essential for the campaign of 1896 and Hay's subsequent attempts to edge Reid out of the running for a high post in the McKinley administration. Some relevant material may also be found in the McKinley papers.

The Hay-Henry Adams relationship has been widely discussed, notably (in addition to the biographies of Hay) in Ernest Samuels, *Henry Adams: The Major Phase* (Cambridge, Massachusetts, 1964) and in *Henry Adams: The Middle Years* (Cambridge, Massachusetts, 1958), and by Herbert Edwards, "Henry Adams: Politician and Statesman," *New England Quarterly* 22 (March, 1949), 49–60. Adams' own, *The Education of Henry Adams* (available in several editions) is, of course, essential. David S. Barry, *Forty Years in Washington* (Boston, 1924), asserts (probably incorrectly) that there was a secret door connecting the adjoining Hay and Adams residences in Washington, D.C.

There is an enormous amount of manuscript material dealing with the Hay-Adams relationship in the Hay papers at the Library of Congress and at Brown University, and in the Adams Family papers, Henry Adams papers, and the Theodore Frelinghuysen Dwight papers at the Massachusetts Historical Society. In addition, there are several published Hay-Adams letters in Worthington C. Ford, ed., *Letters of Henry Adams* (1845–1891)(Boston and New York, 1930); *Letters of Henry Adams (1892–1918)* (Boston and New York, 1938); Harold D. Cater, ed., *Henry Adams and His Friends: A Collection of His Unpublished Letters* (Boston, 1947); Hay, ed., *Letters and Diaries;* and Thayer, *John Hay.*

Although this study did not deal with the Hay-Adams relationship in detail, it appears that previous authors may have made too much of the influence each man had on the other. The relationship was exceedingly intimate on a personal level, but in the sphere of social philosophy, politics, and foreign policy there seems to have been little substantive influence. There was, however, almost complete candor.

Hay's relationship with Theodore Roosevelt should be traced in the Hay and Roosevelt papers at the Library of Congress, and, for their earliest contacts, in the Hay papers at Brown. Morison, ed., *Letters of Roosevelt;* Henry Cabot Lodge, ed., *Selections from the Correspondence of Theodore Roosevelt and Henry Cabot Lodge* (2 vols.: New York, 1925); and Anna Roosevelt Cowles, ed., *Letters from Theodore Roosevelt to Anna Roosevelt 1870–1918* (New York and London, 1924) are also useful. *Theodore Roosevelt: An Autobiography* (New York, 1920) must be used with care, for it suggest that there was no tension at all between Hay and Roosevelt.

There are many secondary works dealing with Roosevelt. Among the most helpful are John M. Blum, *The Republican Roosevelt* (Cambridge, Massachusetts, 1954) whose interpretation of Roosevelt as essentially conservative was foreshadowed in Daniel Aaron, *Men of Good Hope: A Story of American Progressives* (New York, 1951); Howard K. Beale, *Theodore Roosevelt and the Rise of America to World Power* (Baltimore, 1956); and David H. Burton, *Theodore Roosevelt: Confident Imperialist* (Philadelphia, 1968).

Dennett and Thayer deal briefly with Hay's social philosophy in relation to his times and both underestimate the depth of Hay's conservative reaction. Hay's novel, *The Bread-winners*, is very helpful in determining Hay's thought. The best historical analysis of *The Bread-winners* is Frederic Cople Jaher, "Industrialism and the American Aristocrat: A Social Study of John Hay and His Novel, *The Bread-Winners*," *Journal of the Illinois State Historical Society* 65 (Spring, 1972), 69–93. Louis Hacker in "Middle Western Exquisite," *Nation* 137 (November 8, 1933), 545, a sarcastic review of Dennett, *John Hay*, dismisses Hay as one of the lesser tragedies of the Gilded Age.

There is a considerable body of literature on the late nineteenth century though there is not yet an in-depth study of the thought of men like Hay that compares, for example, to Walter Houghton's study of Victorian England, *The Victorian Frame of Mind 1830–1870* (New Haven, 1957). General studies of the age, such as Samuel P. Hays, *The Response to Industrialism, 1885–1914* (Chicago, 1957) and Robert Wiebe, *The Search for Order 1877–1920* (New York, 1967) are essential for background and deal, to some extent, with thought patterns of the age.

There are also a number of specialized studies of nineteenth-century men who shared some of Hay's values. Edward C. Kirkland, *Dream and Thought in the Business Community, 1860–1900* (Ithaca, New York, 1956) is a useful if impressionistic study of its topic. The mugwumps, who were very much like Hay even though he detested them, receive generally sympathetic treatment from Geoffrey Blodgett in *The Gentle Reformers: Massachusetts Democrats in the Cleveland Era* (Cambridge, Massachusetts, 1966), and much less sympathetic treatment from John G. Sproat, who emphasizes their moral arrogance in *"The Best Men": Liberal Reformers in the Gilded Age* (New York, 1968). The early portions of Eric Goldman, *Rendezvous With Destiny: A History of Modern American Reform* (revised edition; New York, 1956) also deals with liberal reformers, while Daniel Aaron's imaginative study, *Men of Good Hope*, deals sympathetically with middle-class socialists and utopian reformers.

The only discussion of Hay's racial views is Kenton J. Clymer, "Anti-Semitism in the Late Nineteenth Century: The Case of John Hay," *American Jewish Historical Quarterly* 60 (June, 1971), 344–54. *Castilian Days, The Bread-winners,* and *Abraham Lincoln* are useful in determining Hay's views of race and ethnicity with *The Bread-winners* being the most significant. His addresses while ambassador to England are also helpful in determining his affinity for Anglo-Saxon cultures and values.

The issue of race and ethnicity during the period of Hay's maturity is dealt with comprehensively in Thomas F. Gossett, *Race: The History of an Idea* (Dallas, 1963). More specialized studies include John Higham, *Strangers in the Land: Patterns of American Nativism* (second edition; New York, 1965) which examines anti-immigrant feeling. The same topic, as it relates specifically to Boston's intellectuals, is dealt with in Barbara M. Solomon, *Ancestors and Immigrants: A Changing New England Tradition* (Cambridge, Massachusetts, 1956), a most helpful study for understanding anti-Irish feelings among the elite. The first chapter of Howard K. Beale, *Roosevelt and the Rise of America to World Power* includes a revealing discussion of racial attitudes, as does chapter four of Bradford Perkins, *The Great Rapprochement: England and the United States, 1895–1914* (New York, 1968) which deals with the concept of Anglo-Saxonism. Richard Hofstadter, *Social Darwinism in American Thought* (revised edition; Boston, 1955) is a comprehensive, sometimes highly technical study of its subject. Works on black-white relations are numerous; C. Vann Woodward's classic, *The Strange Career of Jim Crow* (revised edition; New York, 1957), stands out.

For Hay's views of Europe and especially of Spain during the 1860's and 1870's Hay's poems should be consulted, as well as his two speeches, "The Progress of Democracy in Europe" and "Daybreak in Spain," both of which are available in the Hay collection at Brown University. Some of Hay's early letters and diary entries are readily available in Dennett, ed., *Lincoln and the Civil War*, and Hay's editorials in the *New York Tribune*, many of which can be read in the Hay collection in the Library of Congress, are very helpful especially regarding developments in Spain. *Castilian Days* is, of course, essential.

For developments within Spain during these years, H. Butler Clarke, *Modern Spain 1815–1898* (Cambridge, England, 1906) is adequate if dated. Edgar Holt, *The Carlist Wars in Spain* (Chester Springs, Pennsylvania, 1967) capably discusses men and events as the Carlists saw them. Spanish relations with Cuba are fully treated in Hugh Thomas, *Cuba: The Pursuit of Freedom* (New York, 1971), a work which partially supplants two older diplomatic works, French E. Chadwick, *The Relations of the United States and Spain: Diplomacy* (New York, 1909), and James M. Callahan, *Cuba and International Relations: A Historical Study in American Diplomacy* (Baltimore, 1899). The latter details the diplomacy regarding Cuba in the 1860's and 1870's but in a rather disorganized and dull manner.

There is a very rich literature on American expansionism in the 1890's of which the following are only a selection of some of the most significant. Ernest May, *Imperial Democracy: The Emergence of America as a Great Power* (New York, 1961) is an essential work, admirable in its use of multiarchival research. May's stress on the force of public opinion has been criticized, while his conclusion that American expansion was essentially purposeless seems questionable. William Appleman Williams, on the other hand, perhaps overdoes the purposefulness of American expansion in *The Roots of the Modern American Empire:*

A Study of the Growth and Shaping of Social Consciousness in a Marketplace Society (New York, 1969) and in *The Tragedy of American Diplomacy* (revised edition; New York, 1962). Economic motivations are also stressed in Walter LaFeber, *The New Empire: An Interpretation of American Expansion, 1860–1898* (Ithaca, New York, 1963).

Noneconomic motives for expansion are stressed in Julius W. Pratt, *Expansionists of 1898: The Acquisition of Hawaii and the Spanish Island* (Baltimore, 1935), a classic account; Richard Hofstadter, "Manifest Destiny and the Philippines," in Daniel Aaron, ed., *America in Crisis: Fourteen Crucial Episodes in American History* (New York, 1952); H. Wayne Morgan, *William McKinley and His America* (Syracuse, 1963); and Ernest May, *American Imperialism: A Speculative Essay* (New York, 1968). May stresses the importance of European models for American imperialism. Hay's thought tends to support May's thesis. Other overviews of American expansion include Albert K. Weinberg, *Manifest Destiny: A Study of National Expansion in American History* (Baltimore, 1935), and Charles Vevier, "American Continentalism: An Idea of Expansion, 1845–1910," *American Historical Review* 65 (January, 1960), 323–35. Vevier attempts to refute those who see overseas expansion as a bold departure from American tradition. For additional readings on American expansion consult the fine annotated bibliography in Richard H. Miller, ed., *American Imperialism: The Quest for National Fulfillment* (New York, 1970).

The Spanish American War and the subsequent annexation of the Philippines is dealt with in virtually all of the above mentioned works. In addition, H. Wayne Morgan, ed., *Making Peace with Spain: The Diary of Whitelaw Reid, September–December, 1898* (Austin, 1965) is slightly helpful in understanding Hay's attitude, and the *Foreign Relations* series is useful for understanding the peace negotiations. Subsequent American policy in the Philippines has not received the attention it deserves. It is as if once the Philippines were acquired the issue of imperialism ceased to be a matter of importance to diplomatic historians. Perhaps this is because Americans conceive themselves to have had no colonial history. In any event, a few recent works have helped fill the gap. Most important is Peter W. Stanley, "A Nation in the Making: The United States and the Philippines, 1899–1921" (Ph.D. dissertation, Harvard University, 1970) which is now available in book form from Harvard University Press. John M. Gates, *Schoolbooks and Krags: The United States in the Philippines, 1898–1902* (Westport, Conn., 1973) is a careful study of the army's role, and Oscar M. Alfonso, *Theodore Roosevelt and the Philippines* (Quezon City, 1970), though somewhat unpolished, is the first in-depth study of its topic. Onofre Corpuz, "Western Colonisation and the Filipino Response," *Journal of Southeast Asian History* 3 (1962), 1–22 is an excellent, brief analysis of American-Filipino interaction. Garel A. Grunder and William E. Livezey, *The Philippines and the United States* (Norman, Okla., 1951) is now superceded by Stanley's study. Leon Wolff, *Little Brown Brother: How the United States Purchased and Pacified the Philippine Islands at the Century's Turn* (Garden City, N.Y., 1960) is partially supplanted by Gates' monograph. Wolff's assessment of American action is considerably more negative than Gates', an understandable assessment, but the book's sarcastic tone detracts from its value. There are, in addition, a fairly large number of memoir and semi-memoir materials available. Hay's views are best ascertained from the unpublished exchanges between the State Department and the Schurman Commission.

The basic work on American diplomacy in China remains A. Whitney Griswold, *The Far Eastern Policy of the United States* (New Haven and London, 1938). Marilyn B. Young, *Rhetoric of Empire: American China Policy 1895–1901* (Cambridge, Massachusetts, 1968) is a thoroughly researched work covering the years mentioned. Young emphasizes America's lack of concern for China's welfare, despite the rhetoric to the contrary. Unfortunately, the book is sometimes disjointed. Another new work, Thomas J. McCormick, *China Market: America's Quest for Informal*

Empire 1893–1901 (Chicago, 1967), is a stimulating interpretation arguing that the hope for a China market accounts
for American expansion in the 1890's.

The Open Door notes have evoked much historical
writing. Roy V. Magers in "John Hay and American Traditions in China," *Social Science* 4 (May, 1929), 299–311,
sees the notes as part of long-established American policies
extending back at least to the time of Daniel Webster. Paul
H. Clyde, "The Open-Door Policy of John Hay," *Historical
Outlook* 22 (May, 1931), 210–14, anticipates George F.
Kennan, *American Diplomacy, 1900–1950* (Chicago, 1951)
in arguing that the Open Door notes represent in fact a
truly new departure. Raymond A. Esthus, "The Changing
Concept of the Open Door, 1899–1910," *Mississippi Valley
Historical Review* 46 (December, 1959), 435–54, points out
the substantial broadening of the second note, but he
overdoes his point.

Anglo-American aspects of American China policy are
treated in a number of works with the above-mentioned
works by Griswold, Clyde, Kennan, and Dennett, *John
Hay,* contending that Hay's policy was the result of British
efforts to enlist American aid. More recent research by Paul
Varg, *Open Door Diplomat: The Life of W. W. Rockhill*
(Urbana, 1952); R. G. Neale, *Great Britain and United
States Expansion: 1898–1900* (East Lansing, Michigan,
1966); and Perkins, *The Great Rapprochement,* has shown
that American policy was in fact quite different from British policy and that those Englishmen who did influence
American actions were private citizens whose recommendations were actually somewhat at odds with official British
policy.

Later aspects of America's China policy are traced in
Varg, *Open Door Diplomat* and in chapter one of Raymond
A. Esthus, *Theodore Roosevelt and Japan* (Seattle and
London, 1968), a work which emphasizes the adminis-
tration's anti-Russian attitude. Esthus' work supercedes
Tyler Dennett, *Roosevelt and The Russo-Japanese War . . .*
(Garden City, New York, 1925). The most recent treatment
of the Russo-Japanese War, from the standpoint of Ameri-

can diplomatic involvement, is Eugene P. Trani, *The Treaty of Portsmouth: An Adventure in American Diplomacy* (Lexington, 1969). An excellent, recent account of American Far Eastern policy, which makes use of Japanese sources, is Akira Iriye, *Pacific Estrangement: Japanese and American Expansion, 1897–1911* (Cambridge, Mass., 1972).

Hay's diplomacy as ambassador to England is adequately discussed in Louis M. Sears, "John Hay in London, 1897–1898," *Ohio Historical Quarterly* 65 (October, 1956), 356–75, an article based on the official dispatches. A more impressionistic account is Beckles Willson, *America's Ambassadors to England, 1785–1928* (London, 1928). There are, in addition, a number of contemporary accounts dealing with Hay as ambassador. An unpublished manuscript article by Mrs. Hay, "Our Life in London," in the Hay papers in the Library of Congress, describes the personal life of the ambassador and his family during the early months of Hay's tenure. The unpublished correspondence between Hay and Henry White, Joseph Choate, and Cecil Spring Rice is most helpful.

General accounts of Anglo-American relations include Perkins, *The Great Rapprochement*, a synthesis that brings "nondiplomatic" factors to bear on policy formation. More narrow approaches are taken by Charles S. Campbell, Jr., *Anglo-American Understanding, 1898–1903* (Baltimore, 1957); A[lexander] E. Campbell, *Great Britain and the United States 1895–1903* (Glasgow, 1960); and Neale, *Great Britain and United States Expansion.* Three older works, R[obert] B. Mowat, *The Diplomatic Relations Of Great Britain and the United States* (London, 1925); Lionel Gelber, *The Rise of Anglo-American Friendship* (London, 1938); and Alfred L. P. Dennis, *Adventures in American Diplomacy 1896–1906* (New York, 1928) are still useful, particularly the last. All of these works shed light on Anglo-American relations during the war with Spain, the Alaska boundary dispute, the Hay-Pauncefote treaties, the Boer War, and China policy.

Several more specialized studies are also helpful. Relations during the Spanish American War are dealt with in Bertha A. Reuter, *Anglo-American Relations During the Spanish American War* (New York, 1924), a work that credits Hay with forging the good relationship that developed during the summer of 1898. St. Loe Strachey, *The Adventure of Living*, discusses Hay's attitude during the war with Spain, particularly his contempt for Germany.

The fur seal and Alaska boundary disputes are treated exhaustively and competently in Charles C. Tansill, *Canadian-American Relations, 1875–1911* (New Haven, 1943). Roosevelt's role is described in Thomas A. Bailey, "Theodore Roosevelt and the Alaska Boundary Settlement," *Canadian Historical Review* 18 (June, 1937), 123–30, while Henry Cabot Lodge discusses his role in the delicate final negotiations in Charles G. Washburne, ed., "Memoir of Henry Cabot Lodge," *Massachusetts Historical Society Proceedings* (April, 1925), 324–76. The Canadian side is traced in John W. DaFoe, *Clifford Sifton in Relation to His Times* (Toronto, 1931).

The Hay-Pauncefote Treaty has received intensive study from J. A. S. Grenville in "Great Britain and the Isthmian Canal, 1898–1901," *American Historical Review* 61 (October, 1955), 48–69. Grenville stresses the crucial importance of Britain's decision to permit the United States to build the isthmian canal alone.

The only work dealing exclusively with American policy during the Boer War is John H. Ferguson, *American Diplomacy and the Boer War* (Philadelphia, 1939). Although rather narrowly diplomatic, Ferguson is aware that Hay's Anglophilia influenced his actions. Baron [Hermann] von Eckardstein, *Ten Years at the Court of St. James*, trans. by George Young (London, 1921), is somewhat useful, while John Hays Hammond, *The Autobiography of John Hays Hammond* (2 vols.; New York, 1935) reveals Hay's friendship with Cecil Rhodes.

A number of memoirs and biographies are also useful for the study of Anglo-American relations during this period. Allan Nevins, *Henry White: Thirty Years of American Diplomacy* (New York and London, 1930) is indispensable for a knowledge of Hay and Anglo-American relations. White was secretary of the American embassy in London during Hay's tenure as ambassador and as secretary of state. Robert B. Mowat, *The Life of Lord Pauncefote* (Boston and New York, 1929) is a good account of the British ambassador, while Blanche E. C. Dugdale, *Arthur James Balfour, First Earl of Balfour, K.G., O.M., F.R.S., Etc.* (2 vols.; New York, 1937) deals with another important personage in Anglo-American relations. Both biographies contain some information on Hay. Eckardstein, *Ten Years at the Court of St. James,* is an interesting memoir in this respect, as is George W. Smalley, *Anglo-American Memoirs* (London, 1912). St. Loe Strachey, *The Adventure of Living,* includes some interesting accounts of Hay.

The best general account of the canal is Dwight C. Miner, *The Fight for the Panama Route: The Story of the Spooner Act and the Hay-Herrán Treaty* (New York, 1940). Margaret Clapp, *Forgotten First Citizen: John Bigelow* (Boston, 1947) provides valuable information on the role that Bigelow played in focusing administration attention on the Panama route. Philippe Bunau-Varilla, *Panama: The Creation, Destruction, and Resurrection* (London, 1913) provides background material from the point of view of a partisan; it must be used with care.

Bibliography

PRIMARY SOURCES

Government Records

National Archives:

Records of the Department of State. Diplomatic Instructions: China. Vols. 5–6.
Records of the Department of State. Diplomatic Instructions: Great Britain. Vols. 32–35.
Records of the Department of State. Diplomatic Despatches: Great Britain. Vols. 188–93.
Records of the Department of State. Correspondence from the Department of State to the Schurman Commission.
Records of the Department of State. Correspondence from the Schurman Commission to the Department of State.

Published Government Records:

Department of State. *Papers Relating to the Foreign Relations of the United States.* Washington, D.C.: Government Printing Office, 1897–1903.

John Hay Sources

Manuscript Collections (in order of importance):

John Hay papers, Manuscript Division, Library of Congress.
John Hay papers, John Hay Library, Brown University.
Tyler Dennett collection of material relating to John Hay, Tyler Dennett papers, Manuscript Division, Library of Congress.
John Hay papers, Henry H. Huntington Library, San Marino, Calif.

John Hay papers, Manuscript Division, Butler Library, Columbia University.
John Hay papers, Houghton Library, Harvard University.

Printed Sources:

Brown University, ed. *The Life and Works of John Hay 1838–1905: A Commemorative Catalogue of the Exhibition Shown at the John Hay Library of Brown University in Honor of The Centennial of his Graduation at the Commencement of 1858.* Providence: Brown University Press, 1961.

Dennett, Tyler, ed. *Lincoln and the Civil War in the Diaries and Letters of John Hay.* New York: Dodd, Mead & Co., 1939.

Hay, Clara S., ed. *Letters of John Hay and Extracts from his Diary.* 3 vols. Washington, D.C.: By the editor. 1908.

Hay, Clarence, compiler. *The Complete Poetical Works of John Hay.* Boston and New York: Houghton Mifflin Co., 1917.

[Hay, John], *The Addresses of John Hay.* New York: Century Co., 1906.

_____. *Amasa Stone: Born April 27, 1818. Died May 11, 1883.* [New York: Devinne Press, 1883].

_____. *The Balance Sheet of the Two Parties.* Cleveland: Leader Printing Co., 1880.

_____. *The Bread-winners: A Social Study.* 1883. Reprint. Ridgewood, N. J.: Gregg Press, 1967.

_____. *Castilian Days.* Boston: Osgood & Co., 1871.

_____. *Castilian Days.* 2nd ed. Boston: Houghton Mifflin Co., 1899.

_____. *Castilian Days.* 3rd ed. Boston: Houghton Mifflin Co., 1904.

_____. *Dr. Charles Hay. Born February 7, 1801. Died September 18, 1884.* [New York: By the author, 1885].

_____. "The Mormon Prophet's Tragedy." *Atlantic Monthly* 24 (December, 1869); 669–78.

_____. *The Platform of Anarchy.* [Cleveland, 1896].

[Montague, Amy A. C.], ed. *A College Friendship: A Series of Letters from John Hay to Hannah Angell.* Boston: By the editor, 1938.

Ticknor, Caroline, ed. *A Poet in Exile: Early Letters of John Hay.* Boston: Houghton Mifflin Co., 1910.

Nicolay, John G. and Hay, John. *Abraham Lincoln: A History.* 10 vols. New York: Century Co., 1890.

Related Manuscript Collections

Manuscript Division, Library of Congress. Papers of:

Blaine, James G.
Carnegie, Andrew.
Choate, Joseph H.
Dennett, Tyler.
Dewey, George.
Hood, Edwin Milton.
Foster, John Watson.
Harrison, Benjamin.
McKinley, William.
Mahan, Alfred Thayer.
Mitchell, Silas Weir.
Moore, John Bassett.
Morgan, John T.
Olney, Richard.
Porter, Horace.
Reid, Whitelaw.
Roosevelt, Theodore.
Root, Elihu.
Sherman, John.
Schurz, Carl.
Smalley, George Washburne.
Straus, Oscar S.
Wadsworth Family.
Washington, Booker T.
Watterson, Henry.
White, Henry.
Whitney, William C.
Young, John Russell.

Massachusetts Historical Society. Papers of:

Adams Family.
Adams, Henry.
Dwight, Theodore Frelinghuysen.
Edes, H. H.
Hoar, George F.
Lodge, Henry Cabot.
Long, John D.

Houghton Library, Harvard University. Papers of:

Adams, Brooks.
Howells, William Dean.
Rockhill, William W.

Harvard Archives, Harvard University. Papers of:

Eliot, Charles W.

Manuscript Division, Butler Library, Columbia University. Papers of:

Holls, Frederick W.
Jay Family.
Nevins, Allan.

Manuscript Division, New York Public Library. Papers of:

Carnegie, Andrew.
Ford collection.
Gilder, Richard Watson.
Mitchell, Silas Weir.
Montague collection.
Raymond, Henry J.
Tilden, Samuel J.

University of Virginia Library. Papers of:

Bartlett Literary collection.
Davis, Richard Harding.

Cornell University Library. Papers of:

Schurman, Jacob G.
White, Andrew D.

University of California at Berkeley Library. Papers of:

Twain, Mark.

Manuscript Division, British Museum, London. Papers of:

Balfour, Arthur James.

Related Printed Sources

Adams, Henry. *The Education of Henry Adams.* New York: Random House, Modern Library, 1931.

Barry, David S. *Forty Years in Washington.* Boston: Little, Brown, & Co., 1924.

Beale, Harriet S. Blaine, ed. *Letters of Mrs. James G. Blaine.* 3 vols. New York: Duffield & Co., 1908.

Bigelow, John. *Retrospections of an Active Live.* 5 vols. New York: Baker & Taylor Co., 1909.

Brown University, ed. *The Dedication of the John Hay Library, Brown University, Providence, Rhode Island (November 11, 1910).* Providence, 1911.

Bunau-Varilla, Philippe. *Panama: The Creation, Destruction, and Resurrection.* London: Constable & Co., 1913.

Carnegie, Andrew. *Autobiography of Andrew Carnegie.* Boston and New York: Houghton Mifflin Co., 1920.

Cater, Harold Dean, ed. *Henry Adams and His Friends: A Collection of His Unpublished Letters.* Boston: Houghton Mifflin Co., 1947.

Clemens, Samuel L. *Mark Twain's Autobiography.* 2 vols. New York and London: Harper & Bros., 1924.

Cowles, Anna Roosevelt, ed. *Letters from Theodore Roosevelt to Anna Roosevelt Cowles 1870–1918.* New York and London: Charles Scribner's Sons, 1924.

Cullom, Shelby. *Fifty Years of Public Service: Personal Recollections of Shelby M. Cullom Senior United States Senator from Illinois.* Chicago: A. C. McClurg & Co., 1911.

Dewey, George. *Autobiography of George Dewey: Admiral of the Navy.* New York: Charles Scribner's Sons, 1913.

DeVoto, Bernard, ed. *Mark Twain in Eruption: Hitherto Unpublished Pages about Men and Events by Mark Twain.* New York and London: Harper & Bros. 1940.

Eckardstein, Baron [Hermann] von. *Ten Years at the Court of St. James.* Translated by George Young. London: Thornton Butterworth, 1921.

Ford, Worthington C., ed. *Letters of Henry Adams (1858–1891).* Boston and New York: Houghton Mifflin Co., 1930.

––––––, ed. *Letters of Henry Adams (1892–1918).* Boston and New York: Houghton Mifflin Co., 1938.

Foster, John W. *Diplomatic Memoirs.* 2 vols. Boston and New York: Houghton Mifflin Co., 1909.

Gilder, Rosamond, ed. *Letters of Richard Watson Gilder.* Boston and New York: Houghton Mifflin Co., 1916.

Hammond, John Hays. *The Autobiography of John Hays Hammond.* 2 vols. New York: Farrar & Rinehart, 1935.

Harte, Geoffrey Bret, ed. *The Letters of Bret Harte.* Boston and New York: Houghton Mifflin Co., 1926.

Howells, Mildred, ed. *Life in Letters of William Dean Howells.* 2 vols. Garden City, N. Y.: Doubleday, Doran & Co., 1928.

Irwin, Will, ed. *Letters to Kermit from Theodore Roosevelt 1902–1908.* New York and London: Charles Scribner's Sons, 1946.

[Keenan, Henry F.] *The Money-Makers. A Social Parable.* New York: D. Appleton and Co., 1885.

Lodge, Henry Cabot, ed. *Selections from the Correspondence of Theodore Roosevelt and Henry Cabot Lodge.* 2 vols. New York: Charles Scribner's Sons, 1925.

[McKinley, William.] *Speeches and Addresses of William McKinley from March 1, 1897 to May 30, 1900.* New York: Doubleday & McClure, 1900.

Marcosson, Isaac F. *Adventures in Interviewing.* London and New York: John Lane Co., 1920.

————. *Before I Forget: A Pilgrimage to the Past.* New York: Dodd, Mead & Co., 1959.

Morgan, H. Wayne, ed. *Making Peace with Spain: The Diary of Whitelaw Reid, September–December, 1898.* Austin: University of Texas Press, [1965].

Morison, Elting E., ed. *Cowboys and Kings: Three Great Letters by Theodore Roosevelt.* Cambridge, Mass.: Harvard University Press, 1954.

————, ed. *The Letters of Theodore Roosevelt.* 8 vols. Cambridge, Mass.: Harvard University Press, 1951–54.

Paine, Albert Bigelow, ed. *Mark Twain's Letters.* 2 vols. New York and London: Harper & Bros., 1917.

————, ed. *Mark Twain's Notebook.* New York and London: Harper & Bros., 1935.

Roosevelt, Theodore. *Theodore Roosevelt: An Autobiography.* New York: Charles Scribner's Sons, 1920.

Smith, Henry Nash, and Gibson, William M., ed. *Mark Twain-Howells Letters: The Correspondence of Samuel L. Clemens and William Dean Howells 1872–1910.* 2 vols. Cambridge, Mass.: Harvard University Press, 1960.

St. Loe Strachey, John. *The Adventure of Living: A Subjective Autobiography.* London: Hodder & Stoughton, 1922.

Smalley, George W. *Anglo-American Memoirs.* London: Duckworth & Co., 1912.

Straus, Oscar S. *The American Spirit.* New York: Century Co., 1913.

Thoron, Ward, ed. *The Letters of Mrs. Henry Adams 1865–1883.* Boston: Little, Brown, & Co., 1936.

Traubel, Horace. *With Walt Whitman in Camden.* 5 vols. New York, Philadelphia, and Carbondale, Illinois, 1906–64.

Washburne, Charles G., ed. "Memoir of Henry Cabot Lodge," *Massachusetts Historical Society Proceedings* (April, 1925): 324–76.

Watterson, Henry. *"Marse Henry": An Autobiography.* New York: George H. Doran Co., 1909.

Wecter, Dixon, ed. *Mark Twain to Mrs. Fairbanks.* San Marino, Calif.: Huntington Library, 1949.

SECONDARY MATERIAL

Material Relating to Hay

Books:

Dennett, Tyler, *John Hay: From Poetry to Politics.* Port Washington, N. Y.: Kennikat Press, 1963.

Sears, Lorenzo. *John Hay, Author, Statesman.* New York: Dodd, Mead, & Co., 1914.

Thayer, William R. *The Life and Letters of John Hay.* 2 vols. Boston and New York: Houghton Mifflin Co., 1916.

Ward, St. Ignatius, Sister. *The Poetry of John Hay.* Washington, D.C.: The Catholic University of America, 1930.

Dissertation:

Sherrill, Anne Hummel. "John Hay: Shield of Union." Ph.D. dissertation, University of California, Berkeley, 1967.

Articles and Speeches:

Adams, Brooks. "John Hay." *McClure's Magazine* 19 (June, 1902): 173–82.

Bishop, Joseph B. "A Friendship with John Hay." *Century* 71 (March, 1906): 773–80.

Chapman, A. S. "The Boyhood of John Hay." *Century* 56 (July, 1909): 444–54.

Clemens, Samuel L. "John Hay and the Ballads." *Harper's Weekly* 49 (October 21, 1905): 1530.

Clymer, Kenton J. "Anti-Semitism in the Late Nineteenth Century: The Case of John Hay." *American Jewish Historical Quarterly* 60 (June, 1971): 344–54.

Dennis, Alfred L. P. "John Hay." In *The American Secretaries of State and Their Diplomacy,* edited by Samuel F. Bemis, New York: Alfred A. Knopf, 1927–29.

Dulles, Foster R. "John Hay." In *An Uncertain Tradition: American Secretaries of State in the Twentieth Century,* edited by Norman Graebner, New York: McGraw-Hill, 1961.

Hacker, Louis M. "Middle Western Exquisite." *Nation* 137 (November 8, 1933): 545.

Hicks, Granville. "The Conversion of John Hay." *New Republic* 63 (June 10, 1931): 100–101.

Howells, William D. "John Hay in Literature." *North American Review* 171 (September, 1905): [343]–351.

———. Review of *Castilian Days. Atlantic Monthly* 28 (November, 1871): 336–38.

Jaher, Frederic Cople. "Industrialism and the American Aristocrat: A Social Study of John Hay and His Novel, *The Bread-winners.*" *Journal of the Illinois State Historical Society* 65 (Spring, 1972): 69–93.

[King, Clarence]. "John Hay." *Scribner's Monthly* 7 (April, 1874): 736–39.

Mellen, George F. "John Hay—Littérateur." *Methodist Review* 101 (July, 1918): 547–56.

"Mr. John Hay." *Spectator* 91 (August 22, 1903): 226–67.

Moore, John Bassett. "John Hay." *Political Science Quarterly* 32 (August, 1905): 171–76.

———. "Mr. Hay's Work in Diplomacy." *Review of Reviews* 32 (August, 1905): 171–76.

Moores, Charles W. "John Hay, The Making of a Great Diplomat." *Putnam's* 6 (June, 1909): 297–308.

Root, Elihu. *Address by Elihu Root at the Dedication of the John Hay Library, Brown University, November 11, 1910.* New York: The *Evening Post* Job Printing Office, 1910.

———. *Remarks of Elihu Root on Unveiling a Memorial Window to the Honorable John Hay at the Keneseth Israel, Philadelphia, December 2, 1906.* N.p.: n.d.

Wellman, Walter. "John Hay: An American Gentleman." *Review of Reviews* 32 (August, 1905): [166]–171.

Young John Russell. "John Hay." *Munsey's Magazine 20* (November, 1898): 246–50.

Biographies and Other Accounts
of Individuals

Beale, Howard K. *Theodore Roosevelt and the Rise of America to World Power.* Baltimore: Johns Hopkins Press, 1956.

Blum, John M. *The Republican Roosevelt.* Cambridge, Mass.: Harvard University Press, 1954.

Budd, Louis J. *Mark Twain: Social Philosopher.* Bloomington: Indiana University Press, 1962.

Burton, David H. *Theodore Roosevelt: Confident Imperialist.* Philadelphia: University of Pennsylvania Press, 1968.

Carter, Everett. *Howells and the Age of Realism.* New York and Philadelphia: J. B. Lippincott & Co., 1954.

Clapp, Margaret. *Forgotten First Citizen: John Bigelow.* Boston: Little, Brown & Co., 1947.

Cortissoz, Royal. *The Life of Whitelaw Reid.* 2 vols. New York: Charles Scribner's Sons, 1921.

DaFoe, John W. *Clifford Sifton in Relation to his Times.* Toronto: The Macmillan Co. of Canada, 1931.

Duckett, Margaret. *Mark Twain and Bret Harte.* Norman: University of Oklahoma Press, 1964.

Dugdale, Blanche E. C. *Arthur James Balfour, First Earl of Balfour, K.G., O.M., F.R.S., Etc.,* 2 vols. New York: G. P. Putnam's Sons, 1937.

Edwards, Herbert. "Henry Adams: Politician and Statesman." *New England Quarterly 22* (March, 1949): 49–60.

Ferguson, [John] DeLancey. *Mark Twain: Man and Legend.* Indianapolis and New York: Charter Books, 1963.

Garraty, John A. *Henry Cabot Lodge.* New York: Alfred A. Knopf, 1953.

Gwynn, Stephen. *The Letters and Friendships of Sir Cecil Spring Rice: A Record.* 2 vols. Boston and New York: Houghton Mifflin Co., 1929.

Hacker, Louis M. *The World of Andrew Carnegie: 1865–1901.* Philadelphia and New York: J. B. Lippincott Co., 1968.

Harbaugh, William H. *Power and Responsibility: The Life and Times of Theodore Roosevelt.* New York: Farrar, Straus & Cudahy, 1961.

Kaplan, Justin, *Mr. Clemens and Mark Twain: A Biography.* New York: Simon & Schuster, 1966.

Kirk, Clara M. *W. D. Howells and Art in His Time.* New Brunswick, N. J.: Rutgers University Press, 1965.

Leech, Margaret. *In the Days of McKinley.* New York: Harper & Bros., 1959.

Marcosson, Issac F. *"Marse Henry:" A Biography of Henry Watterson.* New York: Dodd, Mead & Co., 1951.

Martin, Edward S. *The Life of Joseph Hodges Choate as Gathered Chiefly from his Letters.* 2 vols. New York: Charles Scribner's Sons, 1920.

Monteiro, George. *Henry James and John Hay: The Record of A Friendship.* Providence, R. I.: Brown University Press, 1965.

_____. "A Note on the Mark Twain-Whitelaw Reid Relationship," *The Emerson Society Quarterly* 19 (2nd Quarter, 1960); 20–21.

Morgan, H. Wayne. *William McKinley and His America.* Syracuse, N. Y.: Syracuse University Press, 1963.

Mowat, Robert B. *The Life of Lord Pauncefote.* Boston and New York: Houghton Mifflin Co., 1929.

Muzzey, David S. *James G. Blaine: A Political Idol of Other Days.* New York: Dodd, Mead & Co., 1934.

Nevins, Allan. *Henry White: Thirty Years of American Diplomacy.* New York and London: Harper & Bros., 1930.

O'Connor, Richard. *Bret Harte: A Biography.* Boston and Toronto: Little, Brown & Co., 1966.

Olcott, Charles S. *The Life of William McKinley.* 2 vols. Boston and New York: Houghton Mifflin Co., 1916.

Paine, Albert Bigelow. *Mark Twain, A Biography: The Personal and Literary Life of Samuel Langhorne Clemens.* New York and London: Harper & Bros., 1912.

Pemberton, T. Edgar. *The Life of Bret Harte.* New York: Dodd, Mead & Co., 1903.

"Reminiscences of Bret Harte," *Overland Monthly* 40 (September, 1902): [220]–[239].

Samuels, Ernest. *Henry Adams: The Major Phase.* Cambridge, Mass.: Harvard University Press, 1964.

_____. *Henry Adams: The Middle Years.* Cambridge, Mass.: Harvard University Press, 1958.

Stewart, George R., Jr. *Bret Harte: Argonaut and Exile, Being An Account of the Life of the Celebrated American Humorist* . . . . Boston and New York: Houghton Mifflin Co., 1931.

Ticknor, Caroline. *Poe's Helen.* New York: Charles Scribner's Sons, 1916.

Varg, Paul. *Open Door Diplomat: The Life of W. W. Rockhill.* Urbana: The University of Illinois Press, 1952.

Wall, Joseph F. *Henry Watterson: Reconstructed Rebel.* New York: Oxford University Press, 1956.

_____. *Andrew Carnegie.* New York: Oxford University Press, 1970.

Wilkins, Thurman. *Clarence King: A Biography.* New York: Macmillan Co., 1958.

Social and Intellectual Climate of the Late Nineteenth Century

Aaron, Daniel. *Men of Good Hope: A Story of American Progressives.* New York: Oxford University Press, 1951.

Blodgett, Geoffrey. *The Gentle Reformers: Massachusetts Democrats in the Cleveland Era.* Cambridge, Mass.: Harvard University Press, 1966.

Hays, Samuel P. *The Response to Industrialism, 1885–1914.* Chicago: University of Chicago Press, 1957.

Higham, John. "Anti-Semitism in the Gilded Age: A Reinterpretation." *Mississippi Valley Historical Review* 43 (March, 1957):' 559–78.

_____. "The Reorientation of American Culture in the 1890's." In *The Origins of Modern Consciousness,* edited by Paul Weiss. Detroit: Wayne State University Press, 1965.

_____. *Strangers in the Land: Patterns of American Nativism 1860–1925.* 2nd ed. New York: Atheneum, 1965.

Hofstadter, Richard. *The Age of Reform: From Bryan to F.D.R.* New York: Random House, Vintage Books, 1955.

_____. *Social Darwinism in American Thought.* Rev. ed. Boston: Beacon Press, 1955.

Goldman, Eric. *Rendezvous with Destiny: A History of Modern American Reform.* Rev. ed. New York: Random House, Vintage Books, 1956.

Gossett, Thomas F. *Race: The History of an Idea.* Dallas: Southern Methodist University Press, 1963.

Houghton, Walter E. *The Victorian Frame of Mind 1830–1870.* New Haven: Yale University Press, 1957.

Kirkland, Edward C. *Dream and Thought in the Business Community, 1860–1900.* Ithaca, N. Y.: Cornell University Press, 1956.

_____. *Industry Comes of Age: Business, Labor, and Public Policy, 1860–1897.* New York: Holt, Reinhart & Winston, 1961.

McCloskey, Robert G. *American Conservatism in the Age of Enterprise, 1865–1910. A Study of William Graham Sumner, Stephen J. Field and Andrew Carnegie.* Cambridge, Mass.: Harvard University Press, 1951.

MacFarland, Gerald W. "Partisan of Nonpartisanship: Dorman B. Eaton and the Genteel Reform Tradition." *Journal of American History* 54 (March, 1968): 806–22.

Solomon, Barbara M. *Ancestors and Immigrants: A Changing New England Tradition.* Cambridge, Mass.: Harvard University Press, 1956.

Sproat, John G. *"The Best Men": Liberal Reformers in the Gilded Age.* New York: Oxford University Press, 1968.

Wiebe, Robert H. *The Search for Order 1877–1920.* New York: Hill & Wang, 1967.

Spain in the 1860's and 1870's

Callahan, James M. *Cuba and International Relations: A Historical Study in American Diplomacy.* Baltimore: Johns Hopkins Press, 1899.

Chadwick, French E. *The Relations of the United States and Spain: Diplomacy.* New York: Charles Scribner's Sons, 1909.

Clarke, H. Butler. *Modern Spain 1815–1898.* Cambridge: The University Press, 1906.

Holt, Edgar. *The Carlist Wars in Spain.* Chester Springs, Pa.: Dufours Editions, 1967.

General Works on the Diplomacy of the 1890's and Early Twentieth Century

Beisner, Robert. *Twelve Against Empire: The Anti-imperialists, 1898–1900.* New York: McGraw-Hill, 1968.

Dennis, Alfred L. P. *Adventures in American Diplomacy 1896–1906.* New York: E. P. Dutton & Co., 1928.

Grenville, John A. S. and Young, George B. *Politics, Strategy, and American Diplomacy: Studies in Foreign Policy, 1873–1917.* New Haven: Yale University Press, 1966.

Hofstadter, Richard. "Manifest Destiny and the Philippines." In *America in Crisis,* edited by Daniel Aaron. New York: Alfred A. Knopf, 1952.

Huntington, Samuel P. *The Soldier and the State: The Theory and Politics of Civil-Military Relations.* Cambridge, Mass.: Harvard University Press, 1957.

Gibson, William M. "Mark Twain and Howells: Anti-Imperialists." *New England Quarterly* 20 (December, 1947): 435–70.

Kennan, George F. *American Diplomacy, 1900–1950.* Chicago: University of Chicago Press, 1951.

LaFeber, Walter. *The New Empire: An Interpretation of American Expansion, 1860–1898.* Ithaca, N. Y.: Cornell University Press, 1963.

Langer, William. *The Diplomacy of Imperialism 1890–1902.* New York and London: Alfred A. Knopf, 1935.

May, Ernest. *American Imperialism: A Speculative Essay.* New York: Atheneum, 1968.

_____. *Imperial Democracy: The Emergence of America as a Great Power.* New York: Harcourt, Brace & World, 1961.

Osgood, Robert E. *Ideals and Self-Interest in America's Foreign Relations: The Great Transformation of the Twentieth Century.* Chicago: University of Chicago Press, 1953.

Pratt, Julius W. *Expansionists of 1898: The Acquisition of Hawaii and the Spanish Islands.* Baltimore: Johns Hopkins Press, 1935.

Vevier, Charles. "American Continentalism: An Idea of Expansion, 1845–1910." *American Historical Review* 65 (January, 1960): 323–35.

Weinberg, Albert K. *Manifest Destiny: A Study of National Expansion in American History.* Baltimore: Johns Hopkins Press, 1935.

Williams, William A. *The Roots of The Modern American Empire: A Study of the Growth and Shaping of Social Consciousness in a Marketplace Society.* New York: Random House, 1969.

_____. *The Tragedy of American Diplomacy.* Rev. ed. New York: Dell Publishing Co., 1962.

The Spanish American War and the Acquisition and Governance of the Philippines

Alfonso, Oscar M. "Taft's Early Views on the Filipinos." *Solidarity* 4 (June, 1969): 52–58.

_____. *Theodore Roosevelt and the Philippines.* Quezon City: University of the Philippines Press, 1970.

Bryce, James. "British Experience in the Government of Colonies." *Century* 35 (March, 1898): 718–28.

Corpuz, Onofre. "Western Colonisation and the Filipino Response." *Journal of Southeast Asian History* 3 (1962): 1–22.

Gates, John M. *Schoolbooks and Krags: The United States in the Philippines, 1898–1902.* Westport, Conn.: Greenwood Press, 1973.

Grunder, Garel A. and Livezey, William E. *The Philippines and the United States.* Norman: University of Oklahoma Press, 1951.

King, Clarence. "Shall Cuba Be Free?" *Forum* 20 (September, 1895): 50–65.

Schurman, Jacob G. *Philippine Affairs: A Retrospect and Outlook.* New York: Charles Scribner's Sons, 1902.

Stanley, Peter W. *A Nation in the Making: The United States and the Philippines, 1899–1921.* Cambridge, Mass.: Harvard University Press, 1974.

Thomas, Hugh. *Cuba: The Pursuit of Freedom.* New York: Harper & Row, 1971.

Wolff, Leon. *Little Brown Brother: How the United States Purchased and Pacified the Philippine Islands at the Century's Turn.* Garden City, N. Y.: Doubleday & Co., 1960.

Worcester, Dean C. *The Philippines, Past and Present.* New York: Macmillan Co., 1914.

China Policy

Clyde, Paul H. "The Open-Door Policy of John Hay," *Historical Outlook* 22 (May, 1931): 210–14.

Dennett, Tyler. *Roosevelt and the Russo-Japanese War: A Critical Study of American Policy in Eastern Asia in 1902–05, based primarily upon the private papers of Theodore Roosevelt.* Garden City, N. Y.: Doubleday, Page & Co., 1925.

Esthus, Raymond A. "The Changing Concept of the Open Door, 1899–1910." *Mississippi Valley Historical Review* 46 (December, 1959); 435–54.

———. *Theodore Roosevelt and Japan.* Seattle and London: University of Washington Press, 1968.

Fairbank, John King. *The United States and China.* 3rd ed. Cambridge, Mass.: Harvard University Press, 1971.

Griswold, A. Whitney. *The Far Eastern Policy of the United*

States. New Haven and London: Yale University Press, 1938.

Iriye, Akira. *Pacific Estrangement: Japanese and American Expansion, 1897–1911.* Cambridge, Mass.: Harvard University Press, 1972.

Magers, Roy V. "John Hay and American Traditions in China." *Social Science* 4 (May, 1929); 229–311.

McCormick, Thomas J. *China Market: America's Quest for Informal Empire 1893–1901.* Chicago: Quadrangle Books, 1967.

Pressman, Harvey. "Hay, Rockhill, and China's Integrity: A Reappraisal." *Papers on China* [Center for East Asian Studies, Harvard University] 13 (December, 1959): 61–79.

Varg, Paul A. *The Making of a Myth: The United States and China 1897–1912.* East Lansing: Michigan State University Press, 1968.

Young, Marilyn B. *The Rhetoric of Empire: American China Policy 1895–1901.* Cambridge, Mass.: Harvard University Press, 1968.

Anglo-American Relations

"The American Ambassador." *Saturday Review* [London] 86 (August 20, 1898): 231.

Bailey, Thomas A. "Theodore Roosevelt and the Alaska Boundary Settlement." *Canadian Historical Review* 18 (June, 1937): 123–30.

Campbell, A[lexander] E. *Great Britain and the United States 1895–1903.* Glasgow: Robert MacLehose & Co., 1960.

Campbell, Charles S., Jr. *Anglo-American Understanding, 1898–1903.* Baltimore: Johns Hopkins Press, 1957.

Ferguson, John H. *American Diplomacy and the Boer War.* Philadelphia: University of Pennsylvania Press, 1939.

Gelber, Lionel. *The Rise of Anglo-American Friendship.* London: Oxford University Press, 1938.

Grenville, J. A. S. "Great Britain and the Isthmian Canal, 1898–1901." *American Historical Review* 61 (October, 1955): 48–69.

Moore, John Bassett. "The Interoceanic Canal and the Hay-Pauncefote Treaty." *New York Times,* March 4, 1900, p. 23.

Mowat, R[obert] B. *The Diplomatic Relations of Great Britain and the United States.* London: Edward Arnold & Co., 1925.

Neale, R. G. *Great Britain and United States Expansion: 1898–1900.* East Lansing: Michigan State University Press, 1966.
"The New United States Ambassador." *Spectator* 78 (February 27, 1897): 298.
"Our New Ambassador to England." *Critic* 30 (March 20, 1897): 197–98.
Perkins, Bradford. *The Great Rapprochement: England and The United States, 1895–1914.* New York: Atheneum, 1968.
Reuter, Bertha A. *Anglo-American Relations During the Spanish-American War.* New York: Macmillan Co., 1924.
Sears, Louis M. "John Hay in London 1897–1898." *Ohio Historical Quarterly* 65 (October, 1956): 356–75.
Tansill, Charles C. *Canadian-American Relations, 1875–1911.* New Haven: Yale University Press, 1943.
Willson, Beckles. *America's Ambassadors to England (1785–1928): A Narrative of Anglo-American Diplomatic Relations.* London: John Murray, 1928.

The Panama Canal

Miner, Dwight C. *The Fight for the Panama Route: The Story of the Spooner Act and the Hay-Herrán Treaty.* New York: Columbia University Press, 1940.

Index